Annual Editions: U.S. History,
Volume 1: Colonial Through
Reconstruction, 23/e

Edited by: Wendy Maier-Sarti
Oakton Community College

http://create.mcgraw-hill.com

This McGraw-Hill Create text may include materials submitted to
McGraw-Hill for publication by the instructor of this course.
The instructor is solely responsible for the editorial content of such
materials. Instructors retain copyright of these additional materials.

ISBN-10: 1259153290   ISBN-13: 9781259153297

Contents

Unit 4   121

4. The Civil War and Reconstruction   122

Preface

History is rooted in the past, but as a discipline if continues to grow and thrive. Covering pre-contact to the end of Reconstruction, the article selections in this volume demonstrate that individuals and groups seldom covered, or even incorporated into scholarship, are now given serious attention, while time-honored history is still very much respected and included.

Topics that seemed obscure in the past are slowly moving toward mainstream historical study. For example, innovative investigations into gender, marginalized groups, native peoples, or even new economic research challenge previously held notions about many topics. From examining new scholarship into colonial relationships with Native Americans, or deciphering whether or not in the post-Civil War years, because of economic necessity, "the federal government [was] willing to promote business, and with little initial regulation" allowing industrialization to grow at a rapid fire pace, fresh research into topics old and new challenge past conclusions. Current studies on indentured servitude reveals that women were especially vulnerable because of their indentured status. Yet, to move forward we must also respect the past, and not veer, as my esteemed editorial predecessor stated, to "advance agendas [that] authors try to pass off as scholarship." That said, traditional ideas and arguments concerning dominant historical precepts can change and not be agenda-driven, as long as the discipline itself is respected.

However, research continually challenges previously held notions about such topics as women's education, activism via literature, and the national holiday of Thanksgiving. New interpretation of the founding fathers' intent toward states rights versus federal rights continues to emerge in scholarly debate. Innovative arguments consider whether the founding fathers purposely left the issue of education up to individual states. Not all history is found in documents, photos, or oral testimony. Artifacts can describe a generation of people whose cultural ways and practices are lost. These artifacts are especially important when precious little else about a group actually survives. Some histories of the past have also categorized groups as "others", justifying actions committed against them.

This is especially true with Native Americans, who were typically defined as the enemy of the white people of the colonies and then of the newly forming United States. Moreover, as such, Native Americans were often subjected to violence, repression, removal, and, some argue, genocide. Increasingly, scholars take on the very challenging role of defining the past using research, supposition, and past reference materials, while also striving for fairness and objectivity. Yet, striving for this very objectivity can sometimes prove problematic, especially when much of history is based on interpretation of primary evidence, but the interpreter purports that these conclusions are backed up with facts or evidence. We should never interject the present on the past. That said, this edition strives for fairness, balance, and inclusiveness while ensuring that "popular" history does not replace the traditional.

Every revision of *Annual Editions: United States History, Volume I* replaces several of the previous articles with updated or new scholarship. We understand fully that several readers will feel we should have added this or deleted that; this is where your feedback is very helpful to plan the next edition. We try to continually update and improve the quality of the text with every edition. We would especially like to consider alternatives that might not have been included. If you find an article that you think merits inclusion in the next edition, please send it to us (or at least send us the citation, so that the editor can track it down for consideration). We welcome your comments about the readings in this volume. Please feel free to contact us and let us know what you felt were strengths and what were the weaknesses of this particular edition. Your suggestions will be carefully considered and very much appreciated.

Annual Editions: United States History, Volume I is designed for non-specialized survey courses. We have attempted to present a balanced series of articles that reveal the use of newer approaches to the study of history as well as including ones that are more traditional in analysis and scope. Sources consulted for these essays, for the most part, are intended for the general reader: they require no particular expertise to understand them and were chosen to be approachable by a general audience.

This volume contains enhanced pedagogy with a number of features designed to aid students, researchers, and professionals. These include a *Topic Guide* for locating articles on specific subjects; the *table of contents abstracts* that summarize each essay; **Learning Outcomes** at the beginning of each article; and **Critical Thinking** questions and **Internet References** at the end of each article. Articles are organized into four units, each preceded by an overview that provides a background for informed reading of the articles and emphasizes critical issues.

Wendy A. Maier-Sarti
Editor

Editor

Wendy A. Maier-Sarti
Oakton Community College

Wendy A. Maier-Sarti is a professor of history at Oakton Community College. Her work has focused on chronicling the role of women during the Holocaust, with a focus on women's history (imaging of women; female perpetrators of genocide; women and work; women and war). Her book, published in paperback in 2012 by Academica Press, is titled *Women and Nazis: Perpetrators of Genocide and Other Crimes During Hitler's Regime, 1933–1945*. She is also the academic editor for *Annual Editions: United States History, Volume 1 and Volume 2*, published by McGraw Hill.

Maier-Sarti has published over three dozen essays, reference and encyclopedic entries, articles, and book reviews on topics including the Holocaust, Adolf Hitler, Eleanor Roosevelt, Hermann Göring, Harry Truman, Arthur Miller, HRH Edward, Duke of Windsor, Hollywood and World War Two, Betty Grable, and others. In addition to teaching surveys on U.S. History, Western Civilization, and Women's History, she is responsible for developing and teaching several new courses, including History of Genocide, History of the Holocaust; History of Nazi Germany and Women in Non-Western Civilization.

Academic Advisory Board

Correlation Guide

The *Annual Editions* series provides students with convenient, inexpensive access to current, carefully selected articles from the public press. **Annual Editions: United States History, Volume 1: Colonial through Reconstruction, 23/e** is an easy-to-use reader that presents articles on important topics such as *America's First Immigrants, the Revolution, the Civil War, Reconstruction,* and many more. For more information on *Annual Editions* and other *McGraw-Hill Contemporary Learning Series* titles, visit www.mcgrawhillcreate.com.

This convenient guide matches the units in **Annual Editions: United States History, Volume 1, 23/e** with the corresponding chapters in three of our best-selling McGraw-Hill History textbooks by Davidson et al., Davidson et al., and Brinkley.

Annual Editions: United States History, Volume 1, 23/e	United States: A Narrative History, Volume 1: To 1877, 6/e by Davidson et al.	Experience History, Volume 1: To 1877, 8/e by Davidson et al.	American History: Connecting with the Past, Volume 1, 14/e by Brinkley
America's First Immigrants	**Chapter 1:** The First Civilizations of North America **Chapter 2:** Old Worlds, New Worlds (1400–1600) **Chapter 3:** Colonization and Conflict in the South (1600–1750) **Chapter 4:** Colonization and Conflict in the North (1600–1700) **Chapter 5:** The Mosaic of Eighteenth-Century America (1689–1771)	**Chapter 1:** The First Civilizations of North America **Chapter 2:** Old Worlds, New Worlds, 1400–1600 **Chapter 3:** Colonization and Conflict in the South, 1600–1750 **Chapter 4:** Colonization and Conflict in the North, 1600–1700 **Chapter 5:** The Mosaic of Eighteenth-Century America, 1689–1768	**Chapter 1:** The Collision of Cultures **Chapter 2:** Transplantations and Borderlands **Chapter 3:** Society and Culture in Provincial America **Chapter 4:** The Empire in Transition
1491	**Chapter 1:** The First Civilizations of North America **Chapter 2:** Old Worlds, New Worlds (1400–1600) **Chapter 3:** Colonization and Conflict in the South (1600–1750) **Chapter 4:** Colonization and Conflict in the North (1600–1700) **Chapter 5:** The Mosaic of Eighteenth-Century America (1689–1771)	**Chapter 1:** The First Civilizations of North America **Chapter 2:** Old Worlds, New Worlds, 1400–1600 **Chapter 3:** Colonization and Conflict in the South, 1600–1750 **Chapter 4:** Colonization and Conflict in the North, 1600–1700 **Chapter 5:** The Mosaic of Eighteenth-Century America, 1689–1768	**Chapter 1:** The Collision of Cultures **Chapter 2:** Transplantations and Borderlands **Chapter 3:** Society and Culture in Provincial America **Chapter 4:** The Empire in Transition
Massacre in Florida	**Chapter 1:** The First Civilizations of North America **Chapter 2:** Old Worlds, New Worlds (1400–1600) **Chapter 3:** Colonization and Conflict in the South (1600–1750) **Chapter 4:** Colonization and Conflict in the North (1600–1700) **Chapter 5:** The Mosaic of Eighteenth-Century America (1689–1771)	**Chapter 1:** The First Civilizations of North America **Chapter 2:** Old Worlds, New Worlds, 1400–1600 **Chapter 3:** Colonization and Conflict in the South, 1600–1750 **Chapter 4:** Colonization and Conflict in the North, 1600–1700 **Chapter 5:** The Mosaic of Eighteenth-Century America, 1689–1768	**Chapter 1:** The Collision of Cultures **Chapter 2:** Transplantations and Borderlands **Chapter 3:** Society and Culture in Provincial America **Chapter 4:** The Empire in Transition
Representing the Portrayal of Pilgrims in Elementary History Textbooks and the Myth of the Founding of the American Nation	**Chapter 1:** The First Civilizations of North America **Chapter 2:** Old Worlds, New Worlds (1400–1600) **Chapter 3:** Colonization and Conflict in the South (1600–1750) **Chapter 4:** Colonization and Conflict in the North (1600–1700) **Chapter 5:** The Mosaic of Eighteenth-Century America (1689–1771)	**Chapter 1:** The First Civilizations of North America **Chapter 2:** Old Worlds, New Worlds, 1400–1600 **Chapter 3:** Colonization and Conflict in the South, 1600–1750 **Chapter 4:** Colonization and Conflict in the North, 1600–1700 **Chapter 5:** The Mosaic of Eighteenth-Century America, 1689–1768	**Chapter 1:** The Collision of Cultures **Chapter 2:** Transplantations and Borderlands **Chapter 3:** Society and Culture in Provincial America **Chapter 4:** The Empire in Transition
A Pox on the New World	**Chapter 1:** The First Civilizations of North America **Chapter 2:** Old Worlds, New Worlds (1400–1600) **Chapter 3:** Colonization and Conflict in the South (1600–1750) **Chapter 4:** Colonization and Conflict in the North (1600–1700) **Chapter 5:** The Mosaic of Eighteenth-Century America (1689–1771)	**Chapter 1:** The First Civilizations of North America **Chapter 2:** Old Worlds, New Worlds, 1400–1600 **Chapter 3:** Colonization and Conflict in the South, 1600–1750 **Chapter 4:** Colonization and Conflict in the North, 1600–1700 **Chapter 5:** The Mosaic of Eighteenth-Century America, 1689–1768	**Chapter 1:** The Collision of Cultures **Chapter 2:** Transplantations and Borderlands **Chapter 3:** Society and Culture in Provincial America **Chapter 4:** The Empire in Transition

(contir

Indentured Servants and the Pursuits of Happiness	**Chapter 1:** The First Civilizations of North America **Chapter 2:** Old Worlds, New Worlds (1400–1600) **Chapter 3:** Colonization and Conflict in the South (1600–1750) **Chapter 4:** Colonization and Conflict in the North (1600–1700) **Chapter 5:** The Mosaic of Eighteenth-Century America (1689–1771)	**Chapter 1:** The First Civilizations of North America **Chapter 2:** Old Worlds, New Worlds, 1400–1600 **Chapter 3:** Colonization and Conflict in the South, 1600–1750 **Chapter 4:** Colonization and Conflict in the North, 1600–1700 **Chapter 5:** The Mosaic of Eighteenth-Century America, 1689–1768	**Chapter 1:** The Collision of Cultures **Chapter 2:** Transplantations and Borderlands **Chapter 3:** Society and Culture in Provincial America **Chapter 4:** The Empire in Transition
New Amsterdam Becomes New York	**Chapter 1:** The First Civilizations of North America **Chapter 2:** Old Worlds, New Worlds (1400–1600) **Chapter 3:** Colonization and Conflict in the South (1600–1750) **Chapter 4:** Colonization and Conflict in the North (1600–1700) **Chapter 5:** The Mosaic of Eighteenth-Century America (1689–1771)	**Chapter 1:** The First Civilizations of North America **Chapter 2:** Old Worlds, New Worlds, 1400–1600 **Chapter 3:** Colonization and Conflict in the South, 1600–1750 **Chapter 4:** Colonization and Conflict in the North, 1600–1700 **Chapter 5:** The Mosaic of Eighteenth-Century America, 1689–1768	**Chapter 1:** The Collision of Cultures **Chapter 2:** Transplantations and Borderlands **Chapter 3:** Society and Culture in Provincial America **Chapter 4:** The Empire in Transition
Taken by Indians	**Chapter 1:** The First Civilizations of North America **Chapter 2:** Old Worlds, New Worlds (1400–1600) **Chapter 3:** Colonization and Conflict in the South (1600–1750) **Chapter 4:** Colonization and Conflict in the North (1600–1700) **Chapter 5:** The Mosaic of Eighteenth-Century America (1689–1771)	**Chapter 1:** The First Civilizations of North America **Chapter 2:** Old Worlds, New Worlds, 1400–1600 **Chapter 3:** Colonization and Conflict in the South, 1600–1750 **Chapter 4:** Colonization and Conflict in the North, 1600–1700 **Chapter 5:** The Mosaic of Eighteenth-Century America, 1689–1768	**Chapter 1:** The Collision of Cultures **Chapter 2:** Transplantations and Borderlands **Chapter 3:** Society and Culture in Provincial America **Chapter 4:** The Empire in Transition
Blessed and Bedeviled	**Chapter 1:** The First Civilizations of North America **Chapter 2:** Old Worlds, New Worlds (1400–1600) **Chapter 3:** Colonization and Conflict in the South (1600–1750) **Chapter 4:** Colonization and Conflict in the North (1600–1700) **Chapter 5:** The Mosaic of Eighteenth-Century America (1689–1771)	**Chapter 1:** The First Civilizations of North America **Chapter 2:** Old Worlds, New Worlds, 1400–1600 **Chapter 3:** Colonization and Conflict in the South, 1600–1750 **Chapter 4:** Colonization and Conflict in the North, 1600–1700 **Chapter 5:** The Mosaic of Eighteenth-Century America, 1689–1768	**Chapter 1:** The Collision of Cultures **Chapter 2:** Transplantations and Borderlands **Chapter 3:** Society and Culture in Provincial America **Chapter 4:** The Empire in Transition
Pontiac's War	**Chapter 1:** The First Civilizations of North America **Chapter 2:** Old Worlds, New Worlds (1400–1600) **Chapter 3:** Colonization and Conflict in the South (1600–1750) **Chapter 4:** Colonization and Conflict in the North (1600–1700) **Chapter 5:** The Mosaic of Eighteenth-Century America (1689–1771)	**Chapter 1:** The First Civilizations of North America **Chapter 2:** Old Worlds, New Worlds, 1400–1600 **Chapter 3:** Colonization and Conflict in the South, 1600–1750 **Chapter 4:** Colonization and Conflict in the North, 1600–1700 **Chapter 5:** The Mosaic of Eighteenth-Century America, 1689–1768	**Chapter 1:** The Collision of Cultures **Chapter 2:** Transplantations and Borderlands **Chapter 3:** Society and Culture in Provincial America **Chapter 4:** The Empire in Transition
"The Sparck of Rebellion"	**Chapter 6:** Toward the War for American Independence (1754–1776) **Chapter 7:** The American People and the American Revolution (1775–1783) **Chapter 8:** Crisis and Constitution (1776–1789)	**Chapter 6:** Toward the War for American Independence, 1754–1776 **Chapter 7:** The American People: The American Revolution, 1775–1783 **Chapter 8:** Crisis and Constitution, 1776–1789	**Chapter 5:** The American Revolution **Chapter 6:** The Constitution and the New Republic **Chapter 7:** The Jeffersonian Era
The Gain from Thomas Paine	**Chapter 6:** Toward the War for American Independence (1754–1776) **Chapter 7:** The American People and the American Revolution (1775–1783) **Chapter 8:** Crisis and Constitution (1776–1789)	**Chapter 6:** Toward the War for American Independence, 1754–1776 **Chapter 7:** The American People: The American Revolution, 1775–1783 **Chapter 8:** Crisis and Constitution, 1776–1789	**Chapter 5:** The American Revolution **Chapter 6:** The Constitution and the New Republic **Chapter 7:** The Jeffersonian Era

(continued)

One Revolution Two Wars	**Chapter 6:** Toward the War for American Independence (1754–1776) **Chapter 7:** The American People and the American Revolution (1775–1783) **Chapter 8:** Crisis and Constitution (1776–1789)	**Chapter 6:** Toward the War for American Independence, 1754–1776 **Chapter 7:** The American People: The American Revolution, 1775–1783 **Chapter 8:** Crisis and Constitution, 1776–1789	**Chapter 5:** The American Revolution **Chapter 6:** The Constitution and the New Republic **Chapter 7:** The Jeffersonian Era
Equality and Schooling: Laggards, Percentiles and the U.S. Constitution	**Chapter 6:** Toward the War for American Independence (1754–1776) **Chapter 7:** The American People and the American Revolution (1775–1783) **Chapter 8:** Crisis and Constitution (1776–1789)	**Chapter 6:** Toward the War for American Independence, 1754–1776 **Chapter 7:** The American People: The American Revolution, 1775–1783 **Chapter 8:** Crisis and Constitution, 1776–1789	**Chapter 5:** The American Revolution **Chapter 6:** The Constitution and the New Republic **Chapter 7:** The Jeffersonian Era
A Day to Remember: July 4, 1776	**Chapter 6:** Toward the War for American Independence (1754–1776) **Chapter 7:** The American People and the American Revolution (1775–1783) **Chapter 8:** Crisis and Constitution (1776–1789)	**Chapter 6:** Toward the War for American Independence, 1754–1776 **Chapter 7:** The American People: The American Revolution, 1775–1783 **Chapter 8:** Crisis and Constitution, 1776–1789	**Chapter 5:** The American Revolution **Chapter 6:** The Constitution and the New Republic **Chapter 7:** The Jeffersonian Era
Building a Nation from Thirteen States: The Constitutional Convention and Preemption	**Chapter 6:** Toward the War for American Independence (1754–1776) **Chapter 7:** The American People and the American Revolution (1775–1783) **Chapter 8:** Crisis and Constitution (1776–1789)	**Chapter 6:** Toward the War for American Independence, 1754–1776 **Chapter 7:** The American People: The American Revolution, 1775–1783 **Chapter 8:** Crisis and Constitution, 1776–1789	**Chapter 5:** The American Revolution **Chapter 6:** The Constitution and the New Republic **Chapter 7:** The Jeffersonian Era
America's Worst Winter Ever: And Why Mythmakers Chose to Forget It	**Chapter 6:** Toward the War for American Independence (1754–1776) **Chapter 7:** The American People and the American Revolution (1775–1783) **Chapter 8:** Crisis and Constitution (1776–1789)	**Chapter 6:** Toward the War for American Independence, 1754–1776 **Chapter 7:** The American People: The American Revolution, 1775–1783 **Chapter 8:** Crisis and Constitution, 1776–1789	**Chapter 5:** The American Revolution **Chapter 6:** The Constitution and the New Republic **Chapter 7:** The Jeffersonian Era
Franklin Saves the Peace	**Chapter 6:** Toward the War for American Independence (1754–1776) **Chapter 7:** The American People and the American Revolution (1775–1783) **Chapter 8:** Crisis and Constitution (1776–1789)	**Chapter 6:** Toward the War for American Independence, 1754–1776 **Chapter 7:** The American People: The American Revolution, 1775–1783 **Chapter 8:** Crisis and Constitution, 1776–1789	**Chapter 5:** The American Revolution **Chapter 6:** The Constitution and the New Republic **Chapter 7:** The Jeffersonian Era
Madison's Radical Agenda	**Chapter 9:** The Early Republic (1789–1824) **Chapter 10:** The Opening of America (1815–1850) **Chapter 11:** The Rise of Democracy (1824–1840) **Chapter 12:** The Fires of Perfection (1820–1850) **Chapter 13:** The Old South (1820–1860) **Chapter 14:** Western Expansion and the Rise of the Slavery Issue (1820–1850)	**Chapter 9:** The Early Republic, 1789–1824 **Chapter 10:** The Opening of America, 1815–1850 **Chapter 11:** The Rise of Democracy, 1824–1840 **Chapter 12:** The Fires of Perfection, 1820–1850 **Chapter 13:** The Old South, 1820–1850 **Chapter 14:** Western Expansion and the Rise of the Slavery Issue, 1820–1850	**Chapter 8:** Varieties of American Nationalism **Chapter 9:** Jacksonian America **Chapter 10:** America's Economic Revolution **Chapter 11:** Cotton, Slavery, and the Old South **Chapter 12:** Antebellum Culture and Reform **Chapter 13:** The Impending Crisis
Wall Street's First Collapse	**Chapter 9:** The Early Republic (1789–1824) **Chapter 10:** The Opening of America (1815–1850) **Chapter 11:** The Rise of Democracy (1824–1840) **Chapter 12:** The Fires of Perfection (1820–1850) **Chapter 13:** The Old South (1820–1860) **Chapter 14:** Western Expansion and the Rise of the Slavery Issue (1820–1850)	**Chapter 9:** The Early Republic, 1789–1824 **Chapter 10:** The Opening of America, 1815–1850 **Chapter 11:** The Rise of Democracy, 1824–1840 **Chapter 12:** The Fires of Perfection, 1820–1850 **Chapter 13:** The Old South, 1820–1850 **Chapter 14:** Western Expansion and the Rise of the Slavery Issue, 1820–1850	**Chapter 8:** Varieties of American Nationalism **Chapter 9:** Jacksonian America **Chapter 10:** America's Economic Revolution **Chapter 11:** Cotton, Slavery, and the Old South **Chapter 12:** Antebellum Culture and Reform **Chapter 13:** The Impending Crisis
Adams Appoints Marshall	**Chapter 9:** The Early Republic (1789–1824) **Chapter 10:** The Opening of America (1815–1850) **Chapter 11:** The Rise of Democracy (1824–1840) **Chapter 12:** The Fires of Perfection (1820–1850) **Chapter 13:** The Old South (1820–1860) **Chapter 14:** Western Expansion and the Rise of the Slavery Issue (1820–1850)	**Chapter 9:** The Early Republic, 1789–1824 **Chapter 10:** The Opening of America, 1815–1850 **Chapter 11:** The Rise of Democracy, 1824–1840 **Chapter 12:** The Fires of Perfection, 1820–1850 **Chapter 13:** The Old South, 1820–1850 **Chapter 14:** Western Expansion and the Rise of the Slavery Issue, 1820–1850	**Chapter 8:** Varieties of American Nationalism **Chapter 9:** Jacksonian America **Chapter 10:** America's Economic Revolution **Chapter 11:** Cotton, Slavery, and the Old South **Chapter 12:** Antebellum Culture and Reform **Chapter 13:** The Impending Crisis

(continued)

The Revolution of 1803	**Chapter 9:** The Early Republic (1789–1824) **Chapter 10:** The Opening of America (1815–1850) **Chapter 11:** The Rise of Democracy (1824–1840) **Chapter 12:** The Fires of Perfection (1820–1850) **Chapter 13:** The Old South (1820–1860) **Chapter 14:** Western Expansion and the Rise of the Slavery Issue (1820–1850)	**Chapter 9:** The Early Republic, 1789–1824 **Chapter 10:** The Opening of America, 1815–1850 **Chapter 11:** The Rise of Democracy, 1824–1840 **Chapter 12:** The Fires of Perfection, 1820–1850 **Chapter 13:** The Old South, 1820–1850 **Chapter 14:** Western Expansion and the Rise of the Slavery Issue, 1820–1850	**Chapter 8:** Varieties of American Nationalism **Chapter 9:** Jacksonian America **Chapter 10:** America's Economic Revolution **Chapter 11:** Cotton, Slavery, and the Old South **Chapter 12:** Antebellum Culture and Reform **Chapter 13:** The Impending Crisis
Dolley Madison Saves the Day	**Chapter 9:** The Early Republic (1789–1824) **Chapter 10:** The Opening of America (1815–1850) **Chapter 11:** The Rise of Democracy (1824–1840) **Chapter 12:** The Fires of Perfection (1820–1850) **Chapter 13:** The Old South (1820–1860) **Chapter 14:** Western Expansion and the Rise of the Slavery Issue (1820–1850)	**Chapter 9:** The Early Republic, 1789–1824 **Chapter 10:** The Opening of America, 1815–1850 **Chapter 11:** The Rise of Democracy, 1824–1840 **Chapter 12:** The Fires of Perfection, 1820–1850 **Chapter 13:** The Old South, 1820–1850 **Chapter 14:** Western Expansion and the Rise of the Slavery Issue, 1820–1850	**Chapter 8:** Varieties of American Nationalism **Chapter 9:** Jacksonian America **Chapter 10:** America's Economic Revolution **Chapter 11:** Cotton, Slavery, and the Old South **Chapter 12:** Antebellum Culture and Reform **Chapter 13:** The Impending Crisis
Abigail Adams' Last Act of Defiance	**Chapter 9:** The Early Republic (1789–1824) **Chapter 10:** The Opening of America (1815–1850) **Chapter 11:** The Rise of Democracy (1824–1840) **Chapter 12:** The Fires of Perfection (1820–1850) **Chapter 13:** The Old South (1820–1860) **Chapter 14:** Western Expansion and the Rise of the Slavery Issue (1820–1850)	**Chapter 9:** The Early Republic, 1789–1824 **Chapter 10:** The Opening of America, 1815–1850 **Chapter 11:** The Rise of Democracy, 1824–1840 **Chapter 12:** The Fires of Perfection, 1820–1850 **Chapter 13:** The Old South, 1820–1850 **Chapter 14:** Western Expansion and the Rise of the Slavery Issue, 1820–1850	**Chapter 8:** Varieties of American Nationalism **Chapter 9:** Jacksonian America **Chapter 10:** America's Economic Revolution **Chapter 11:** Cotton, Slavery, and the Old South **Chapter 12:** Antebellum Culture and Reform **Chapter 13:** The Impending Crisis
Fashioning Slavery: Slaves and Clothing in the United States South, 1830–1865	**Chapter 9:** The Early Republic (1789–1824) **Chapter 10:** The Opening of America (1815–1850) **Chapter 11:** The Rise of Democracy (1824–1840) **Chapter 12:** The Fires of Perfection (1820–1850) **Chapter 13:** The Old South (1820–1860) **Chapter 14:** Western Expansion and the Rise of the Slavery Issue (1820–1850)	**Chapter 9:** The Early Republic, 1789–1824 **Chapter 10:** The Opening of America, 1815–1850 **Chapter 11:** The Rise of Democracy, 1824–1840 **Chapter 12:** The Fires of Perfection, 1820–1850 **Chapter 13:** The Old South, 1820–1850 **Chapter 14:** Western Expansion and the Rise of the Slavery Issue, 1820–1850	**Chapter 8:** Varieties of American Nationalism **Chapter 9:** Jacksonian America **Chapter 10:** America's Economic Revolution **Chapter 11:** Cotton, Slavery, and the Old South **Chapter 12:** Antebellum Culture and Reform **Chapter 13:** The Impending Crisis
Circumcision of the Female Intellect: 19th Century Women Who Opposed Scholarly Education	**Chapter 9:** The Early Republic (1789–1824) **Chapter 10:** The Opening of America (1815–1850) **Chapter 11:** The Rise of Democracy (1824–1840) **Chapter 12:** The Fires of Perfection (1820–1850) **Chapter 13:** The Old South (1820–1860) **Chapter 14:** Western Expansion and the Rise of the Slavery Issue (1820–1850)	**Chapter 9:** The Early Republic, 1789–1824 **Chapter 10:** The Opening of America, 1815–1850 **Chapter 11:** The Rise of Democracy, 1824–1840 **Chapter 12:** The Fires of Perfection, 1820–1850 **Chapter 13:** The Old South, 1820–1850 **Chapter 14:** Western Expansion and the Rise of the Slavery Issue, 1820–1850	**Chapter 8:** Varieties of American Nationalism **Chapter 9:** Jacksonian America **Chapter 10:** America's Economic Revolution **Chapter 11:** Cotton, Slavery, and the Old South **Chapter 12:** Antebellum Culture and Reform **Chapter 13:** The Impending Crisis
Education and Access to Christian Thought in the Writing of Harriet Beecher Stowe and Anna Julia Cooper	**Chapter 9:** The Early Republic (1789–1824) **Chapter 10:** The Opening of America (1815–1850) **Chapter 11:** The Rise of Democracy (1824–1840) **Chapter 12:** The Fires of Perfection (1820–1850) **Chapter 13:** The Old South (1820–1860) **Chapter 14:** Western Expansion and the Rise of the Slavery Issue (1820–1850)	**Chapter 9:** The Early Republic, 1789–1824 **Chapter 10:** The Opening of America, 1815–1850 **Chapter 11:** The Rise of Democracy, 1824–1840 **Chapter 12:** The Fires of Perfection, 1820–1850 **Chapter 13:** The Old South, 1820–1850 **Chapter 14:** Western Expansion and the Rise of the Slavery Issue, 1820–1850	**Chapter 8:** Varieties of American Nationalism **Chapter 9:** Jacksonian America **Chapter 10:** America's Economic Revolution **Chapter 11:** Cotton, Slavery, and the Old South **Chapter 12:** Antebellum Culture and Reform **Chapter 13:** The Impending Crisis

(continued)

The Holdouts	**Chapter 9:** The Early Republic (1789–1824) **Chapter 10:** The Opening of America (1815–1850) **Chapter 11:** The Rise of Democracy (1824–1840) **Chapter 12:** The Fires of Perfection (1820–1850) **Chapter 13:** The Old South (1820–1860) **Chapter 14:** Western Expansion and the Rise of the Slavery Issue (1820–1850)	**Chapter 9:** The Early Republic, 1789–1824 **Chapter 10:** The Opening of America, 1815–1850 **Chapter 11:** The Rise of Democracy, 1824–1840 **Chapter 12:** The Fires of Perfection, 1820–1850 **Chapter 13:** The Old South, 1820–1850 **Chapter 14:** Western Expansion and the Rise of the Slavery Issue, 1820–1850	**Chapter 8:** Varieties of American Nationalism **Chapter 9:** Jacksonian America **Chapter 10:** America's Economic Revolution **Chapter 11:** Cotton, Slavery, and the Old South **Chapter 12:** Antebellum Culture and Reform **Chapter 13:** The Impending Crisis
A Unique Northern Plains Ceramic Vessel in the Museum's Lewis and Clark Collection	**Chapter 9:** The Early Republic (1789–1824) **Chapter 10:** The Opening of America (1815–1850) **Chapter 11:** The Rise of Democracy (1824–1840) **Chapter 12:** The Fires of Perfection (1820–1850) **Chapter 13:** The Old South (1820–1860) **Chapter 14:** Western Expansion and the Rise of the Slavery Issue (1820–1850)	**Chapter 9:** The Early Republic, 1789–1824 **Chapter 10:** The Opening of America, 1815–1850 **Chapter 11:** The Rise of Democracy, 1824–1840 **Chapter 12:** The Fires of Perfection, 1820–1850 **Chapter 13:** The Old South, 1820–1850 **Chapter 14:** Western Expansion and the Rise of the Slavery Issue, 1820–1850	**Chapter 8:** Varieties of American Nationalism **Chapter 9:** Jacksonian America **Chapter 10:** America's Economic Revolution **Chapter 11:** Cotton, Slavery, and the Old South **Chapter 12:** Antebellum Culture and Reform **Chapter 13:** The Impending Crisis
Deadweight Loss and the American Civil War: The Political Economy of Slavery, Secession, and Emancipation	**Chapter 15:** The Union Broken (1850–1861) **Chapter 16 :** Total War and the Republic (1861–1865) **Chapter 17:** Reconstructing the Union (1865–1877)	**Chapter 15:** The Union Broken, 1850–1861 **Chapter 16 :** Total War and the Republic, 1861–1865 **Chapter 17:** Reconstructing the Union, 1865–1877	**Chapter 14:** The Civil War **Chapter 15:** Reconstruction and the New South
What the Founders *Really* Thought About Race	**Chapter 15:** The Union Broken (1850–1861) **Chapter 16 :** Total War and the Republic (1861–1865) **Chapter 17:** Reconstructing the Union (1865–1877)	**Chapter 15:** The Union Broken, 1850–1861 **Chapter 16 :** Total War and the Republic, 1861–1865 **Chapter 17:** Reconstructing the Union, 1865–1877	**Chapter 14:** The Civil War **Chapter 15:** Reconstruction and the New South
John Brown's Raid on Harpers Ferry	**Chapter 15:** The Union Broken (1850–1861) **Chapter 16 :** Total War and the Republic (1861–1865) **Chapter 17:** Reconstructing the Union (1865–1877)	**Chapter 15:** The Union Broken, 1850–1861 **Chapter 16 :** Total War and the Republic, 1861–1865 **Chapter 17:** Reconstructing the Union, 1865–1877	**Chapter 14:** The Civil War **Chapter 15:** Reconstruction and the New South
Free at Last	**Chapter 15:** The Union Broken (1850–1861) **Chapter 16 :** Total War and the Republic (1861–1865) **Chapter 17:** Reconstructing the Union (1865–1877)	**Chapter 15:** The Union Broken, 1850–1861 **Chapter 16 :** Total War and the Republic, 1861–1865 **Chapter 17:** Reconstructing the Union, 1865–1877	**Chapter 14:** The Civil War **Chapter 15:** Reconstruction and the New South
There Goes the South	**Chapter 15:** The Union Broken (1850–1861) **Chapter 16 :** Total War and the Republic (1861–1865) **Chapter 17:** Reconstructing the Union (1865–1877)	**Chapter 15:** The Union Broken, 1850–1861 **Chapter 16 :** Total War and the Republic, 1861–1865 **Chapter 17:** Reconstructing the Union, 1865–1877	**Chapter 14:** The Civil War **Chapter 15:** Reconstruction and the New South
Lincoln and the Constitutional Dilemma of Emancipation	**Chapter 15:** The Union Broken (1850–1861) **Chapter 16 :** Total War and the Republic (1861–1865) **Chapter 17:** Reconstructing the Union (1865–1877)	**Chapter 15:** The Union Broken, 1850–1861 **Chapter 16 :** Total War and the Republic, 1861–1865 **Chapter 17:** Reconstructing the Union, 1865–1877	**Chapter 14:** The Civil War **Chapter 15:** Reconstruction and the New South
Why Was the Confederacy Defeated?	**Chapter 15:** The Union Broken (1850–1861) **Chapter 16 :** Total War and the Republic (1861–1865) **Chapter 17:** Reconstructing the Union (1865–1877)	**Chapter 15:** The Union Broken, 1850–1861 **Chapter 16 :** Total War and the Republic, 1861–1865 **Chapter 17:** Reconstructing the Union, 1865–1877	**Chapter 14:** The Civil War **Chapter 15:** Reconstruction and the New South
Steven Hahn Sings the Slaves Triumphant	**Chapter 15:** The Union Broken (1850–1861) **Chapter 16 :** Total War and the Republic (1861–1865) **Chapter 17:** Reconstructing the Union (1865–1877)	**Chapter 15:** The Union Broken, 1850–1861 **Chapter 16 :** Total War and the Republic, 1861–1865 **Chapter 17:** Reconstructing the Union, 1865–1877	**Chapter 14:** The Civil War **Chapter 15:** Reconstruction and the New South
A Slave's Audacious Bid for Freedom	**Chapter 15:** The Union Broken (1850–1861) **Chapter 16 :** Total War and the Republic (1861–1865) **Chapter 17:** Reconstructing the Union (1865–1877)	**Chapter 15:** The Union Broken, 1850–1861 **Chapter 16 :** Total War and the Republic, 1861–1865 **Chapter 17:** Reconstructing the Union, 1865–1877	**Chapter 14:** The Civil War **Chapter 15:** Reconstruction and the New South

(concluded)

A Graceful Exit	**Chapter 15:** The Union Broken (1850–1861) **Chapter 16 :** Total War and the Republic (1861–1865) **Chapter 17:** Reconstructing the Union (1865–1877)	**Chapter 15:** The Union Broken, 1850–1861 **Chapter 16 :** Total War and the Republic, 1861–1865 **Chapter 17:** Reconstructing the Union, 1865–1877	**Chapter 14:** The Civil War **Chapter 15:** Reconstruction and the New South
How the West Was Lost	**Chapter 15:** The Union Broken (1850–1861) **Chapter 16 :** Total War and the Republic (1861–1865) **Chapter 17:** Reconstructing the Union (1865–1877)	**Chapter 15:** The Union Broken, 1850–1861 **Chapter 16 :** Total War and the Republic, 1861–1865 **Chapter 17:** Reconstructing the Union, 1865–1877	**Chapter 14:** The Civil War **Chapter 15:** Reconstruction and the New South
'It Was We, the People; Not We, the White Males'	**Chapter 15:** The Union Broken (1850–1861) **Chapter 16 :** Total War and the Republic (1861–1865) **Chapter 17:** Reconstructing the Union (1865–1877)	**Chapter 15:** The Union Broken, 1850–1861 **Chapter 16 :** Total War and the Republic, 1861–1865 **Chapter 17:** Reconstructing the Union, 1865–1877	**Chapter 14:** The Civil War **Chapter 15:** Reconstruction and the New South
Foul Lines: Teaching Race in Jim Crow America through Baseball History	**Chapter 15:** The Union Broken (1850–1861) **Chapter 16 :** Total War and the Republic (1861–1865) **Chapter 17:** Reconstructing the Union (1865–1877)	**Chapter 15:** The Union Broken, 1850–1861 **Chapter 16 :** Total War and the Republic, 1861–1865 **Chapter 17:** Reconstructing the Union, 1865–1877	**Chapter 14:** The Civil War **Chapter 15:** Reconstruction and the New South

Topic Guide

This topic guide suggests how the selections in this book relate to the subjects covered in your course. You may want to use the topics listed on these pages to search the Web more easily.

All the articles that relate to each topic are listed below the bold-faced term.

Adams, Abigail
Abigail Adams' Last Act of Defiance

Adams, John
Adams Appoints Marshall

African Americans
John Brown's Raid on Harpers Ferry
Free at Last
Lincoln and the Constitutional Dilemma of Emancipation

American Revolution
America's Worst Winter Ever: And Why Mythmakers Chose to Forget It
Building a Nation from Thirteen States: The Constitutional Convention and Preemption
Franklin Saves the Peace
The Gain from Thomas Paine
"The Sparck of Rebellion"
One Revolution Two Wars

Anthony, Susan B.
'It Was We, the People; Not We, the White Males'

Boston Tea Party
"The Sparck of Rebellion"

Brown, John
John Brown's Raid on Harpers Ferry

Business
Wall Street's First Collapse

Civil War
A Graceful Exit
Deadweight Loss and the American Civil War: The Political Economy of Slavery, Secession, and Emancipation
Lincoln and the Constitutional Dilemma of Emancipation
Why Was the Confederacy Defeated?

Colonial America
Blessed and Bedeviled
Indentured Servants and the Pursuits of Happiness
Massacre in Florida
New Amsterdam Becomes New York
Pontiac's War
A Pox on the New World
Representing the Portrayal of Pilgrims in Elementary History Textbooks and the Myth of the Founding of the American Nation
Taken by Indians

Constitution
Adams Appoints Marshall
Building a Nation from Thirteen States: The Constitutional Convention and Preemption
Equality and Schooling: Laggards, Percentiles and the U.S. Constitution
Madison's Radical Agenda

Culture
America's First Immigrants
Blessed and Bedeviled
1491
Indentured Servants and the Pursuits of Happiness
Representing the Portrayal of Pilgrims in Elementary History Textbooks and the Myth of the Founding of the American Nation

Declaration of Independence
A Day to Remember: July 4, 1776

Education
Circumcision of the Female Intellect: 19th Century Women Who Opposed Scholarly Education
Equality and Schooling: Laggards, Percentiles and the U.S. Constitution

Emancipation Proclamation
Lincoln and the Constitutional Dilemma of Emancipation
There Goes the South
A Slave's Audacious Bid for Freedom
Steven Hahn Sings the Slaves Triumphant

Environment
1491

Exploration
America's First Immigrants
1491
Massacre in Florida

Franklin, Benjamin
Franklin Saves the Peace

French Colonists
Massacre in Florida

Government
Adams Appoints Marshall
Building a Nation from Thirteen States: The Constitutional Convention and Preemption
The Holdouts
Lincoln and the Constitutional Dilemma of Emancipation
Madison's Radical Agenda
'It Was We, the People, Not We, the White Males'

Hamilton, Alexander
Wall Street's First Collapse

Jackson, Andrew
The Holdouts

Jefferson, Thomas
The Revolution of 1803
Wall Street's First Collapse

Lee, Robert E.
A Graceful Exit

Unit 1

UNIT

Prepared by: Wendy A. Maier-Sarti, *Oakton Community College*

The New Land

Europeans had been fascinated with the "New World" long before they were able to mount expeditions to actually go there. Artists and writers imagined all sorts of exotic plants and animals, and depicted human inhabitants as ranging from the most brutal savages to races of highly advanced peoples. These latter were reputed to have constructed cities of great splendor, where fabulous treasures of precious metals and jewels lay for the taking. The "age of exploration" had to await the sufficient accumulation of capital to finance expeditions and the advanced technology to make them feasible. Motives were mixed in undertaking such ventures: the desire to explore the unknown, national rivalries, the quest for routes to the Far East, converting the heathens to Christianity, and pure greed were among them. Spain and Portugal led the way, followed by France and England.

The "new world," of course, was new only to Europeans. The inhabitants had lived here for a long time without even knowing (let alone caring) that Europe existed. For decades, the conventional wisdom was that what were, and are still, called "Native Americans," emigrated here from Asia across the Bering land bridge to Alaska. Archaeologists have found settlements dating from at least 1,000 years before this migration is supposed to have occurred, challenging the understanding of when North America was indeed really settled. Estimates are that there were from 80 to 100 million people living in the Western Hemisphere at the time the European explorations began. In the region that became the United States, there were no powerful empires such as those developed by the Aztecs in Mexico or the Incas in Peru. There were, however, fairly sophisticated settlements such as the small town of Cahokia, located near present-day St. Louis, Missouri. European incursions often proved catastrophic for peoples at whatever stage of civilization. Not only did some of the explorers treat indigenous peoples with genocidal brutality, they brought with them a variety of deadly diseases against which natives had no defenses. Therefore, once European contact began, one of the immediate consequences was the impact that communicable diseases had on Native Americans. Successive diseases also swept through European settlements as well as those of the Indians. The expansion of Europe, therefore, came at the expense of millions of unfortunates in the new world.

Developments in history often have an air of inevitability about them. Additionally, matters of chance or actions that have unanticipated consequences play an important role. One such incident that had unanticipated consequences occurred in 1565, when the French and Spanish engaged in conflict. One of the ramifications of this relatively brief military encounter later led to English settlement along the Atlantic coastline. English settlement was not exactly what has been historically portrayed. For example, the early Pilgrims and their alleged interactions with Native Americans have fallen into American historical legend, with the story of these interactions represented in the Thanksgiving holiday. Legend overshadows truisms; such myths often mask the fact that these interactions between native peoples and the English were violent and oppressive. Native populations also sometimes captured or kidnapped white settlers, and few settlers survived. As settlements grew, so did conflicts within differing socioeconomic classes and also along gender lines.

Indentured servitude has seldom been covered in detail, and students of history often leave their classes with preconceived notions of how white servitude was constructed and carried out. Over 100,000 indentured servants came to America, and women were especially marginalized. Their exclusion from the public sphere was not necessarily warranted, but because of their gender, they were often singled out for abuse, sale, or ongoing servitude. Gender conflicts continued and the epitome of this struggle came when the Salem Witch Trials began. The idea that witches existed was commonly held in New England during the seventeenth century, as it was elsewhere. While men were also found "guilty" of witchcraft, the accused were typically marginalized, even if one was a wealthy widow or an innocent man. The staggering number of witchcraft trials reveals a much darker side of early American settlements. Settlers were not the only targets, as native peoples were often seen as subversive and wrongly designated by many colonialists as a collective group; one to control. Native Americans resisted attempts to remove them, sometimes, but not typically, with results in their favor.

When looking at resistance on a mass scale, one must consider what happened when native peoples were murdered or grievously harmed. European actions sometimes touched off wars. Native Americans resisted and resented being under the control of the white colonists. In other instances, when Native Americans were harmed—whether intentionally (war, forced relocation) or unintentionally (legal codes)—they rose up in protest, sometimes resorting to violence to get their point across. Because so many skirmishes broke out, with and without warning, new policies were drawn up to deal with the Native Americans. This was because the British wanted to avoid a protracted conflict, and quite often uneasy alliances began to form. A consequence of treating Native Americans as allies was that many of these same tribes remained loyal to the British when the Americans launched their own rebellion.

Article   Prepared by: Wendy A. Maier-Sarti, *Oakton Community College*

America's First Immigrants

You were probably taught that the hemisphere's first people came from Siberia across a long-gone land bridge. Now a sea route looks increasingly likely, from Asia or even Europe.

Evan Hadingham

Learning Outcomes

After reading this article, you will be able to:

- Describe from where our first inhabitants migrated.

- Explain the evidence that supports the claim that Native Americans resided in North America well before others crossed a now-submerged land bridge from Siberia.

About four miles from the tiny cattle town of Florence, Texas, a narrow dirt road winds across parched limestone, through juniper, prickly pear and stunted oaks, and drops down to a creek. A lush parkland of shade trees offers welcome relief from the 100-degree heat of summer. Running beside the creek for almost half a mile is a swath of chipped, gray stone flakes and soil blackened by cooking fires—thousands of years of cooking fires. This blackened earth, covering 40 acres and almost six feet thick in places, marks a settlement dating back as far as the last ice age 13,000 years ago, when mammoths, giant sloths and saber-toothed cats roamed the North American wilderness.

Since archaeologists began working here systematically seven years ago, they have amassed an astonishing collection of early prehistoric artifacts—nearly half a million so far. Among these are large, stone spearheads skillfully flaked on both sides to give an elegant, leaf-shaped appearance. These projectiles, found by archaeologists throughout North America and as far south as Costa Rica, are known as Clovis points, and their makers, who lived roughly 12,500 to 13,500 years ago, are known as Clovis people, after the town in New Mexico near where the first such point was identified some seven decades ago.

A visit to the Gault site—named after the family who owned the land when the site was first investigated in 1929—along the cottonwood- and walnut-shaded creek in central Texas raises two monumental questions. The first, of course, is, Who were these people? The emerging answer is that they were not simple-minded big-game hunters as they have often been depicted. Rather, they led a less nomadic and more sophisticated life than previously believed.

The second question—Where did they come from?—lies at the center of one of archaeology's most contentious debates. The standard view holds that Clovis people were the first to enter the Americas, migrating from Siberia 13,500 years ago by a now-submerged land bridge across the Bering Strait. This view has been challenged recently by a wide range of discoveries, including an astonishingly well-preserved site in South America predating the supposed migration by at least 1,000 years.

Researchers delving into the origins question have sought to make sense of archaeological finds far and wide, from Canada, California and Chile; from Siberia; and even, most controversially, from France and Spain. The possibility that the first people in the Americas came from Europe is the boldest proposal among a host of new ideas. According to University of Texas at Austin archaeologist Michael Collins, the chief excavator of the Gault site, "you couldn't have a more exciting time to be involved in the whole issue of the peopling of the Americas. You can't write a paper on it and get it published before it's out of date. Surprising new finds keep rocking the boat and launching fresh waves of debate."

In 1932, an American archaeologist identified distinctive spearheads associated with mammoth skeletons near Clovis, New Mexico. The discovery supported an emerging realization that humans lived with now-extinct ice age creatures in North America.

For prehistoric people, one of the chief attractions of the Gault site was a knobby outcrop of a creamy white rock called chert, which conceals a fine, gray, glasslike interior. If struck expertly with a stone or antler tool, the rock fractures in predictable ways, yielding a Clovis point. In the end, each spearhead has distinctive grooves, or "flutes," at the base of each face and was fastened to a wooden shaft with sinew and resin.

Ancient pollen and soil clues tell archaeologists that the climate in Clovis-era Texas was cooler, drier and more tolerable than today's summertime cauldron. Vast herds of mammoths, bison, horses and antelope ranged on the grasslands southeast of Gault, and deer and turkeys inhabited the plateau to the west. Along the creek, based on bones found at the site, Clovis hunters also preyed on frogs, birds, turtles and other small animals.

This abundance of food, coupled with the exceptional quality of the chert, drew people to Gault in large numbers. Unlike the majority of Clovis sites, which are mostly the remains of temporary camps, Gault appears to have been inhabited over long periods and thus contradicts the standard view that Clovis people were always highly mobile, nomadic hunters. Michael Collins says that of the vast quantity of artifacts found at the site, many are tool fragments, left behind by people who'd stuck around long enough to not only break their tools but also to salvage and rework them. The researchers also unearthed a seven by seven foot square of gravel—perhaps the floor of a house—and a possible well, both signs of more than a fleeting presence.

Another clue was concealed on a 13,000-year-old Clovis blade about the size of a dinner knife. Under a magnifying lens, the blade's edge is glossy, rounded and smooth. Marilyn Shoberg, a stone tool analyst on the Gault team who has experimented with replicas, says the blade's polish probably came from cutting grass. This grass could have been used for basketry, bedding, or thatching to make roofs for huts.

Among the most unusual and tantalizing finds at the Gault site are a hundred or so fragments of limestone covered with lightly scratched patterns. Some resemble nets or basketry, while a few could be simple outlines of plants or animals. Although only a dozen can be securely dated to Clovis times, these enigmatic rocks are among the very few surviving artworks from ice age America.

"What this site tells us is that Clovis folks were not specialized mammoth hunters constantly wandering over the landscape," says Collins. "They exploited a variety of animals, they had tools for gathering plants and working wood, stone and hide, and they stayed through the useful life of those tools. All these things are contrary to what you'd expect if they were highly nomadic, dedicated big-game hunters." Yet this unexpected complexity sheds only a feeble glimmer on the more contentious issue of where the Clovis people came from and how they got here.

In the old scenario, still popular in classrooms and picture books, fur-clad hunters in the waning moments of the last ice age, when so much seawater was locked up in the polar ice caps that the sea level was as much as 300 feet lower than today, ventured across a land bridge from Siberia to Alaska. Then, pursuing big game, the hunters trekked south through present-day Canada. They passed down a narrow, 1,000-mile-long treeless corridor bounded by the towering walls of retreating ice sheets until they reached the Great Plains, which

teemed with prey. The human population exploded, and the hunters soon drove into extinction some 35 genera of big animals (see box). All of these were supposedly dispatched by the Clovis point, a Stone Age weapon of mass destruction.

Digging at the Gault site in central Texas, according to project director Michael Collins, has almost doubled the number of Clovis artifacts excavated in North America. Researchers there have also uncovered evidence of ice age art.

For more than half a century, this plausible, "big-game" theory carried with it an appealing, heroic image. As James Adovasio of Mercyhurst College puts it in his book *The First Americans,* it was as if the ice sheets had parted "like the Red Sea for some Clovis Moses to lead his intrepid band of spear-toting, mammoth-slaying wayfarers to the south." But recent discoveries are indicating that almost everything about the theory could be wrong. For one thing, the latest studies show that the ice-free corridor didn't exist until around 12,000 years ago—too late to have served as the route for the very first people to come to America.

Clovis people buried caches of tools. Some stashed points were crafted from exotic stone; others seem too big and thin to have functioned as weapons. One cache was found with a child's bones, suggesting that burying tools could be a ritual act.

Perhaps the strongest ammunition against the old scenario comes from Monte Verde, an archaeological site on a remote terrace, which is today some 40 miles from the Pacific in southern Chile. Here, about 14,500 years ago, a hunting-and-gathering band lived year-round beside a creek in a long, oval hide tent, partitioned with logs. Archaeologist Tom Dillehay of Vanderbilt University began probing Monte Verde in 1977, unearthing the surface of the ancient encampment, complete with wood, plants and even remains of food, all preserved under a layer of waterlogged peat. Dillehay recovered three human footprints, two chunks of uneaten mastodon meat and possibly even traces of herbal medicine (indicated by nonfood plants still used by healers in the Andes). The dating of these extraordinary finds, at least 1,000 years before the earliest Clovis sites in North America, aroused skepticism for two decades until, in 1997, a group of leading archaeologists inspected the site and vindicated Dillehay's meticulous work.

No such triumph has emerged for any of the dozen or so sites in North America claimed to predate Clovis. But among the most intriguing is a rock overhang in Pennsylvania called

Meadowcroft, where a 30-year campaign of excavation suggests that hunters may have reached the Northeast 3,000 or 4,000 years before the Clovis era.

Saber-toothed cats prowled North America for millions of years. For some reason, they died out about 13,000 years ago.

Meanwhile, genetics studies are pointing even more strongly to an early entry into the continent. By analyzing the mitochondrial DNA of living Native Americans, Douglas Wallace, a geneticist at the University of California at Irvine, and his colleagues have identified five distinct lineages that stretch back like family trees. Mitochondria are the cells' energy factories. Their DNA changes very little from one generation to the next, altered only by tiny variations that creep in at a steady and predictable rate. By counting the number of these variations in related lineages, Wallace's team can estimate their ages. When the team applied this technique to the DNA of Native Americans, they reached the stunning conclusion that there were at least four separate waves of prehistoric migration into the Americas, the earliest well over 20,000 years ago.

If the first Americans did arrive well before the oldest known Clovis settlements, how did they get here? The most radical theory for the peopling of the New World argues that Stone Age mariners journeyed from Europe around the southern fringes of the great ice sheets in the North Atlantic. Many archaeologists greet this idea with head-shaking scorn, but the proposition is getting harder to dismiss outright.

Dennis Stanford, a Clovis expert at the Smithsonian Institution's Department of Anthropology who delights in prodding his colleagues with unconventional thinking, was a longtime supporter of the land bridge scenario. Then, with the end of the cold war came the chance to visit archaeological sites and museums in Siberia—museums that should have been filled with tools that were predecessors of the Clovis point. "The result was a big disappointment," says Stanford. "What we found was nothing like we expected, and I was surprised that the technologies were so different." Instead of a single leaf-shaped Clovis spearhead, ice age Siberian hunters made projectiles that were bristling with rows of tiny razor-like blades embedded in wooden shafts. To Stanford, that meant no Siberian hunters armed with Clovis technology had walked to the Americas.

Meanwhile, Bruce Bradley, a prehistoric stone tool specialist at Britain's University of Exeter, had noticed a strong resemblance between Clovis points and weapons from ice age Europe. But the idea that the two cultures might be directly connected was heretical. "It certainly wasn't part of the scientific process at that point," Bradley says. "There was no possibility, forget it, don't even think about it." Bradley eventually pursued it to the storerooms of the Musée National de Préhistoire in Les Eyzies-de-Tayac in southwest France, where he pored through boxes of local prehistoric stone tools and waste flakes. "I was absolutely flabbergasted," he recalls. "If somebody had brought out a box of this stuff in the United States and set it down in front of me, I'd have said, 'Man, where did you get all that great Clovis stuff?'" But the material was the work of a culture called the Solutrean that thrived in southwest France and northern Spain during the coldest spell of the ice age, from around 24,000 to 19,000 years ago.

Thousands of years before their successors created the masterworks of Lascaux and Altamira, Solutrean-age artists began painting vivid murals in the depths of caves such as Cougnac and Cosquer. They made delicate, eyed sewing needles out of bone, enabling them to stitch tightfitting skin garments to repel the cold. They devised the *atlatl,* or spear thrower, a hooked bone or wood handle that extends the reach of the hunter's arm to multiply throwing power. But their most distinctive creation was a stone spearhead shaped like a laurel leaf.

Apart from the absence of a fluted base, the Solutrean laurel leaf strongly resembles the Clovis point and was made using the same, highly skillful flaking technique. Both Clovis and Solutrean stone crafters practiced controlled overshot flaking, which involved trimming one edge by striking a flake off the opposite side, a virtuoso feat of handiwork rarely seen in other prehistoric cultures. To Bradley, "there had to be some sort of historic connection" between the Solutrean and Clovis peoples.

Dennis Stanford and Bruce Bradley say that similarities between Clovis and Solutrean finds are overwhelming.

Critics of the theory point to a yawning gap between the two peoples: roughly 5,000 years divide the end of Solutrean culture and the emergence of Clovis. But Stanford and Bradley say that recent claims of pre-Clovis sites in the southeastern United States may bridge the time gap. In the mid-1990s at Cactus Hill, the remains of an ancient sand dune overlooking the Nottoway River on Virginia's coastal plain, project director Joseph McAvoy dug down a few inches beneath a Clovis layer and uncovered simple stone blades and projectile points associated with a hearth, radiocarbon dated to some 17,000 to 19,000 years ago. This startlingly early date has drawn skeptical fire, but the site's age was recently confirmed by an independent dating technique. Stanford and Bradley suggest that the early people at Cactus Hill were Clovis forerunners who had not yet developed the full-blown Clovis style. They are convinced that many more sites like Cactus Hill will turn up on the East Coast. But the burning question is, Did these ice age Virginians invent the Clovis point all by themselves, or were they descendants of Solutreans who brought the point with them from Europe?

Many archaeologists ridicule the notion that people made an arduous, 3,000-mile journey during the bleakest period of

Hunted to Extinction?

At the end of the last ice age, 35 genera of big animals, or "megafauna," went extinct in the Americas, including mammoths, mastodons, giant ground sloths, giant beavers, horses, short-faced bears and saber-toothed cats. Archaeologists have argued for decades that the arrival of hunters wielding Clovis spear points at around the same time was no coincidence. Clovis hunters pursued big game—their signature stone points are found with the bones of mammoths and mastodons at 14 kill sites in North America. Experiments carried out with replica spears thrust into the corpses of circus elephants indicate that the Clovis point could have penetrated a mammoth's hide. And computer simulations suggest that large, slow-breeding animals could have easily been wiped out by hunting as the human population expanded.

But humans might not be entirely to blame. The rapidly cycling climate at the end of the ice age may have changed the distribution of plants that the big herbivores grazed on, leading to a population crash among meat-eating predators too. New research on DNA fragments recovered from ice age bison bones suggests that some species were suffering a slow decline in diversity—probably caused by dwindling populations—long before any Clovis hunters showed up. Indigenous horses are now thought to have died out in Alaska about 500 years before the Clovis era. For mammoths and other beasts who did meet their demise during the Clovis times, many experts believe that a combination of factors—climate change plus pressure from human hunters—drove them into oblivion.

Amid all the debate, one point is clear: the Clovis hunter wasn't as macho as people once thought. Bones at the Gault site in central Texas reveal that the hunters there were feeding on less daunting prey—frogs, birds, turtles and antelope—as well as mammoth, mastodon and bison. As the late, renowned archaeologist Richard (Scotty) MacNeish is said to have remarked, "Each Clovis generation probably killed one mammoth, then spent the rest of their lives talking about it."

A different critique of the out-of-Europe theory dismisses the resemblance between Solutrean and Clovis points. Many archaeologists suggest that similarities between Clovis and Solutrean artifacts are coincidental, the result of what they call convergence. "These were people faced with similar problems," says Solutrean expert Lawrence Straus of the University of New Mexico. "And the problems involved hunting large- and medium-sized game with a similar, limited range of raw materials—stone, bone, ivory, antler, wood and sinew. They're going to come up with similar solutions."

More tellingly, in Straus' view, is that he can find little evidence of seafaring technology in the Solutrean sites he has dug in northern Spain. Although rising sea levels have drowned sites on the ice age coastline, Straus has investigated surviving inland cave sites no more than a couple of hours' walk from the beach. "There's no evidence of deep-sea fishing," says Straus, "no evidence of marine mammal hunting, and consequently no evidence, even indirect, for their possession of seaworthy boats."

And David Meltzer, an archaeologist at Southern Methodist University and a critic of the European-origins idea, is struck more by the differences between the Solutrean and Clovis cultures than their similarities—particularly the near-absence of art and personal ornaments from Clovis. Still, he says, the controversy is good for the field. "In the process of either killing or curing" the theory, "we will have learned a whole lot more about the archaeological record, and we'll all come out smarter than we went in."

Besides crossing the land bridge from Asia and traveling to ice age America from Europe by boat, a third possible entryway is a sea route down the west coast. Using maritime skills later perfected by the Inuit, prehistoric south Asians might have spread gradually around the northern rim of the Pacific in small skin-covered boats. They skirt the southern edge of the Bering land bridge and paddle down the coast of Alaska, dodging calving glaciers and icebergs as they pursue seals and other marine mammals. They keep going all the way to the beaches of Central and South America. They arrive at Monte Verde, inland from the Chilean coast, some 14,500 years ago. Each new generation claims fresh hunting grounds a few miles beyond the last, and in a matter of centuries these first immigrants have populated the entire west coast of the Americas. Soon the hunters start moving inland and, in the north, their descendants become the Clovis people.

Clovis people may well have reached North America via sea route. Seals and other marine prey may have sustained them until they found New World hunting grounds.

Many archaeologists now accept the west coast theory as a likely solution to the origin of the earliest Americans. On Prince of Wales Island in southeastern Alaska, inside the aptly named On Your Knees Cave, University of South Dakota

the ice age, when the Atlantic would have been much colder and stormier than today. Stanford believes that traditional Inuit technology suggests otherwise; he has witnessed traditional seagoing skills among Inupiat communities in Barrow, Alaska. Inupiat hunters still build large skin-covered canoes, or *umiaks,* which enable them to catch seals, walrus and other sea mammals that abound along the frozen edges of the pack ice. When twilight arrives or storms threaten, the hunters pull their boats up on the ice and camp beneath them. Ronald Brower of the Inupiat Heritage Center in Barrow says, "There's nothing that would have prevented . . . people from crossing the Atlantic into the Americas 19,000 years ago. It would be a perfectly normal situation from my perspective."

paleontologist Timothy Heaton and University of Colorado at Boulder archaeologist E. James Dixon recovered an accumulation of animal bones from the last ice age. When mile-high ice sheets still straddled the interior of the continent 17,000 years ago, ringed seals, foxes and seabirds made their home on the island. "Humans could easily have survived there," Heaton says.

The ultimate evidence for the western sea route would be the discovery of pre-Clovis human remains on the coast. No such luck. Dixon and Heaton have found human jaw fragments and other remains in the On Your Knees Cave, but those date to about 11,000 years ago—too recent to establish the theory. And what may be the oldest-known human remains in North America—leg bones found on Santa Rosa Island, off the California coast—are from 13,000 years ago, the heart of the Clovis era. Still, those remains hint that by then people were plying the waters along the Pacific Coast.

If the trail of the very earliest Americans remains elusive, so, too, does the origin of the Clovis point. "Although the technology needed to produce a Clovis point was found among other cultures during the ice age," says Ken Tankersley of Northern Kentucky University, "the actual point itself is unique to the Americas, suggesting that it was invented here in the New World." If so, the spearhead would be the first great American invention—the Stone Age equivalent of the Swiss Army Knife, a trademark tool that would be widely imitated. The demand for the weapon and the high-quality stone it required probably encouraged Clovis people to begin long-distance trading and social exchanges. The spearhead may also have delivered a new level of hunting proficiency and this, in turn, would have fueled a population spurt, giving Clovis people their lasting presence in the archaeological record.

Sheltering from the broiling heat under the cottonwoods at Gault, Michael Collins told me of his conviction that the Clovis people who flocked to the shady creek were not pioneers but had profited from a long line of forebears. "Clovis represents the end product of centuries, if not millennia, of learning how to live in North American environments," he said. "The Clovis culture is too widespread, is found in too many environments, and has too much evidence for diverse activities to be the leavings of people just coming into the country." Collins reminded me that his team has investigated less than 10 percent of the enormous site. And archaeologists have barely scratched the surface of a handful of other Gault-size, Clovis-era sites—Williamsburg, in Virginia, for instance, or Shoop, in Pennsylvania. "One thing you can be sure," he said, beaming, "there'll be great new discoveries just around the corner."

Critical Thinking

1. Discuss where the early Native American people came from and include an analysis as to why this remains controversial.

2. How can archaeological findings dispute historical claims?

Create Central

www.mhhe.com/createcentral

Internet References

Who Were the First Americans?
http://csfa.tamu.edu/who.php

Tracing the First North American Hunters
http://news.ku.dk/all_news/2011/2011.10/tracing-the-first-north-american-hunters/

Does Skull Prove That the First Americans Came from Europe?
www.utexas.edu/courses/stross/ant322m_files/1stpersons.htm

EVAN HADINGHAM is the senior science editor of the PBS series NOVA and the author of books on prehistory.

Article   Prepared by: Wendy A. Maier-Sarti, *Oakton Community College*

1491

[handwritten: Thesis]; then compare

Before it became the New World, the Western Hemisphere was vastly more populous and sophisticated than has been thought—an altogether more salubrious place to live at the time than, say, Europe. New evidence of both the extent of the population and its agricultural advancement leads to a remarkable conjecture: the Amazon rain forest may be largely a human artifact.

CHARLES C. MANN

Learning Outcomes

After reading this article, you will be able to:

- Explain why the author believes that native tribes lived in the western hemisphere longer than previously thought.
- Analyze the level of sophistication of the early native communities.
- Discuss the impact that the Europeans had on the natural environment as well as on the Native peoples.

The plane took off in weather that was surprisingly cool for north-central Bolivia and flew east, toward the Brazilian border. In a few minutes the roads and houses disappeared, and the only evidence of human settlement was the cattle scattered over the savannah like jimmies on ice cream. Then they, too, disappeared. By that time the archaeologists had their cameras out and were clicking away in delight.

Below us was the Beni, a Bolivian province about the size of Illinois and Indiana put together, and nearly as flat. For almost half the year rain and snowmelt from the mountains to the south and west cover the land with an irregular, slowly moving skin of water that eventually ends up in the province's northern rivers, which are sub-subtributaries of the Amazon. The rest of the year the water dries up and the bright-green vastness turns into something that resembles a desert. This peculiar, remote, watery plain was what had drawn the researchers' attention, and not just because it was one of the few places on earth inhabited by people who might never have seen Westerners with cameras.

Clark Erickson and William Balée, the archaeologists, sat up front. Erickson is based at the University of Pennsylvania; he works in concert with a Bolivian archaeologist, whose seat in the plane I usurped that day. Balée is at Tulane University, in New Orleans. He is actually an anthropologist, but as native peoples have vanished, the distinction between anthropologists and archaeologists has blurred. The two men differ in build, temperament, and scholarly proclivity, but they pressed their faces to the windows with identical enthusiasm.

Indians were here in greater numbers than previously thought, and they imposed their will on the landscape. Columbus set foot in a hemisphere thoroughly dominated by humankind.

Dappled across the grasslands below was an archipelago of forest islands, many of them startlingly round and hundreds of acres across. Each island rose ten or thirty or sixty feet above the floodplain, allowing trees to grow that would otherwise never survive the water. The forests were linked by raised berms, as straight as a rifle shot and up to three miles long. It is Erickson's belief that this entire landscape—30,000 square miles of forest mounds surrounded by raised fields and linked by causeways—was constructed by a complex, populous society more than 2,000 years ago. Balée, newer to the Beni, leaned toward this view but was not yet ready to commit himself.

Erickson and Balée belong to a cohort of scholars that has radically challenged conventional notions of what the Western Hemisphere was like before Columbus. When I went to high school, in the 1970s, I was taught that Indians came to the Americas across the Bering Strait about 12,000 years ago, that they lived for the most part in small, isolated groups, and that they had so little impact on their environment that even after millennia of habitation it remained mostly wilderness. My son picked up the same ideas at his schools. One way to summarize the views of people like Erickson and Balée would be to say that in their opinion this picture of Indian life is wrong in almost every aspect. Indians were here far longer than previously thought, these researchers believe, and in much greater numbers. And they were so successful at imposing their will on the landscape that in 1492 Columbus set foot in a hemisphere thoroughly dominated by humankind.

Given the charged relations between white societies and native peoples, inquiry into Indian culture and history is inevitably contentious. But the recent scholarship is especially controversial. To begin with, some researchers—many but not all from an older generation—deride the new theories as fantasies arising from an almost willful misinterpretation of data and a perverse kind of political correctness. "I have seen no evidence that large numbers of people ever lived in the Beni," says Betty J. Meggers, of the Smithsonian Institution. "Claiming otherwise is just wishful thinking." Similar criticisms apply to many of the new scholarly claims about Indians, according to Dean R. Snow, an anthropologist at Pennsylvania State University. The problem is that "you can make the meager evidence from the ethnohistorical record tell you anything you want," he says. "It's really easy to kid yourself."

More important are the implications of the new theories for today's ecological battles. Much of the environmental movements is animated, consciously or not, by what William Denevan, a geographer at the University of Wisconsin, calls, polemically, "the pristine myth"—the belief that the Americas in 1491 were an almost unmarked, even Edenic land, "untrammeled by man," in the words of the Wilderness Act of 1964, one of the nation's first and most important environmental laws. As the University of Wisconsin historian William Cronon has written, restoring this long-ago, putatively natural state is, in the view of environmentalists, a task that society is morally bound to undertake. Yet if the new view is correct and the work of humankind was pervasive, where does that leave efforts to restore nature?

The Beni is a case in point. In addition to building up the Beni mounds for houses and gardens, Erickson says, the Indians trapped fish in the seasonally flooded grassland. Indeed, he says, they fashioned dense zigzagging networks of earthen fish weirs between the causeways. To keep the habitat clear of unwanted trees and undergrowth, they regularly set huge areas on fire. Over the centuries the burning created an intricate ecosystem of fire-adapted plant species dependent on native pyrophilia. The current inhabitants of the Beni still burn, although now it is to maintain the savannah for cattle. When we flew over the areas, the dry season had just begun, but mile-long lines of flame were already on the march. In the charred areas behind the fires were the blackened spikes of trees—many of them one assumes, of the varieties that activists fight to save in other parts of Amazonia.

After we landed, I asked Balée, Should we let people keep burning the Beni? Or should we let the trees invade and create a verdant tropical forest in the grasslands, even if one had not existed here for millennia?

Balée laughed. "You're trying to trap me, aren't you?" he said.

Like a Club between the Eyes

According to family lore, my great-grandmother's great-grandmother's great-grandfather was the first white person hanged in America. His name was John Billington. He came on the *Mayflower*, which anchored off the coast of Massachusetts on November 9, 1620. Billington was not a Puritan; within six months of arrival he also became the first white person in America to be tried for complaining about the police. "He is a knave," William Bradford, the colony's governor, wrote to Billington, "and so will live and die." What one historian called Billington's "troublesome career" ended in 1630, when he was hanged for murder. My family has always said that he was framed—but we *would* say that, wouldn't we?

A few years ago it occurred to me that my ancestor and everyone else in the colony had voluntarily enlisted in a venture that brought them to New England without food or shelter six weeks before winter. Half the 102 people on the *Mayflower* made it through to spring, which to me was amazing. How, I wondered, did they survive?

In his history of Plymouth Colony, Bradford provided the answer: by robbing Indian houses and graves. The *Mayflower* first hove to at Cape Cod. An armed company staggered out. Eventually it found a recently deserted Indian settlement. The newcomers—hungry, cold, sick—dug up graves and ransacked houses, looking for underground stashes of corn. "And sure it was God's good providence that we found this corn," Bradford wrote, "for else we know not how we should have done." (He felt uneasy about the thievery, though.) When the colonists came to Plymouth, a month later, they set up shop in another deserted Indian village. All through the coastal forest the Indians had "died on heapes, as they lay in their houses," the English trader Thomas Morton noted. "And the bones and skulls upon the several places of their habitations made such a spectacle" that to Morton the Massachusetts woods seemed to be "a new found Golgotha"—the hill of executions in Roman Jerusalem.

To the Pilgrims' astonishment, one of the corpses they exhumed on Cape Cod had blond hair. A French ship had been wrecked there several years earlier. The Patuxet Indians imprisoned a few survivors. One of them supposedly learned enough of the local language to inform his captors that God would destroy them for their misdeeds. The Patuxet scoffed at the threat. But the Europeans carried a disease, and they bequeathed it to their jailers. The epidemic (probably of viral hepatitis, according to a study by Arthur E. Spiess, an archaeologist at the Maine Historic Preservation Commission, and Bruce D. Spiess, the director of clinical research at the Medical College of Virginia) took years to exhaust itself and may have killed 90 percent of the people in coastal New England. It made huge differences to American history. "The good hand of God favored our beginnings," Bradford mused, by "sweeping away great multitudes of the natives . . . that he might make room for us."

By the time my ancestor set sail on the *Mayflower*, Europeans had been visiting New England for more than a hundred years. English, French, Italian, Spanish, and Portuguese mariners regularly plied the coastline, trading what they could, occasionally kidnapping the inhabitants for slaves. New England, the Europeans saw, was thickly settled and well defended. In 1605 and 1606 Samuel de Champlain visited Cape Cod, hoping to establish a French base. He abandoned the idea. Too many people already lived there. A year later Sir Ferdinand Gorges—British despite his name—tried to establish

English community in southern Maine. It had more founders than Plymouth and seems to have been better organized. Confronted by numerous well-armed local Indians, the settlers abandoned the project within months. The Indians at Plymouth would surely have been an equal obstacle to my ancestor and his ramshackle expedition had disease not intervened.

Faced with such stories, historians have long wondered how many people lived in the Americas at the time of contact. "Debated since Columbus attempted a partial census on Hispaniola in 1496," William Denevan has written, this "remains one of the great inquiries of history." (In 1976 Denevan assembled and edited an entire book on the subject, *The Native Population of the Americas in 1492.*) The first scholarly estimate of the indigenous population was made in 1910 by James Mooney, a distinguished ethnographer at the Smithsonian Institution. Combing through old documents, he concluded that in 1491 North America had 1.15 million inhabitants. Mooney's glittering reputation ensured that most subsequent researchers accepted his figure uncritically.

That changed in 1966, when Henry F. Dobyns published "Estimating Aboriginal American Population: An Appraisal of Techniques With a New Hemispheric Estimate," in the journal *Current Anthropology*. Despite the carefully neutral title, his argument was thunderous, its impact long-lasting. In the view of James Wilson, the author of *The Earth Shall Weep* (1998), a history of indigenous Americans, Dobyns's colleagues "are still struggling to get out of the crater that paper left in anthropology." Not only anthropologists were affected. Dobyns's estimate proved to be one of the opening rounds in today's culture wars.

Dobyns began his exploration of pre-Columbian Indian demography in the early 1950s, when he was a graduate student. At the invitation of a friend, he spent a few months in northern Mexico, which is full of Spanish-era missions. There he poked through the crumbling leather-bound ledgers in which Jesuits recorded local births and deaths. Right away he noticed how many more deaths there were. The Spaniards arrived, and then Indians died—in huge numbers at incredible rates. It hit him, Dobyns told me recently, "like a club right between the eyes."

It took Dobyns eleven years to obtain his PhD. Along the way he joined a rural-development project in Peru, which until colonial times was the seat of the Incan empire. Remembering what he had seen at the northern fringe of the Spanish conquest, Dobyns decided to compare it with figures for the south. He burrowed into the papers of the Lima cathedral and read apologetic Spanish histories. The Indians in Peru, Dobyns concluded, had faced plagues from the day the conquistadors showed up—in fact, before then: smallpox arrived around 1525, seven years ahead of the Spanish. Brought to Mexico apparently by a single sick Spaniard, it swept south and eliminated more than half the population of the Incan empire. Smallpox claimed the Incan dictator Huayna Capac and much of his family, setting off a calamitous war of succession. So complete was the chaos that Francisco Pizarro was able to seize an empire the size of Spain and Italy combined with a force of 168 men.

Smallpox was only the first epidemic. Typhus (probably) in 1546, influenza and smallpox together in 1558, smallpox again in 1589, diphtheria in 1614, measles in 1618—all ravaged the remains of Incan culture. Dobyns was the first social scientist to piece together this awful picture, and he naturally rushed his findings into print. Hardly anyone paid attention. But Dobyns was already working on a second, related question: If all those people died, how many had been living there to begin with? Before Columbus, Dobyns calculated, the Western Hemisphere held ninety to 112 million people. Another way of saying this is that in 1491 more people lived in the Americas than in Europe.

His argument was simple but horrific. It is well known that Native Americans had no experience with many European diseases and were therefore immunologically unprepared—"virgin soil," in the metaphor of epidemiologists. What Dobyns realized was that such diseases could have swept from the coastlines initially visited by Europeans to inland areas controlled by Indians who had never seen a white person. The first whites to explore many parts of the Americas may therefore have encountered places that were already depopulated. Indeed, Dobyns argued, they must have done so.

Peru was one example, the Pacific Northwest another. In 1792 the British navigator George Vancouver led the first European expedition to survey Puget Sound. He found a vast charnel house: human remains "promiscuously scattered about the beach, in great numbers." Smallpox, Vancouver's crew discovered, had preceded them. Its few survivors, second lieutenant Peter Puget noted, were "most terribly pitted . . . indeed many have lost their Eyes." In *Pox Americana* (2001), Elizabeth Fenn, a historian at George Washington University, contends that the disaster on the northwest coast was but a small part of a continental pandemic that erupted near Boston in 1774 and cut down Indians from Mexico to Alaska.

Because smallpox was not endemic in the Americas, colonials, too, had not acquired any immunity. The virus, an equal-opportunity killer, swept through the Continental Army and stopped the drive into Quebec. The American Revolution would be lost, Washington and other rebel leaders feared, if the contagion did to the colonists what it had done to the Indians. "The small Pox! The small Pox!" John Adams wrote to his wife, Abigail. "What shall We do with it?" In retrospect, Fenn says, "One of George Washington's most brilliant moves was to inoculate the army against smallpox during the Valley Forge winter of '78." Without inoculation smallpox could easily have given the United States back to the British.

So many epidemics occurred in the Americas, Dobyns argued, that the old data used by Mooney and his successors represented population nadirs. From the few cases in which before-and-after totals are known with relative certainty, Dobyns estimated that in the first 130 years of contact about 95 percent of the people in the Americas died—the worst demographic calamity in recorded history.

Dobyns's ideas were quickly attacked as politically motivated, a push from the hate-America crowd to inflate the toll of imperialism. The attacks continue to this day. "No question about it, some people want those higher numbers," says

Shepard Krech III, a Brown University anthropologist who is the author of *The Ecological Indian* (1999). These people, he says, were thrilled when Dobyns revisited the subject in a book, *Their Numbers Become Thinned* (1983)—and revised his own estimates upward. Perhaps Dobyns's most vehement critic is David Henige, a bibliographer of Africana at the University of Wisconsin, whose *Numbers from Nowhere* (1998) is a landmark in the literature of demographic fulmination. "Suspect in 1966, it is no less suspect nowadays," Henige wrote of Dobyns's work. "If anything, it is worse."

When Henige wrote *Numbers From Nowhere,* the fight about pre-Columbian populations had already consumed forests' worth of trees; his bibliography is ninety pages long. And the dispute shows no sign of abating. More and more people have jumped in. This is partly because the subject is inherently fascinating. But more likely the increased interest in the debate is due to the growing realization of the high political and ecological stakes.

Inventing by the Millions

On May 30, 1539, Hernando de Soto landed his private army near Tampa Bay, in Florida. Soto, as he was called, was a novel figure: half warrior, half venture capitalist. He had grown very rich very young by becoming a market leader in the nascent trade for Indian slaves. The profits had helped to fund Pizarro's seizure of the Incan empire, which had made Soto wealthier still. Looking quite literally for new worlds to conquer, he persuaded the Spanish Crown to let him loose in North America. He spent one fortune to make another. He came to Florida with 200 horses, 600 soldiers, and 300 pigs.

From today's perspective, it is difficult to imagine the ethical system that would justify Soto's actions. For four years his force, looking for gold, wandered through what is now Florida, Georgia, North and South Carolina, Tennessee, Alabama, Mississippi, Arkansas, and Texas, wrecking almost everything it touched. The inhabitants often fought back vigorously, but they had never before encountered an army with horses and guns. Soto died of fever with his expedition in ruins; along the way his men had managed to rape, torture, enslave, and kill countless Indians. But the worst thing the Spaniards did, some researchers say, was entirely without malice—bring the pigs.

According to Charles Hudson, an anthropologist at the University of Georgia who spent fifteen years reconstructing the path of the expedition, Soto crossed the Mississippi a few miles downstream from the present site of Memphis. It was a nervous passage: the Spaniards were watched by several thousand Indian warriors. Utterly without fear, Soto brushed past the Indian force into what is now eastern Arkansas, through thickly settled land—"very well peopled with large towns," one of his men later recalled, "two or three of which were to be seen from one town." Eventually the Spaniards approached a cluster of small cities, each protected by earthen walls, sizeable moats, and deadeye archers. In his usual fashion, Soto brazenly marched in, stole food, and marched out.

After Soto left, no Europeans visited this part of the Mississippi Valley for more than a century. Early in 1682 whites appeared again, this time Frenchmen in canoes. One of them was René-Robert Cavelier, Sieur de la Salle. The French passed through the area where Soto had found cities cheek by jowl. It was deserted—La Salle didn't see an Indian village for 200 miles. About fifty settlements existed in this strip of the Mississippi when Soto showed up, according to Anne Ramenofsky, an anthropologist at the University of New Mexico. By La Salle's time the number had shrunk to perhaps ten, some probably inhabited by recent immigrants. Soto "had a privileged glimpse" of an Indian world, Hudson says. "The window opened and slammed shut. When the French came in and the record opened up again, it was a transformed reality. A civilization crumbled. The question is, how did this happen?"

Swine alone can disseminate anthrax, brucellosis, leptospirosis, trichinosis, and tuberculosis. Only a few of Hernando de Soto's pigs would have had to wander off to infect the forest.

The question is even more complex than it may seem. Disaster of this magnitude suggests epidemic disease. In the view of Ramenofsky and Patricia Galloway, an anthropologist at the University of Texas, the source of the contagion was very likely not Soto's army but its ambulatory meat locker: his 300 pigs. Soto's force itself was too small to be an effective biological weapon. Sicknesses like measles and smallpox would have burned through his 600 soldiers long before they reached the Mississippi. But the same would not have held true for the pigs, which multiplied rapidly and were able to transmit their diseases to wildlife in the surrounding forest. When human beings and domesticated animals live close together, they trade microbes with abandon. Over time mutation spawns new diseases: Avian influenza becomes human influenza, bovine rinderpest becomes measles. Unlike Europeans, Indians did not live in close quarters with animals—they domesticated only the dog, the llama, the alpaca, the guinea pig, and here and there, the turkey and the Muscovy duck. In some ways this is not surprising: the New World had fewer animal candidates for taming than the Old. Moreover, few Indians carry the gene that permits adults to digest lactose, a form of sugar abundant in milk. Non-milk-drinkers, one imagines, would be less likely to work at domesticating milk-giving animals. But this is guesswork. The fact is that what scientists call zoonotic disease was little known in the Americas. Swine alone can disseminate anthrax, brucellosis, leptospirosis, taeniasis, trichinosis, and tuberculosis. Pigs breed exuberantly and can transmit diseases to deer and turkeys. Only a few of Soto's pigs would have had to wander off to infect the forest.

Indeed, the calamity wrought by Soto apparently extended across the whole Southeast. The Coosa city-states, in western Georgia, and the Caddoan-speaking civilization, centered on the Texas-Arkansas border, disintegrated soon after Soto appeared. The Caddo had had a taste for monumental architecture: public plazas, ceremonial platforms, mausoleums. After Soto's army left, notes Timothy K. Perttula, an archaeological consultant in Austin, Texas, the Caddo stopped building community centers and began digging community cemeteries. Between Soto's and La Salle's visits, Perttula believes, the Caddoan population fell from about 200,000 to about 8,500—a drop of nearly 96 percent. In the eighteenth century the tally shrank further, to 1,400. An equivalent loss today in the population of New York City would reduce it to 56,000—not enough to fill Yankee Stadium. "That's one reason whites think of Indians as nomadic hunters," says Russell Thornton, an anthropologist at the University of California at Los Angeles. "Everything else— all the heavily populated urbanized societies—was wiped out."

Could a few pigs truly wreak this much destruction? Such apocalyptic scenarios invite skepticism. As a rule, viruses, microbes, and parasites are rarely lethal on so wide a scale—a pest that wipes out its host species does not have a bright evolutionary future. In its worst outbreak, from 1347 to 1351, the European Black Death claimed only a third of its victims. (The rest survived, though they were often disfigured or crippled by its effects.) The Indians in Soto's path, if Dobyns, Ramenofsky, and Perttula are correct, endured losses that were incomprehensibly greater.

One reason is that Indians were fresh territory for many plagues, not just one. Smallpox, typhoid, bubonic plague, influenza, mumps, measles, whooping cough—all rained down on the Americas in the century after Columbus. (Cholera, malaria, and scarlet fever came later.) Having little experience with epidemic diseases, Indians had no knowledge of how to combat them. In contrast, Europeans were well versed in the brutal logic of quarantine. They boarded up houses in which plague appeared and fled to the countryside. In Indian New England, Neal Salisbury, a historian at Smith college, wrote in *Manitou and Providence* (1982), family and friends gathered with the shaman at the sufferer's bedside to wait out the illness—a practice that "could only have served to spread the disease more rapidly."

Indigenous biochemistry may also have played a role. The immune system constantly scans the body for molecules that it can recognize as foreign—molecules belonging to an invading virus, for instance. No one's immune system can identify all foreign presences. Roughly speaking, an individual's set of defensive tools is known as his MHC type. Because many bacteria and viruses mutate easily, they usually attack in the form of several slightly different strains. Pathogens win when MHC types miss some of the strains and the immune system is not stimulated to act. Most human groups contain many MHC types; a strain that slips by one person's defenses will be nailed by the defenses of the next. But, according to Francis L. Black, an epidemiologist at Yale University, Indians are characterized by unusually homogeneous MHC types. One out of three South American Indians have similar MHC types; among Africans the corresponding figure is one in 200. The cause is a matter for Darwinian speculation, the effects less so.

In 1966 Dobyns's insistence on the role of disease was a shock to his colleagues. Today the impact of European pathogens on the New World is almost undisputed. Nonetheless, the fight over Indian numbers continues with undiminished fervor. Estimates of the population of North America in 1491 disagree by an order of magnitude—from 18 million, Dobyns's revised figure, to 1.8 million, calculated by Douglas H. Ubelaker, an anthropologist at the Smithsonian. To some "high counters," as David Henige calls them, the low counters' refusal to relinquish the vision of an empty continent is irrational or worse. "Non-Indian 'experts' always want to minimize the size of aboriginal populations," says Lenore Stiffarm, a Native American-education specialist at the University of Saskatchewan. The smaller the numbers of Indians, she believes, the easier it is to regard the continent as having been up for grabs. "It's perfectly acceptable to move into unoccupied land," Stiffarm says. "And land with only a few 'savages' is the next best thing."

"Most of the arguments for the very large numbers have been theoretical," Ubelaker says in defense of low counters. "When you try to marry the theoretical arguments to the data that are available on individual groups in different regions, it's hard to find support for those numbers." Archaeologists, he says, keep searching for the settlements in which those millions of people supposedly lived, with little success. "As more and more excavation is done, one would expect to see more evidence for dense populations than has thus far emerged." Dean Snow, the Pennsylvania State anthropologist, examined Colonial-era Mohawk Iroquois sites and found "no support for the notion that ubiquitous pandemics swept the region." In his view, asserting that the continent was filled with people who left no trace is like looking at an empty bank account and claiming that it must once have held millions of dollars.

The low counters are also troubled by the Dobynsian procedure for recovering original population numbers: applying an assumed death rate, usually 95 percent, to the observed population nadir. Ubelaker believes that the lowest point for Indians in North America was around 1900, when their numbers fell to about half a million. Assuming a 95 percent death rate, the pre-contact population would have been 10 million. Go up one percent, to a 96 percent death rate, and the figure jumps to 12.5 million—arithmetically creating more than two million people from a tiny increase in mortality rates. At 98 percent the number bounds to 25 million. Minute changes in baseline assumptions produce wildly different results.

"It's an absolutely unanswerable question on which tens of thousands of words have been spent to no purpose," Henige says. In 1976 he sat in on a seminar by William Denevan, the Wisconsin geographer. An "epiphanic moment" occurred when he read shortly afterward that scholars had "uncovered" the existence of eight million people in Hispaniola. *Can you just invent millions of people?* he wondered. "We can make of the historical record that there was depopulation and movement of people from internecine warfare and diseases," he says. "But as for how much, who knows? When we start putting numbers to something like that—applying large figures like ninety-five percent—we're saying things we shouldn't say. The number implies a level of knowledge that's impossible."

Nonetheless, one must try—or so Denevan believes. In his estimation the high counters (though not the highest counters) seem to be winning the argument, at least for now. No definitive data exist, he says, but the majority of the extant evidentiary scraps support their side. Even Henige is no low counter. When I asked him what he thought the population of the Americas was before Columbus, he insisted that any answer would be speculation and made me promise not to print what he was going to say next. Then he named a figure that forty years ago would have caused a commotion.

To Elizabeth Fenn, the smallpox historian, the squabble over numbers obscures a central fact. Whether one million or 10 million or 100 million died, she believes, the pall of sorrow that engulfed the hemisphere was immeasurable. Languages, prayers, hopes, habits, and dreams—entire ways of life hissed away like steam. The Spanish and the Portuguese lacked the germ theory of disease and could not explain what was happening (let alone stop it). Nor can we explain it; the ruin was too long ago and too all-encompassing. In the long run, Fenn says, the consequential finding is not that many people died but that many people once lived. The Americas were filled with a stunningly diverse assortment of peoples who had knocked about the continents for millennia. "You have to wonder," Fenn says. "What were all those people *up* to in all that time?"

Buffalo Farm

In 1810 Henry Brackenridge came to Cahokia, in what is now southwest Illinois, just across the Mississippi from St. Louis. Born close to the frontier, Brackenridge was a budding adventure writer; his *Views of Louisiana,* published three years later, was a kind of nineteenth-century *Into Thin Air,* with terrific adventure but without tragedy. Brackenridge had an eye for archaeology, and he had heard that Cahokia was worth a visit. When he got there, trudging along the desolate Cahokia River, he was "struck with a degree of astonishment." Rising from the muddy bottomland was a "stupendous pile of earth," vaster than the Great Pyramid at Giza. Around it were more than a hundred smaller mounds, covering an area of five square miles. At the time, the area was almost uninhabited. One can only imagine what passed through Brackenridge's mind as he walked alone to the ruins of the biggest Indian city north of the Rio Grande.

To Brackenridge, it seemed clear that Cahokia and the many other ruins in the Midwest had been constructed by Indians. It was not so clear to everyone else. Nineteenth-century writers attributed them to, among others, the Vikings, the Chinese, the "Hindoos," the ancient Greeks, the ancient Egyptians, lost tribes of Israelites, and even straying bands of Welsh. (This last claim was surprisingly widespread; when Lewis and Clark surveyed the Missouri, Jefferson told them to keep an eye out for errant bands of Welsh-speaking white Indians.) The historian George Bancroft, dean of his profession, was a dissenter: the earthworks, he wrote in 1840, were purely natural formations.

Bancroft changed his mind about Cahokia, but not about Indians. To the end of his days he regarded them as "feeble barbarians, destitute of commerce and of political connection." His characterization lasted, largely unchanged, for more than a century. Samuel Eliot Morison, the winner of two Pulitzer Prizes, closed his monumental *European Discovery of America* (1974) with the observation that Native Americans expected only

"short and brutish lives, void of hope for any future." As late as 1987 *American History: A Survey,* a standard high school textbook by three well-known historians, described the Americas before Columbus as "empty of mankind and its works." The story of Europeans in the New World, the book explained, "is the story of the creation of a civilization where none existed."

Alfred Crosby, a historian at the University of Texas, came to other conclusions. Crosby's *The Columbian Exchange: Biological Consequences of 1492* caused almost as much of a stir when it was published, in 1972, as Henry Dobyns's calculation of Indian numbers six years earlier, though in different circles. Crosby was a standard names-and-battles historian who became frustrated by the random contingency of political events. "Some trivial thing happens and you have this guy winning the presidency instead of that guy," he says. He decided to go deeper. After he finished his manuscript, it sat on his shelf—he couldn't find a publisher willing to be associated with his new ideas. It took him three years to persuade a small editorial house to put it out. *The Columbian Exchange* has been in print ever since; a companion, *Ecological Imperialism: The Biological Expansion of Europe, 900–1900,* appeared in 1986.

Human history, in Crosby's interpretation, is marked by two world-altering centers of invention: the Middle East and central Mexico, where Indian groups independently created nearly all of the Neolithic innovations, writing included. The Neolithic Revolution began in the Middle East about 10,000 years ago. In the next few millennia humankind invented the wheel, the metal tool, and agriculture. The Sumerians eventually put these inventions together, added writing, and became the world's first civilization. Afterward Sumeria's heirs in Europe and Asia frantically copied one another's happiest discoveries; innovations ricocheted from one corner of Eurasia to another, stimulating technological progress. Native Americans, who had crossed to Alaska before Sumeria, missed out on the bounty. "They had to do everything on their own," Crosby says. Remarkably, they succeeded.

When Columbus appeared in the Caribbean, the descendants of the world's two Neolithic civilizations collided, with overwhelming consequences for both. American Neolithic development occurred later than that of the Middle East, possibly because the Indians needed more time to build up the requisite population density. Without beasts of burden they could not capitalize on the wheel (for individual workers on uneven terrain skids are nearly as effective as carts for hauling), and they never developed steel. But in agriculture they handily outstripped the children of Sumeria. Every tomato in Italy, every potato in Ireland, and every hot pepper in Thailand came from this hemisphere. Worldwide, more than half the crops grown today were initially developed in the Americas.

Maize, as corn is called in the rest of the world, was a triumph with global implications. Indians developed an extraordinary number of maize varieties for different growing conditions, which meant that the crop could and did spread throughout the planet. Central and Southern Europeans became particularly dependent on it; maize was the staple of Serbia, Romania, and Moldavia by the nineteenth century. Indian crops dramatically reduced hunger, Crosby says, which led to an Old World population boom.

In the Aztec capital Tenochtitlán the Spaniards gawped like hayseeds at the side streets, ornately carved buildings, and markets bright with goods from hundreds of miles away.

Along with peanuts and manioc, maize came to Africa and transformed agriculture there, too. "The probability is that the population of Africa was greatly increased because of maize and other American Indian crops," Crosby says. "Those extra people helped make the slave trade possible." Maize conquered Africa at the time when introduced diseases were leveling Indian societies. The Spanish, the Portuguese, and the British were alarmed by the death rate among Indians, because they wanted to exploit them as workers. Faced with a labor shortage, the Europeans turned their eyes to Africa. The continent's quarrelsome societies helped slave traders to siphon off millions of people. The maize-fed population boom, Crosby believes, let the awful trade continue without pumping the well dry.

Back home in the Americas, Indian agriculture long sustained some of the world's largest cities. The Aztec capital of Tenochtitlán dazzled Hernán Cortés in 1519; it was bigger than Paris, Europe's greatest metropolis. The Spaniards gawped like hayseeds at the wide streets, ornately carved buildings, and markets bright with goods from hundreds of miles away. They had never before seen a city with botanical gardens, for the excellent reason that none existed in Europe. The same novelty attended the force of a thousand men that kept the crowded streets immaculate. (Streets that weren't ankle-deep in sewage! The conquistadors had never heard of such a thing.) Central America was not the only locus of prosperity. Thousands of miles north, John Smith, of Pocahontas fame, visited Massachusetts in 1614, before it was emptied by disease, and declared that the land was "so planted with Gardens and Corne fields, and so well inhabited with a goodly, strong and well proportioned people . . . [that] I would rather live here than any where."

Smith was promoting colonization, and so had reason to exaggerate. But he also knew the hunger, sickness, and oppression of European life. France—"by any standards a privileged country," according to its great historian, Fernand Braudel—experienced seven nationwide famines in the fifteenth century and thirteen in the sixteenth. Disease was hunger's constant companion. During epidemics in London the dead were heaped onto carts "like common dung" (the simile is Daniel Defoe's) and trundled through the streets. The infant death rate in London orphanages, according to one contemporary source, was 88 percent. Governments were harsh, the rule of law arbitrary. The gibbets poking up in the background of so many old paintings were, Braudel observed, "merely a realistic detail."

The Earth Shall Weep, James Wilson's history of Indian America, puts the comparison bluntly: "the western hemisphere was larger, richer, and more populous than Europe." Much of it was freer, too. Europeans, accustomed to the serfdom that thrived from Naples to the Baltic Sea, were puzzled and alarmed by the democratic spirit and respect for human rights in many Indian societies, especially those in North America. In theory, the sachems of New England Indian groups were absolute monarchs. In practice, the colonial leader Roger Williams wrote, "they will not conclude of ought . . . unto which the people are averse."

Pre-1492 America wasn't a disease-free paradise, Dobyns says, although in his "exuberance as a writer," he told me recently, he once made that claim. Indians had ailments of their own, notably parasites, tuberculosis, and anemia. The daily grind was wearing; life-spans in America were only as long as or a little longer than those in Europe, if the evidence of indigenous graveyards is to be believed. Nor was it a political utopia—the Inca, for instance, invented refinements to totalitarian rule that would have intrigued Stalin. Inveterate practitioners of what the historian Francis Jennings described as "state terrorism practiced horrifically on a huge scale," the Inca ruled so cruelly that one can speculate that their surviving subjects might actually have been better off under Spanish rule.

I asked seven anthropologists, archaeologists, and historians if they would rather have been a typical Indian or a typical European in 1491. Every one chose to be an Indian.

I asked seven anthropologists, archaeologists, and historians if they would rather have been a typical Indian or a typical European in 1491. None was delighted by the question, because it required judging the past by the standards of today—a fallacy disparaged as "presentism" by social scientists. But every one chose to be an Indian. Some early colonists gave the same answer. Horrifying the leaders of Jamestown and Plymouth, scores of English ran off to live with the Indians. My ancestor shared their desire, which is what led to the trumped-up murder charges against him—or that's what my grandfather told me, anyway.

As for the Indians, evidence suggests that they often viewed Europeans with disdain. The Hurons, a chagrined missionary reported, thought the French possessed "little intelligence in comparison to themselves." Europeans, Indians said, were physically weak, sexually untrustworthy, atrociously ugly, and just plain dirty. (Spaniards, who seldom if ever bathed, were amazed by the Aztec desire for personal cleanliness.) A Jesuit reported that the "Savages" were disgusted by handkerchiefs: "They say, we place what is unclean in a fine white piece of linen, and put it away in our pockets as something very precious, while they throw it upon the ground." The Micmac scoffed at the notion of French superiority. If Christian civilization was so wonderful, why were its inhabitants leaving?

Like people everywhere, Indians survived by cleverly exploiting their environment. Europeans tended to manage land by breaking it into fragments for farmers and herders. Indians often worked on such a grand scale that the scope of their ambition can be hard to grasp. They created small plots, as Europeans did (about 1.5 million acres of terraces still exist in the Peruvian Andes), but they also reshaped entire landscapes to suit their purposes. A principal tool was fire, used to keep down underbrush and create the open, grassy conditions favorable for game. Rather than domesticating animals for meat, Indians retooled whole ecosystems to grow bumper crops of elk, deer, and bison. The first white settlers in Ohio found forests as open as English parks—they could drive carriages through the woods. Along the Hudson River the annual fall burning lit up the banks for miles on end; so flashy was the show that the Dutch in New Amsterdam boated upriver to goggle at the blaze like children at fireworks. In North America, Indian torches had their biggest impact on the Midwestern prairie, much or most of which was created and maintained by fire. Millennia of exuberant burning shaped the plains into vast buffalo farms. When Indian societies disintegrated, forest invaded savannah in Wisconsin, Illinois, Kansas, Nebraska, and the Texas Hill Country. Is it possible that the Indians changed the Americas more than the invading Europeans did? "The answer is probably yes for most regions for the next 250 years or so" after Columbus. William Denevan wrote, "and for some regions right up to the present time."

Amazonia has become *the* emblem of vanishing wilderness—an admonitory image of untouched Nature. But the rain forest itself may be a cultural artifact—that is, an artificial object.

When scholars first began increasing their estimates of the ecological impact of Indian civilization, they met with considerable resistance from anthropologists and archaeologists. Over time the consensus in the human sciences changed. Under Denevan's direction, Oxford University Press has just issued the third volume of a huge catalogue of the "cultivated landscapes" of the Americas. This sort of phrase still provokes vehement objection—but the main dissenters are now ecologists and environmentalists. The disagreement is encapsulated by Amazonia, which has become *the* emblem of vanishing wilderness—an admonitory image of untouched Nature. Yet recently a growing number of researchers have come to believe that Indian societies had an enormous environmental impact on the jungle. Indeed, some anthropologists have called the Amazon forest itself a cultural artifact—that is, an artificial object.

Green Prisons

Northern visitors' first reaction to the storied Amazon rain forest is often disappointment. Ecotourist brochures evoke the immensity of Amazonia but rarely dwell on its extreme flatness. In the river's first 2,900 miles the vertical drop is only 500 feet. The river oozes like a huge runnel of dirty metal through a landscape utterly devoid of the romantic crags, arroyos, and heights that signify wilderness and natural spectacle to most North Americans. Even the animals are invisible, although sometimes one can hear the bellow of monkey choruses. To the untutored eye—mine, for instance—the forest seems to stretch out in a monstrous green tangle as flat and incomprehensible as a printed circuit board.

The area east of the lower-Amazon town of Santarém is an exception. A series of sandstone ridges several hundred feet high reach down from the north, halting almost at the water's edge. Their tops stand drunkenly above the jungle like old tombstones. Many of the caves in the buttes are splattered with ancient petroglyphs—renditions of hands, stars, frogs, and human figures, all reminiscent of Miró, in overlapping red and yellow and brown. In recent years one of these caves, La Caverna da Pedra Pintada (Painted Rock Cave), has drawn attention in archaeological circles.

Wide and shallow and well lit, Painted Rock Cave is less thronged with bats than some of the other caves. The arched entrance is twenty feet high and lined with rock paintings. Out front is a sunny natural patio suitable for picnicking, edged by a few big rocks. People lived in this cave more than 11,000 years ago. They had no agriculture yet, and instead ate fish and fruit and built fires. During a recent visit I ate a sandwich atop a particularly inviting rock and looked over the forest below. The first Amazonians, though, must have done more or less the same thing.

In college I took an introductory anthropology class in which I read *Amazonia: Man and Culture in a Counterfeit Paradise* (1971), perhaps the most influential book ever written about the Amazon, and one that deeply impressed me at the time. Written by Betty J. Meggers, the Smithsonian archaeologist, *Amazonia* says that the apparent lushness of the rain forest is a sham. The soils are poor and can't hold nutrients—the jungle flora exists only because it snatches up everything worthwhile before it leaches away in the rain. Agriculture, which depends on extracting the wealth of the soil, therefore faces inherent ecological limitations in the wet desert of Amazonia.

As a result, Meggers argued, Indian villages were forced to remain small—any report of "more than a few hundred" people in permanent settlements, she told me recently, "makes my alarm bells go off." Bigger, more complex societies would inevitably overtax the forest soils, laying waste to their own foundations. Beginning in 1948 Meggers and her late husband, Clifford Evans, excavated a chiefdom on Marajó, an island twice the size of New Jersey that sits like a gigantic stopper in the mouth of the Amazon. The Marajóara, they concluded, were failed offshoots of a sophisticated culture in the Andes. Transplanted to the lush trap of the Amazon, the culture choked and died.

Green activists saw the implication: development in tropical forests destroys both the forests and their developers. Meggers's account had enormous public impact—*Amazonia* is one of the wellsprings of the campaign to save rain forests.

Then Anna C. Roosevelt, the curator of archaeology at Chicago's Field Museum of Natural History, re-excavated Marajó. Her complete report, *Moundbuilders of the Amazon*

(1991), was like the anti-matter version of *Amazonia.* Marajó, she argued, was "one of the outstanding indigenous cultural achievements of the New World," a powerhouse that lasted for more than a thousand years, had "possibly well over 100,000" inhabitants, and covered thousands of square miles. Rather than damaging the forest, Marajó's "earth construction" and "large, dense populations" had *improved* it: the most luxuriant and diverse growth was on the mounds formerly occupied by the Marajóara. "If you listened to Meggers's theory, these places should have been ruined," Roosevelt says.

Meggers scoffed at Roosevelt's "extravagant claims," "polemical tone," and "defamatory remarks." Roosevelt, Meggers argued, had committed the beginner's error of mistaking a site that had been occupied many times by small, unstable groups for a single, long-lasting society. "[Archaeological remains] build up on areas of half a kilometer or so," she told me, "because [shifting Indian groups] don't land exactly on the same spot. The decorated types of pottery don't change much over time, so you can pick up a bunch of chips and say, 'Oh, look, it was all one big site!' Unless you know what you're doing, of course." Centuries after the conquistadors, "the myth of El Dorado is being revived by archaeologists," Meggers wrote last fall in the journal *Latin American Antiquity,* referring to the persistent Spanish delusion that cities of gold existed in the jungle.

The dispute grew bitter and personal; inevitable in a contemporary academic context, it has featured vituperative references to colonialism, elitism, and employment by the CIA. Meanwhile, Roosevelt's team investigated Painted Rock Cave. On the floor of the cave what looked to me like nothing in particular turned out to be an ancient midden: a refuse heap. The archaeologists slowly scraped away sediment, traveling backward in time with every inch. When the traces of human occupation vanished, they kept digging. ("You always go a meter past sterile," Roosevelt says.) A few inches below they struck the charcoal-rich dirt that signifies human habitation—a culture, Roosevelt said later, that wasn't supposed to be there.

For many millennia the cave's inhabitants hunted and gathered for food. But by about 4000 years ago they were growing crops—perhaps as many as 140 of them, according to Charles R. Clement, an anthropological botanist at the Brazilian National Institute for Amazonian Research. Unlike Europeans, who planted mainly annual crops, the Indians, he says, centered their agriculture on the Amazon's unbelievably diverse assortment of trees: fruits, nuts, and palms. "It's tremendously difficult to clear fields with stone tools," Clement says. "If you can plant trees, you get twenty years of productivity out of your work instead of two or three."

Planting their orchards, the first Amazonians transformed large swaths of the river basin into something more pleasing to human beings. In a widely cited article from 1989, William Balée, the Tulane anthropologist, cautiously estimated that about 12 percent of the nonflooded Amazon forest was of anthropogenic origin—directly or indirectly created by human beings. In some circles this is now seen as a conservative position. "I basically think it's all human-created," Clement told me in Brazil. He argues that Indians changed the assortment

and density of species throughout the region. So does Clark Erickson, the University of Pennsylvania archaeologist, who told me in Bolivia that the lowland tropical forests of South America are among the finest works of art on the planet. "Some of my colleagues would say that's pretty radical," he said, smiling mischievously. According to Peter Stahl, an anthropologist at the State University of New York at Binghamton, "lots" of botanists believe that "what the eco-imagery would like to picture as a pristine, untouched Urwelt [primeval world] in fact has been managed by people for millennia." The phrase "built environment," Erickson says, "applies to most, if not all, Neotropical landscapes."

"Landscape" in this case is meant exactly—Amazonian Indians literally created the ground beneath their feet. According to William I. Woods, a soil geographer at Southern Illinois University, ecologists' claims about terrible Amazonian land were based on very little data. In the late 1990s Woods and others began careful measurements in the lower Amazon. They indeed found lots of inhospitable terrain. But they also discovered swaths of *terra preta*—rich, fertile "black earth" that anthropologists increasingly believe was created by human beings.

Terra preta, Woods guesses, covers at least 10 percent of Amazonia, an area the size of France. It has amazing properties, he says. Tropical rain doesn't leach nutrients from *terra preta* fields; instead the soil, so to speak, fights back. Not far from Painted Rock Cave is a 300-acre area with a two-foot layer of *terra preta* quarried by locals for potting soil. The bottom third of the layer is never removed, workers there explain, because over time it will re-create the original soil layer in its initial thickness. The reason, scientists suspect, is that *terra preta* is generated by a special suite of microorganisms that resists depletion. "Apparently," Woods and the Wisconsin geographer Joseph M. McCann argued in a presentation last summer, "at some threshold level . . . dark earth attains the capacity to perpetuate—even *regenerate* itself—thus behaving more like a living 'super'-organism than an inert material."

In as yet unpublished research the archaeologists Eduardo Neves, of the University of São Paulo; Michael Heckenberger, of the University of Florida; and other colleagues examined *terra preta* in the upper Xingu, a huge southern tributary of the Amazon. Not all Xingu cultures left behind this living earth, they discovered. But the ones that did generated it rapidly—suggesting to Woods that *terra preta* was created deliberately. In a process reminiscent of dropping microorganism-rich starter into plain dough to create sourdough bread, Amazonian peoples, he believes, inoculated bad soil with a transforming bacterial charge. Not every group of Indians there did this, but quite a few did, and over an extended period of time.

When Woods told me this, I was so amazed that I almost dropped the phone. I ceased to be articulate for a moment and said things like "wow" and "gosh." Woods chuckled at my reaction, probably because he understood what was passing through my mind. Faced with an ecological problem, I was thinking, the Indians *fixed* it. They were in the process of terraforming the Amazon when Columbus showed up and ruined everything.

Scientists should study the microorganisms in *terra preta*, Woods told me, to find out how they work. If that could be learned, maybe some version of Amazonian dark earth could be used to improve the vast expanses of bad soil that cripple agriculture in Africa—a final gift from the people who brought us tomatoes, corn, and the immense grasslands of the Great Plains.

"Betty Meggers would just die if she heard me saying this," Woods told me. "Deep down her fear is that this data will be misused." Indeed, Meggers's recent *Latin American Antiquity* article charged that archaeologists who say the Amazon can support agriculture are effectively telling "developers [that they] are entitled to operate without restraint." Resuscitating the myth of El Dorado, in her view, "makes us accomplices in the accelerating pace of environmental degradation." Doubtless there is something to this—although, as some of her critics responded in the same issue of the journal, it is difficult to imagine greedy plutocrats "perusing the pages of *Latin American Antiquity* before deciding to rev up the chain saws." But the new picture doesn't automatically legitimize paving the forest. Instead it suggests that for a long time big chunks of Amazonia were used nondestructively by clever people who knew tricks we have yet to learn.

Environmentalists want to preserve as much of the world's land as possible in a putatively intact state. But "intact" may turn out to mean "run by human beings for human purposes."

I visited Painted Rock Cave during the river's annual flood, when it wells up over its banks and creeps inland for miles. Farmers in the floodplain build houses and barns on stilts and watch pink dolphins sport from their doorsteps. Ecotourists take shortcuts by driving motorboats through the drowned forests. Guys in dories chase after them, trying to sell sacks of incredibly good fruit.

All of this is described as "wilderness" in the tourist brochures. It's not, if researchers like Roosevelt are correct. Indeed, they believe that fewer people may be living there now than in 1491. Yet when my boat glided into the trees, the forest shut out the sky like the closing of an umbrella. Within a few hundred years the human presence seemed to vanish. I felt alone and small, but in a way that was curiously like feeling exalted. If that place was not wilderness, how should I think of it? Since the fate of the forest is in our hands, what should be our goal for its future?

Novel Shores

Hernando de Soto's expedition stomped through the Southeast for four years and apparently never saw bison. More than a century later, when French explorers came down the Mississippi, they saw "a solitude unrelieved by the faintest trace of man," the nineteenth-century historian Francis Parkman wrote. Instead the French encountered bison, "grazing in herds on the great prairies which then bordered the river."

To Charles Kay, the reason for the buffalo's sudden emergence is obvious. Kay is a wildlife ecologist in the political-science department at Utah State University. In ecological terms, he says, the Indians were the "keystone species" of American ecosystems. A keystone species, according to the Harvard biologist Edward O. Wilson, is a species "that affects the survival and abundance of many other species." Keystone species have a disproportionate impact on their ecosystems. Removing them, Wilson adds, "results in a relatively significant shift in the composition of the [ecological] community."

When disease swept Indians from the land, Kay says, what happened was exactly that. The ecological ancient régime collapsed, and strange new phenomena emerged. In a way this is unsurprising; for better or worse, humankind is a keystone species everywhere. Among these phenomena was a population explosion in the species that the Indians had kept down by hunting. After disease killed off the Indians, Kay believes, buffalo vastly extended their range. Their numbers more than sextupled. The same occurred with elk and mule deer. "If the elk were here in great numbers all this time, the archaeological sites should be chock-full of elk bones," Kay says. "But the archaeologists will tell you the elk weren't there." On the evidence of middens the number of elk jumped about 500 years ago.

Passenger pigeons may be another example. The epitome of natural American abundance, they flew in such great masses that the first colonists were stupefied by the sight. As a boy, the explorer Henry Brackenridge saw flocks "ten miles in width, by one hundred and twenty in length." For hours the birds darkened the sky from horizon to horizon. According to Thomas Neumann, a consulting archaeologist to Lilburn, Georgia, passenger pigeons "were incredibly dumb and always roosted in vast hordes, so they were very easy to harvest." Because they were readily caught and good to eat, Neumann says, archaeological digs should find many pigeon bones in the pre-Columbian strata of Indian middens. But they aren't there. The mobs of birds in the history books, he says, were "outbreak populations—always a symptom of an extraordinarily disrupted ecological system."

Throughout eastern North America the open landscape seen by the first Europeans quickly filled in with forest. According to William Cronon, of the University of Wisconsin, later colonists began complaining about how hard it was to get around. (Eventually, of course, they stripped New England almost bare of trees.) When Europeans moved west, they were preceded by two waves: one of disease, the other of ecological disturbance. The former crested with fearsome rapidity; the later sometimes took more than a century to quiet down. Far from destroying pristine wilderness, European settlers bloodily *created* it. By 1800 the hemisphere was chockablock with new wilderness. If "forest primeval" means a woodland unsullied by the human presence, William Denevan has written, there was much more of it in the late eighteenth century than in the early sixteenth.

Cronon's *Changes in the Land: Indians, Colonists, and the Ecology of New England* (1983) belongs on the same shelf as works by Crosby and Dobyns. But it was not until one of his articles was excerpted in *The New York Times* in 1995 that people outside the social sciences began to understand the implications of this view of Indian history. Environmentalists and ecologists vigorously attacked the anti-wilderness scenario, which they described as infected by postmodern philosophy. A small academic brouhaha ensued, complete with hundreds of footnotes. It precipitated *Reinventing Nature?* (1995), one of the few academic critiques of postmodernist philosophy written largely by biologists. *The Great New Wilderness Debate* (1998), another lengthy book on the subject, was edited by two philosophers who earnestly identified themselves as "Euro-American men [whose] cultural legacy is patriarchal Western civilization in its current postcolonial, globally hegemonic form."

It is easy to tweak academics for opaque, self-protective language like this. Nonetheless, their concerns were quite justified. Crediting Indians with the role of keystone species has implications for the way the current Euro-American members of that keystone species manage the forests, watersheds, and endangered species of America. Because a third of the United States is owned by the federal government, the issue inevitably has political ramifications. In Amazonia, fabled storehouse of biodiversity, the stakes are global.

Guided by the pristine myth, mainstream environmentalists want to preserve as much of the world's land as possible in a putatively intact state. But "intact," if the new research is correct, means "run by human beings for human purposes." Environmentalists dislike this, because it seems to mean that anything goes. In a sense they are correct. Native Americans managed the continent as they saw fit. Modern nations must do the same. If they want to return as much of the landscape as possible to its 1491 state, they will have to find it within themselves to create the world's largest garden.

Critical Thinking

1. How sophisticated were the Native Americans before European conquest?
2. Were the Native Americans egalitarian in terms of their approach to women and community duties?
3. Could the later actions of the European conquerors be considered genocidal? Why or why not?

Create Central

www.mhhe.com/createcentral

Internet References

1492: An Ongoing Voyage
www.loc.gov/exhibits/1492/america.html

The Pristine Myth: The Landscape of the Americas in 1492
http://jan.ucc.nau.edu/~alcoze/for398/class/pristinemyth.html

Health Conditions before Columbus: Palepathology of Native North Americans
www.ncbi.nlm.nih.gov/pmc/articles/PMC1071659/

What Did Europeans Bring To America?
http://people.umass.edu/hist383/class%20notes/european%20pathogens.htm

Overview of the First Americans
www.digitalhistory.uh.edu/era.cfm

Article   Prepared by: Wendy A. Maier-Sarti, *Oakton Community College*

Massacre in Florida

Spain's attack on Fort Caroline and brutal slaughter of its inhabitants ended France's colonial interests on the East Coast.

ANDRÉS RESÉNDEZ

Learning Outcomes

After reading this article, you will be able to:

- Recount the Spanish massacre of the French settlers at the mouth of the St. John River.

- Explain why the Spanish did not take over the fort.

- List the countries that took over as colonizers in Florida.

In June 1564, 300 French colonists arrived at the mouth of the St. Johns River near present-day Jacksonville, Florida, after an arduous voyage across the Atlantic. Among these *colons* were men from some of France's greatest noble houses, bedecked in bright clothes and suits of gilded armor, accompanied by a train of artisans and laborers. They built a triangular outer wall on the southern bank, dragged several cannon into it, and set about raising a village, which soon contained houses, a mill, and a bakery. At first the local Timucua were friendly, furnishing them with food and giving them advice about survival.

France had so far established only rugged outposts along what would become known as the St. Lawrence, to harvest fish and furs and probe for the Northwest Passage. Yet these lowly stations soon fell short of satisfying France's grand ambitions for the New World.

This new settlement—Fort Caroline—represented France's first permanent colony in what would later become the United States, a continental foothold in the strategic Florida peninsula. From here French colonists had access to the sugar plantations and gold fields of the Caribbean and a chance to prey on bullion-bearing Spanish galleons coming from Mexico and Peru. The French crown had big plans for that muddy bank in northeast Florida.

Like the English pilgrims, most of the French settlers were spirited Protestants—Huguenots who saw the New World as a refuge and an opportunity to establish a model community. But unlike their English counterparts, the French pioneers also counted on direct royal patronage. The Huguenots had come to occupy key positions under the monarchy, and the main backer of the venture, Gaspard de Coligny, was a close adviser to the royal family, admiral of the French navy, and the undisputed Huguenot leader. He moved swiftly to resupply Fort Caroline the following year, dispatching seven ships, a thousand men, and provisions. Meanwhile, the situation at Fort Caroline had become dire as relations with the Indians had grown strained and the incipient French settlement had experienced mutinies. Just as the colonists were about to leave, the relief expedition finally arrived in the summer of 1565.

Hearing of this intrusion, Spain had dispatched Pedro Menéndez de Avilés with an armada under sweeping orders to "take the Florida coast." After the two fleets brushed briefly, Menéndez prudently retreated southward, where he broke ground for a new stronghold, St. Augustine, which has gone on to prosper and is today the oldest European-founded town in the continental United States.

Luck favored the Spanish. The French ships, which were roughly twice as numerous and much better supplied, ran into a hurricane, which blew some out to sea and forced others aground. Meanwhile Menéndez sent his men overland against Fort Caroline. At dawn on September 20, 1565, he and 500 men armed with arquebuses, pikes, and targets surprised the fort and overran it. Such men over 15 not killed at the outset were summarily executed. Only women, girls, and young boys were spared. Over the next few weeks Spanish soldiers mopped up the Florida coast, putting to death any French sailors who had managed to survive the storm and shipwreck.

Men over 15 not killed at the outset were summarily executed.

The French would come back to the Florida coast and exact harsh retribution, slaughtering Spaniards. But the damage to French interests on the East Coast had already been done. The French had been driven into the distant north, leaving a vacuum of settlement on the Atlantic coast for the English, Dutch, and

Swedish settlers who arrived half a century later when Spanish power was already passing into decline. Had Fort Caroline prospered, a sizable French-speaking area such as Quebec could well exist in Florida today. But the events of 1565 steered the history of North America in a different direction.

Critical Thinking

1. Why did the massacre occur?
2. How did the Spanish actions in Florida lead to an opening in areas along the Atlantic coastline?

Create Central

www.mhhe.com/createcentral

Internet References

French Colony
http://fcit.usf.edu/florida/docs/f/frenchcol.htm

Fort Caroline National Memorial Jacksonville Florida
www.nps.gov/history/nr/travel/american_latino_heritage/Fort_Caroline_National_Memorial.html

The Americas
www.historyfiles.co.uk/KingListsAmericas/ColoniesFlorida.htm

St. Elena History
http://artsandsciences.sc.edu/sciaa/staff/depratterc/hstory1.html

ANDRÉS RESÉNDEZ, author of *A Land So Strange: The Epic Journey of Cabeza de Vaca* (Basic Books 2009), is an associate professor of history at the University of California at Davis.

Reséndez, Andrés. From *American Heritage*, Winter 2010, pp. 24–25. Copyright © 2010 by American Heritage, Inc. Reprinted by permission of American Heritage Publishing and Andrés Reséndez.

Representing the Portrayal of Pilgrims in Elementary History Texts & the Myth of the Founding of the American Nation by Cecelia L. Parks

31

Article

Prepared by: Wendy A. Maier-Sarti, *Oakton Community College*

Representing the Portrayal of Pilgrims in Elementary History Textbooks and the Myth of the Founding of the American Nation

CECELIA L. PARKS

Learning Outcomes

After reading this article, you will be able to:

- Recount the three elements of the Pilgrim story.

- Characterize the Pilgrims as they really were.

- Identify at least three negative impacts the Pilgrims had on the native tribes.

Every American knows something about the Pilgrims: they were Puritans (or Separatists) who emigrated from England to freely practice their own form of Protestantism. They went first to the Dutch Republic, but about thirty-five members of the party desired complete separation from other religions. These thirty-five Puritans, along with sixty-seven other emigrants, set out in the *Mayflower* for the New World, ostensibly for Virginia. They landed instead in Massachusetts in November of 1620 and chose a site for a settlement, which they named Plymouth. Plymouth lay outside the jurisdiction of the Virginia Company, with whom the Pilgrims were contracted, so they created the Mayflower Compact, which set up what is often seen as a democratic system of government. Unfortunately, because the settlers arrived in November, they were unable to grow food and about half of the group died in the first winter. Luckily for them, however, Squanto, a Native American—and later others—came to help. They taught the settlers how to grow crops and gather food in their new environment. Squanto and his allies also acted as ambassadors and translators to the other Native Americans in the area. At the end of the harvest that year, the Pilgrims celebrated the "First Thanksgiving" with their Native American friends.

This paper will examine how this common representation of Pilgrims in elementary history textbooks reflects and disseminates an American nationalist mythology. This representation communicates this myth specifically through the portrayal of Thanksgiving, the relationship with the Native Americans, and the Pilgrims' "American ideals." Many historical facts are omitted or distorted in this depiction of the Pilgrims' story. The representation of the Pilgrims is examined in two elementary United States history textbooks, *Social Studies: United States History,* published by Houghton Mifflin in 2004, and *United States History: Beginnings to 1877,* published by Holt McDougal in 2010. These texts' presentation of the Pilgrims' story prevents a true understanding of America's complex history and identity.

The theory of invented tradition plays a significant role in the discussion of the Pilgrims and their representation in history textbooks. Eric Hobsbawm and Terence Ranger define invented tradition as "a set of practices, normally governed by overtly or tacitly accepted rules...these ritual or symbolic acts seek to inculcate certain values and norms of behavior by repetition...implying continuity with the past."[1] Importantly, an invented tradition does not have to be a specific event, such as a holiday, though it often takes the form of one. "Tradition" can also mean a longstanding set of beliefs or a doctrine that is woven into the fabric of society. The representation of Pilgrims in textbooks constitutes just such a series of invented traditions.

Textbooks are a particularly effective way to examine the representation of the Pilgrims because they play an integral role in teaching United States history. Frances FitzGerald notes in her seminal examination of history textbooks, "Children have to read textbooks; they usually have to read all of each textbook and are rarely asked to criticize it for style or point of view."[2] Classroom curricula are often based in textbooks, ensuring that the books' representation of the facts will be spread even if the students do not specifically engage with the text. Additionally, the public sees textbooks as a reliable source of correct information about the subject. They purport to contain an unbiased presentation of the facts that students can easily reference. The

American Textbook Council, an independent research organization dedicated to reviewing history texts, addresses this important role of textbooks:

> American history textbooks are the official portraits of our country's past that are purchased by local and state governments and that are assigned to students with the foreknowledge that these students will someday participate in public affairs. How much these students know and what they think about their nation and world will indelibly affect civic character.[3]

Students learn much of what they know about the United States from history textbooks; therefore, the representation of events in this nation's past in textbooks is key to students' perception of those events.

Both textbooks analyzed here are credible examples of the norm in elementary United States history textbooks. The Houghton Mifflin textbook is on the American Textbook Council's list of most widely used elementary history textbooks in the country.[4] Both books convey essentially the same basic information about the Pilgrims (although the Holt McDougal book devotes slightly more text to them), as well as providing similar resources for teachers, such as online lesson plans provided by websites like TeacherLINK.[5]

American national mythology is spread in part by the portrayal of the Pilgrims in elementary United States history textbooks. One of the most prominent examples is the myth of Thanksgiving. Most people perceive the First Thanksgiving as a celebration by the Pilgrims of a successful harvest with their Native American friends. Textbooks represent it as a three-day-long feast with about ninety Native Americans, including Massasoit and Squanto. Most Americans see the First Thanksgiving as a celebration of the Pilgrims' hard work and perseverance through their first year in Plymouth.

Today, Americans celebrate Thanksgiving each year on the fourth Thursday in November. It is a time to remember the Pilgrims, spend time with family, eat turkey, watch football, and (in some cases) actually give thanks. When we celebrate the Pilgrims, we celebrate the values they supposedly upheld. Waters comments, "Today's uniquely positive American values like the rule of law, freedom of religion, cultural diversity, farming, and hard work are logically celebrated by acknowledging the role Pilgrims and Indians played in developing the new society."[6]

This role, however, is largely an invented tradition. The Pilgrims did not actually have a Thanksgiving tradition, and if they had celebrated a day of thanks, it probably would have included prayer and fasting rather than feasting. In fact, Thanksgiving did not become a national holiday until the Civil War, when America desperately needed a holiday to inspire feelings of patriotism and solidarity.[7] Thanksgiving, in its current incarnation, provided the perfect solution. Many Americans think of Thanksgiving as an organic tradition; rather, it was invented to remind a war-torn nation of its roots and to reunite the country.

However, none of this information is mentioned in elementary history textbooks. All the Houghton Mifflin text says of Thanksgiving is, "People in the United States remember this feast during Thanksgiving, a national holiday celebrated every November."[8] When people "remember this feast," they also

remember the Pilgrims, and all of the values and ideals that, according to Waters, are attached to the Pilgrims.

The Houghton Mifflin text credits Squanto, saying, "Squanto taught the Pilgrims to plant crops such as maize (corn), pumpkins, and beans ... By the fall of 1621, the colony had become more successful."[9] The message sent here is that if the students work hard and persevere, they will be rewarded with help and a good harvest in whatever endeavors they are pursuing. These are the quintessential American values of hard work and equal opportunity.

The Holt McDougal text is more explicit in its presentation of Thanksgiving as an invented tradition. It reads, "This feast became known as the first Thanksgiving ... This event marked the survival of the Pilgrims in the new colony."[10] By referring to the celebration as the "first Thanksgiving," the textbook sets Thanksgiving up as an organic tradition started by the Pilgrims and continued by the rest of the nation, not a one-time event that was capitalized on during the Civil War.

Thanksgiving was formally instituted as a national holiday around the same time policies towards Native Americans became much harsher. In the late nineteenth century, especially in the frontier states, "Exterminate or Banish" became a popular slogan regarding Native American policy.[11] This exterminatory rhetoric translated to significant violence against Native Americans throughout the United States. Ironically the Pilgrims' story and Thanksgiving, in which friendliness to the Native Americans plays a key role, rose to national prominence in this time in which general opinion and actions were anything but friendly to Native Americans. Mann posits that genocidal policies such as the ones practiced by the American government in the nineteenth century are "the dark side of democracy," because he has found that ethnic cleansing occurs more in democratic regimes than authoritarian regimes.[12] Since Democratic government also plays a key role in the myth of the Pilgrims, the institution of Thanksgiving as a national holiday demonstrates Lincoln's need for a device that not only unified his people but also highlighted national mythology to ease the people's conscience concerning Native American policy.

Most American schoolchildren are taught that the Pilgrims coexisted peacefully with the Native Americans. The myth is that the Pilgrims were generous, magnanimous settlers who were willingly helped by the friendly Native Americans. Though the settler-Native American relations were generally peaceful from the time of settlement until the Pequot War of 1637, the events that took place before Plymouth was founded were not so benign. Though the exact effect is difficult to quantify, a high percentage of Native Americans died as a result of European contact. Jennings cites an account of a settler:

> In 1656, Adriaen Van der Donck wrote from his experience in New Netherland that "the Indians ... affirm, that before the arrival of the Christians, and before the small pox broke out amongst them, they were ten times as numerous as they are now, and that their population had been melted down by this disease, whereof nine-tenths of them have died."[13]

The Native Americans often cooperated with the settlers because their numbers had been so diminished by disease that they felt they had no other option. Loewen remarks, "Indeed,

Representing the Portrayal of Pilgrims in Elementary History Texts & the Myth of the Founding of the American Nation by Cecelia L. Parks

33

the plague helped prompt the legendary warm reception Plymouth enjoyed from the Wampanoags."[14] In fact, Plymouth was built over an abandoned Native American village called Patuxet that had been decimated by sickness. Another aspect of the myth of the Pilgrims is that "America was a virgin land, or wilderness, inhabited by people called savages...that civilization was required by divine sanction...to conquer the wilderness and make it a garden."[15] America was already inhabited when the Pilgrims arrived; instead of forging new territory in a wilderness, they had to displace the current occupants and resettle the land. Pilgrims also were known to steal from the houses and graves of Native Americans.[16] Without the Native Americans, the settlement at Plymouth would almost certainly have failed, because in spite of poor treatment by Europeans, the Native Americans helped the settlers grow crops and gather food as well as establish trading posts for the furs they trapped. However, this side of the European-Native American relationship is not often discussed, because Westerners try to avoid the image of mass murderers who essentially wiped out entire populations. The myth of the Europeans' good relations with the Native Americans is an invented tradition perpetuated to show the European-Americans in general and the Pilgrims in particular as inherently good people who cohabitated harmoniously with the native peoples.

Notes

1. Eric J. Hobsbawm and Terence O. Ranger, "Introduction: Inventing Traditions" in *The Invention of Tradition,* (New York: Cambridge University Press, 1992), 1.

2. Frances FitzGerald, *America Revised: History Schoolbooks in the Twentieth Century,* (Boston: Little, Brown, 1979), 27.

3. Gilbert T. Sewall, *History Textbooks at the New Century: A Report of the American Textbook Council,* (New York: American Textbook Council, 2000), 2.

4. "Widely Adopted History Textbooks," *American Textbook Council,* accessed October 25, 2010, http://www .historytextbooks.org/adopted.htm.

5. "Lesson Plan—Thanksgiving—A Focus on Clothing," *TeacherLINK @ Utah State University,* accessed October 25, 2010, http://teacherlink.ed.usu.edu/tlresources/units/ Byrnescelebrations/Thanksgiving.html.

6. Tony Waters, "Why Students Think There Are Two Kinds of American History," *The History Teacher* 39, no. 1 (2005): 18.

7. Arthur Quinn, "The Miracle Harvest," *The New York Times,* November 24, 1994, 33, *Academic Search Complete* (accessed January 25, 2012).

8. "European Settlements," in *United States History 5: Houghton Mifflin Social Studies* (Boston: Houghton Mifflin Company, 2004), 138.

9. Ibid.

10. "The English Colonies," in *United States History: Beginnings to 1877* (Austin: Holt McDougal, 2010), 79.

11. Michael Mann, *The Dark Side of Democracy: Explaining Ethnic Cleansing,* (New York: Cambridge, 2005), 91.

12. Ibid., 2.

13. Francis Jennings, *The Invasion of America: Indians, Colonialism, and the Cant of Conquest,* (Chapel Hill: University of North Carolina Press, 1975), 24.

14. James W. Loewen, *Lies My Teacher Told Me: Everything Your American History Textbook Got Wrong,* (New York: Touchstone, 2007), 72.

15. Ibid., 15.

16. Loewen, *Lies My Teacher Told Me,* 75.

Critical Thinking

1. How do you think the myths around the Pilgrims got started?

2. What other intepreations could be applied to the impact that the Pilgrims and Puritans had on Native American cultures?

3. How do the myths and the reality of the Pilgrms differ?

Create Central

www.mhhe.com/createcentral

Internet References

The Pilgrims' Real First Thanksgiving
www.defense.gov/News/NewsArticle.aspx?ID=43005

Embarkation of the Pilgrims
www.aoc.gov/capitol-hill/historic-rotunda-paintings/embarkation-pilgrims

America's First True "Pilgrims"
www.smithsonianmag.com/history-archaeology/hidden-history-excerpt .html#ixzz2dyVRjES8

Pilgrims and Purtains: Background
http://xroads.virginia.edu/~cap/puritan/purhist.html

Parks, Cecelia L. (2012) "Representing the Portrayal of Pilgrims in Elementary History Textbooks and the Myth of the Founding of the American Nation," *Papers and Publications: Interdisciplinary Journal of Undergraduate Research*: vol. 1: iss. 1, article 10. Available at: http://digitalcommons.northgeorgia.edu/papersandpubs/vol1/iss1/10

Article   Prepared by: Wendy A. Maier-Sarti, *Oakton Community College*

A Pox on the New World

As much as nine-tenths of the indigenous population of the Americas died in less than a generation from European pathogens.

CHARLES C. MANN

Learning Outcomes

After reading this article, you will be able to:

- Explain the biological impact that the European settlers had on native populations.

- Explain the reasons why the biological impact was so severe.

- Explain why the biological transfer was not the same from the natives to the Europeans.

In the summer of 1605 the French explorer Samuel de Champlain sailed along the coast of New England, looking for a likely spot to place a colony—a place more hospitable than the upper St. Lawrence River, which he had previously explored. Halfway down the Maine coast he began to find spots with good harbors, abundant supplies of freshwater, and big spreads of cleared land. The problem was that these parcels were already occupied. The peoples there were happy to barter with him and treat his sailors to fine dinners. But none were interested in providing free real estate. A skirmish in Nauset Bay, halfway down Cape Cod, convinced Champlain that he had no hope of starting a colony in this area. Too many people already lived there.

Fifteen years later, a band of English voyagers showed up in Massachusetts. The Pilgrims were everything that Champlain was not: inexperienced, poorly supplied, and lacking in basic survival skills. Arriving on the cusp of winter, they anchored offshore, planted their metaphorical flag on some choice land, and quickly set about the business of dying en masse. Surprisingly, the Pilgrims made it through the winter; within a few years, they were prospering. Why did the land's original inhabitants, so clear about their rejection of the French, allow the English company to stay?

Pilgrim writings provide the answer. Colonist William Bradford learned that three or four years before the *Mayflower* landed, shipwrecked French seamen had set up shop on Cape

Cod. Unwilling to countenance a long-term foreign presence, no matter how unintended, the Indians of Nauset, Bradford recounted, "never left watching & dogging them till they got advantage, and *kild them all but 3. or 4.*" Even this limited mercy proved a mistake. One of the French carried a disease not known in the Americas. He bequeathed it to his captors, who passed it on to their friends and families. As the epidemic spread, the healthy fled from the sick, unwittingly carrying the disease with them to neighboring communities. All along the New England coast, the English poet-adventurer Thomas Morton reported, Indians "died in heapes, as they lay in their houses." So many perished so quickly that the living had no time to bury the dead. Morton, who settled in Massachusetts in 1624, found native skeletons still littering the woods. The Pilgrims fared better than Champlain because they were moving into land that was now largely unoccupied.

So many perished so quickly that the living had no time to bury the dead.

Their story was no exception. Although Europeans had firearms, steel blades, and horses, none of which existed in the Americas, their biggest weapon was biological. By a quirk of evolutionary history, the Western Hemisphere had few epidemic diseases—no smallpox, influenza, measles, or malaria. When these illnesses hitchhiked to the Americas aboard European ships, somewhere between two-thirds and nine-tenths of the native population of the Americas died. Arguably, this is the single most powerful explanatory fact in the entire history of the Americas post-1492.

Consider the two assaults by Hernán Cortés on Mexico's great Triple Alliance (many historians view the term "Aztec" as a 19th-century invention). A brilliant commander who wielded the advantages of guns, swords, horses, and battalions of Alliance-hating indigenous soldiers, Cortés was able to occupy the capital of Tenochtitlán by seizing the empire's supreme military leader. The Alliance was as stunned as Spain would have been if an Indian force had abducted the king of Spain. Eventually there was a counterattack in which most of the Spaniards died, along with their horses. Cortés was reported to have sat weeping at the ruin of his hopes. With no other options, he readied a second assault, this one with far fewer horses, swords, and guns. But he had acquired an additional weapon: smallpox, which was apparently brought over by a Spanish slave. Packed into crowded cities and carrying no resistance, the people of central Mexico died in huge numbers, including most of the imperial court. Cortés's second assault, launched in the wake of the epidemic, was successful.

Disease preceded successful European colonization of the Americas in almost every instance. But it played a later role, too. Carried over in the bodies of colonists from the feverish fens of southwest England, malaria rapidly became endemic from Virginia to Florida. Killing or driving away natives and newcomers alike, it helped to create a labor shortage that fed the demand for African slaves. (Most West Africans are genetically immune to the type of malaria that was imported from England.) During the American Revolution, British general Charles Cornwallis occupied the Carolinas, hoping to inspire a loyalist rebellion—the "southern strategy," as it was known. Alas, the Carolinas were filled with rice paddies, a recent introduction. Mosquitoes thrived in this new environment, as did the malaria parasite inside them. With half his army sick, Cornwallis was ordered to retreat to Yorktown, Virginia, which he regarded as an "unhealthy swamp." (Correctly—malaria was probably introduced in nearby Jamestown.) There the rest of his army fell prey to the disease. His surrender soon followed, effectively ending the war.

George Washington's courage, tenacity, and political deftness were vital to the successful outcome of the American Revolution.

No history would be complete without taking them into account. But equally vital was the grinding, constantly rising toll of mosquito-borne disease. Here, as in so many other instances, examination of the landmarks of human history reveals its inextricable entanglement with the nonhuman world.

Critical Thinking

1. Why did disease spread so fast once European contact with the native populations began?
2. Did European governments react to the widespread deaths? Why or why not?

Create Central

www.mhhe.com/createcentral

Internet References

Virgin Soils Revisited
www2.hawaii.edu/~rrath/hist460/Jones-VirginSoilsRevisited-WMQ60.4Oct2003.html

Were American Indians Victims of Genocide?
http://hnn.us/article/7302

Diseases
http://public.gettysburg.edu/~tshannon/hist106web/site19/diseases.htm

The Persistence of American Indian Health Disparities
www.ncbi.nlm.nih.gov/pmc/articles/PMC1698152/

CHARLES C. MANN, author of *1491: New Revelations of the Americas Before Columbus,* is a correspondent for *Science* and *The Atlantic Monthly* living in Amherst, Massachusetts.

Mann, Charles C. From *American Heritage,* Winter 2010, pp. 23–24. Copyright © 2010 by American Heritage, Inc. Reprinted by permission of American Heritage Publishing and the Charles C. Mann.

Article   Prepared by: Wendy A. Maier-Sarti, *Oakton Community College*

Indentured Servants and the Pursuits of Happiness

CRANDALL SHIFFLETT

Learning Outcomes

After reading this article, you will be able to:

- Articulate the difference in male and female experience as indentured servants.

- Analyze the impact indentured servants had on creating the culture.

- Articulate the reasons behind people becoming indentured servants.

Indentured servants have a long history in America. Since slaves replaced servants as the major source of labor in the late seventeenth century, we tend to forget that indentured servants continued to work into the early nineteenth century. Indentured servants have an even greater longevity as first symbols of the American dream, early icons in the persistent discourse of American exceptionalism. Who were these men and women who made up the ranks of indentured servants? How were they treated and how did this experience in the formative period of their lives shape the attitudes of later generations? These questions raise the much larger issue of Jamestown's place in the formation of an early American culture.

Indentures were mortgages on the future, a promise made to work for the person who paid one's freight and guaranteed passage to the New World. The written contract, if it existed, was a legally enforceable agreement. Its terms usually meant a period of service—typically four to seven years—in exchange for the cost of transportation, sustenance, and shelter. By one estimate, three-fourths of the white population were dependent laborers when they arrived in the New World. But for a variety of reasons, many sailed without a contract in hand and took their chances on working out an agreement once they arrived in Virginia or Maryland. If they found no suitable employer, the ship's captain could sell them to anyone he pleased.

Labor recruiters promoted Virginia as a paradise on earth and an open society where laborers were sure to become landholders. Yet in 1623, Richard Frethorne, writing from Martin's Hundred, a settlement about ten miles from Jamestown, begged his parents to redeem him or send him food. He wrote in the immediate aftermath of one of the bloodiest Indian assaults in a series of retaliatory attacks on settlements along the James River. Frethorne provided dramatic first-person testimony of the settlers' fears of leaving the fort to seek food, having become virtual hostages of local Indians who were angry over unkept promises, encroachments upon their economy, and threats to their culture. Frethorne made the bitter claim that many Englishmen would give one of their limbs to be back in England. Granted this was a low point in the history of the colony; nevertheless it is a reminder that after a decade-and-a-half of settlement, indentured servants were far from realizing the dream of a better life in the Chesapeake Bay region, the dream that had lured many to mortgage their futures.

The indentured servants' chances for success improved substantially after the Virginia Company period. In 1624, after eighteen years of settlement, Jamestown's population numbered only 1,200 people. But after 1625 and until the end of the 1650s, a bullish tobacco market and high labor demand drove the immigration rates upward to almost 2,000 per year. With cheap land and low fixed-capital costs for tools and equipment, a man could start at the bottom and with hard work, thrift, avoidance of legal troubles, and good luck become a landholder and, perhaps, an officeholder. Even without statistical evidence to measure how many fulfilled their terms of service and became landholders, enough servants achieved status gains to satisfy the aspirations of most and keep the dream alive. In the last quarter of the seventeenth century, the switch to slavery further added to the servants' sense of achievement, redemption through hard work, and a new-found sense of superiority over black labor.

Historians have sifted the evidence on the social origins of Chesapeake servants. Although the record is thin—we have evidence on about 15,000 of the roughly 120,000 indentured servants who came to Virginia and Maryland in the seventeenth century—we do know that they played a substantial role in the formation of what might be called the charter culture. Most were young (15–24), male (six men to every woman in 1635; three men to every woman at the close of the century), and single. Mostly they came from the same regions of England: London, the Southeast, and counties extending from the Thames Valley to the West country. Common laborers, skilled artisans, husbandmen, yeomen, and even an occasional gentleman formed the occupational ranks of servants. In other words, they came from a broad spectrum of working men and women, from the ranks of the destitute and homeless through the lower-middle classes and sometimes beyond. The Bristol registration, a remarkable official record of the emigrant's name, length of indenture, occupation, sex, place of origin and destination, owner's name, and name of ship—provides information on the largest single group (10,000). The record was maintained at the Bristol port from 1654 until 1676 and, although incomplete, no earlier records exist of comparable value. Population growth, conversion of arable land to pasturage, and recession in the cloth industry drove thousands to consider emigration while the Virginia Company in 1619 lured many of them with its misleading offer of a headright: fifty acres of land to any servant who fulfilled the terms of the contract. Many servants failed to understand that the headright went to the person who paid the transportation.

The terms of their contracts, laws regulating their behavior, and court records and newspaper advertisements on those who ran away promise to open additional windows on the conditions of indentured servitude. A number of laws enacted in the seventeenth century governed the behavior of masters and servants. These laws tell us a good deal about such matters as the place of bonded labor in the social hierarchy, when race and slavery came to be connected, and of the role of race and gender in early Virginia. Restrictions had to be placed both upon masters against "barbarous" treatment of their servants and upon servants against "fornication" and "unapproved" marriages. Additionally, distinctions evolved in the laws between Indians, slaves, and servants, between the baptized and un-baptized, or Christians and heathens, and so between freedom and slavery. The laws show as much if not more conflict between masters and servants as between servants and slaves. Often slaves and servants ran away together.

For most of the seventeenth century the lives of white indentured servants and enslaved blacks were similar. They worked together in the fields; they ate together and slept in the same part of a building. The changes in day-to-day conditions really came after Nathaniel Bacon's rebellion in 1676. But indentured servitude differed from slavery in one very substantial way. Bondage in perpetuity carried with it (after 1662 in Virginia) the condition of inheritance for every child born of a slave mother. This set slavery apart from indentured servitude however similar were the physical conditions of their lives. And, obviously, indenture was contractual and consensual; slavery was forced and involuntary, usually the result of capture and sale. Finally, the right of self-possession and full control over the labor of one's hands cannot be overestimated.

In the practice of indenture, not uncommonly, owners treated servants like slaves. Even those who did have contracts often found themselves at the mercy of masters who abused them (especially in the case of women), provided the bare minimum in terms of food, clothing and shelter, and took their fifty-acre headright. Historians have noted how such abuse and degradation was bound to shape attitudes of young servants who, as they grew older, helped set later patterns of labor exploitation.

Not surprisingly, servants ran away. Without a published newspaper in the seventeenth century, it is difficult to assess the extent of flight by indentured servants. Court records will need to be thoroughly examined before we can take a full measure of such unrest. But it is already clear from a perusal of some county records that running away was taken quite seriously by colonial officials and was met with harsh treatment, different from that given to resistant slaves only in terms of when it was carried out. Runaway servant entries in York County, Virginia records, for example, reveal punishments of twenty, thirty, or more "lashes on his bare shoulders" for a runaway servant, or additions of years, sometimes twice the original number or more, to the first contract. The leniency of treating the first sentence as a warning did distinguish indentured servants from slaves. But it did little to stop runaways. In the eighteenth century, hundreds of advertisements in the Virginia Gazette newspaper provide a treasure trove of richly detailed information on servant and slave runaways. When all of this evidence is examined carefully, historians will have a fuller picture of the practice of indentured servitude. Then we can begin to assess how the practice shaped the attitudes and values of white laboring men and women whose experience as servants certainly ingrained them to accept black labor exploitation as a common feature of the American experience.

Suggestions for Further Reading

Bailyn, Bernard. *Voyagers to the West: A Passage in the Peopling of America on the Eve of the Revolution.* New York: Alfred Knopf, 1986.

Breen, T. H. and Stephen Innes. *"Myne Owne Ground:" Race and Freedom on Virginia's Eastern Shore, 1640–1676.* New York: Oxford University Press, 1980.

Campbell, Mildred. "Social Origins of Some Early Americans." In *Seventeenth-Century America: Essays in Colonial History.* Edited by James Morton Smith. Chapel Hill: University of North Carolina Press, 1959.

Galenson, David W. *White Servitude in Colonial America: An Economic Analysis.* New York: Cambridge University Press, 1981.

Greene, Jack P. *Pursuits of Happiness: The Social Development of Early Modern British Colonies and the Formation of American Culture.* Chapel Hill: University of North Carolina Press, 1988.

Horn, James. *Adapting to a New World: English Society in the Seventeenth-Century Chesapeake.* Chapel Hill: University of North Carolina Press, 1994.

Kupperman, Karen Ordahl. "The Founding Years of Virginia and the United States." *The Virginia Magazine of History and Biography,* 104 (1996): 103–112.

Sacks, David Harris. *The Widening Gate: Bristol and the Atlantic Economy, 1450–1700.* Berkeley: University of California Press, 1991.

Critical Thinking

1. Why were the male and female experiences different as indentured servants?

2. What was the biggest impact indentured servants had on developing the culture?

3. Given the terms of servitude, was it worth it to become an indentured servant?

Create Central

www.mhhe.com/createcentral

Internet References

African American Heritage and Ethnography
www.nps.gov/ethnography/aah/aaheritage/histContextsF.htm

Slavery and Indentured Servants
http://memory.loc.gov/ammem/awhhtml/awlaw3/slavery.html

White Servitude
www.montgomerycollege.edu/Departments/hpolscrv/whiteser.html

Shifflett, Crandall. From *Virginia Tech*, 2000, pp. 1–3. Copyright © 2000 by Virginia Tech. Reprinted by permission.

Article   Prepared by: Wendy A. Maier-Sarti, *Oakton Community College*

New Amsterdam Becomes New York

The British seize Manhattan from the Dutch—and alter the trajectory of North American history.

RUSSELL SHORTO

Learning Outcomes

After reading this article, you will be able to:

• Explain why the Dutch surrendered the city to the British.

• Explain what impact the Dutch had on the culture of the newly named New York.

On September 5, 1664, two men faced one another across a small stretch of water. Onshore, just outside the fort at the southern tip of Manhattan Island, stood Peter Stuyvesant, director-general of the Dutch colony of New Netherland, his 52-year-old frame balanced on the wooden stump where he had lost a leg in battle a quarter century earlier. Approaching him aboard a small rowboat flying a flag of truce was John Winthrop, governor of the Connecticut colony, until very recently a man Stuyvesant had called his friend.

For 17 years Stuyvesant had managed the Dutch settlement in North America. The colony's origins dated to 1609, when Englishman Henry Hudson had charted the area on behalf of the Dutch East India Company and the Dutch had laid claim to a wide swath of the East Coast. At its height, New Netherland covered an area encompassing all or parts of five future states: New York, New Jersey, Connecticut, Pennsylvania, and Delaware. From its second city, Beverwijck—the future Albany—residents traded for beaver pelts and other furs with Indians. Goods traveled down the Hudson River to the capital of New Amsterdam on Manhattan Island for transshipment to Europe. The colonists also grew tobacco for the European market, and New Amsterdam functioned as a port for English ships from Virginia and New England.

The colony existed in a state of constant struggle. Indians threatened it, and so did the English. Thanks largely to the English Civil Wars, people had fled England in large numbers for the colonies in New England and Virginia, and as their numbers swelled they encroached on the boundaries of New Netherland.

Stuyvesant, meanwhile, had to work with an unusually mixed society. In the 1640s the 500 colonists in New Amsterdam communicated in 18 languages. To deal with this diversity, the city's elders formulated an official policy of tolerance, a genuine anomaly in Europe at the time. Along with tolerance, the Dutch also introduced 17th-century capitalism. The inhabitants were vigorous traders: carpenters, wheelwrights, and even prostitutes bought shares in shipments of goods being transported to the home country.

In addition to mediating between inhabitants and the company officials, Stuyvesant found himself begging Amsterdam for soldiers and ships to protect the colony from encroachment. Failing to get these, he negotiated treaties with the New England governors; his most trusted ally became Winthrop.

He had believed Winthrop's claim in 1661 that the English had no designs on the colony. But in London other plans were afoot. In the wake of the restoration of the Stuart monarchy, Charles II had set about reorganizing the American colonies. He intended to restrict the power of the Puritans and also to make a play for the Dutch colony. The Puritan Winthrop found the first part of this strategy hard to swallow. But he understood the new political reality, fell in line behind the king, and agreed to be an emissary for the crown. Charles granted his brother James, the Duke of York, title over the land that encompassed the Dutch colony. He sent a flotilla of four ships and 2,000 men.

Stuyvesant was clearly outmatched: he could muster only 150 soldiers and had no gunpowder for his cannons. A letter arrived from Richard Nicolls, commander of the flotilla, demanding surrender. Despite the odds, Stuyvesant wanted to fight.

At that moment, Winthrop rowed ashore and handed his former friend a letter granting generous terms. When the townsfolk learned of the offer, they wanted to surrender. Stuyvesant argued against it, but he was forced to capitulate in the end.

As it happened, it was fortunate for the city—whose name was changed forthwith to New York after the duke's title—that it had gotten its start under the Dutch. The Dutch imprinted their tolerance and free trading into its DNA, ensuring that New York would grow along a different trajectory from the rest of British North America. In time these dynamics would lead to New York's distinctively multiethnic, upwardly mobile culture.

And because New York would have a vast impact on the growing United States, the seeds of that Dutch influence would take root in places thousands of miles from where they had originally been sown, and grow in ways that Stuyvesant and Winthrop, as they came together on that late summer day in 1664, could not possibly have foreseen.

Critical Thinking

1. What would cause the Dutch to hand over the city of New Amsterdam without more of a struggle?
2. Why did the Dutch have such a signficant impact on the cultural development of New York?
3. What if the Dutch refused to turn over the city? How would that have impacted the developing culture?

Create Central

www.mhhe.com/createcentral

Internet References

How New Amsterdam became New York
http://digital.library.upenn.edu/women/marshall/country/country-IV-36.html

Columbia University and the City of New York
http://c250.columbia.edu/c250_events/symposia/history_newyork_timeline.html

Dutch Colonies
www.nps.gov/nr/travel/kingston/colonization.htm

RUSSELL SHORTO, author of *Island at the Center of the World: The Epic Story of Dutch Manhattan and the Forgotten Colony That Shaped America* (Random House 2004), is the director of the John Adams Institute in Amsterdam.

Article Prepared by: Wendy A. Maier-Sarti, *Oakton Community College*

Taken by Indians

KEVIN SWEENEY

Learning Outcomes

After reading this article, you will be able to:

- Recount the emotional experience of being captured by Indians and ransomed.
- Explain the importance of first person accounts in history.

At sunrise on this cold winter's day, 39-year-old Mary Rowlandson awoke to the sound of musket fire rippling across her remote town in north central Massachusetts. A peek out of her family's fortified house revealed her worst nightmare: a large number of Indians descending on the small village of 50 to 60 families, firing houses and killing anyone who set foot outside. A wounded man pleaded for his life. The Indians "knocked [him] in [the] head, and stripped him naked, and split open his bowels," she recalled. Methodically, the Indians moved toward her house.

For two hours, "they shot against the House, so that the Bullets seemed to fly like hail . . . [and] "wounded one man among us, then another, and then a third." The Indians set fire to flax and hemp they had jammed against the house's outer walls. Her housemates found themselves "fighting for their lives, others wallowing in their blood, the House on fire over our heads, and the bloody Heathen ready to knock us on the head, if we stirred to [go] out."

But they had no choice as the fire roared up behind them, so Rowlandson, cradling her six-year-old daughter, Sarah, stepped over the threshold only to see her brother-in-law cut down in front of her in a fusillade of bullets; a ball pierced her side, another penetrated her daughter's bowels. "Thus we were butchered by those merciless heathen, standing amazed, with the blood running down to our heels." The house's front compound now contained "many Christians lying in their blood, some here, and some there, like a company of sheep torn by wolves, all of them stripped naked by a company of hell-hounds, roaring, singing, ranting, and insulting, as if they would have torn our very hearts out." In all, 14 men, women, and children staying in Rowlandson's garrison house perished, "some shot, some stab'd with their Spears, some knock'd down with their Hatchets."

Rowlandson, mother of three and wife of the town's absent minister, the Reverend Joseph Rowlandson, was one of a score of survivors who now found themselves force-marched to the Nipmuc town of Menamest, about 25 miles southwest of Lancaster.

The Indians and their captives spent the first night upon a hill within sight of the town. "Oh the roaring, and singing and dancing, and yelling of those black creatures in the night, which made the place a lively resemblance of hell," she remembered. Over the next 82 days, Rowlandson's trek through a "vast and howling Wilderness" in midwinter would cover more than 150 miles. Each "Remove," as she called a stage of her forced journey, took her farther from her familiar world and into that of her captors: "My Children gone, my Relations and Friends gone, our House and home and all our comforts within door, and without all gone (except my life) and I knew not but the next moment that might go too."

Her captors were Algonquian Indians: Wampanoags from Plymouth Colony; neighboring Nipmucs from central Massachusetts; and Narragansetts from what is today southern Rhode Island. In June 1675, Plymouth Colony's mounting threats to Wampanoag lands and independence had set off a series of raids that erupted into sustained warfare. Some Nipmuc warriors and other tribesmen combined to attack colonial villages, and the conflict, later called King Philip's War after the Wampanoag leader, spread to the colonies of Massachusetts and Connecticut. A preemptive assault on the Narragansett by colonial militiamen in December 1675 brought the Indians and the colony of Rhode Island into the war. In January the Indian allies had resolved to regain the initiative and strike a decisive blow by attacking five frontier towns, beginning with the February assault on Lancaster.

For Rowlandson, raised in Puritan New England and married to a minister, her journey into the "desolate wilderness" was spiritual as well as physical. On the ninth day of her captivity, during their "Third Remove," her daughter Sarah died "in this miserable condition, without any refreshing of one nature or other, except a little cold water." Rowlandson wrote, "I have thought since of the wonderful goodness of God to me in preserving me in the use of my reason and senses in that distressed time, that I did not use wicked and violent means to end my own miserable life."

Wounded, starving, but still strong, Mary Rowlandson carried her six-year-old daughter, Sarah, for the first nine days of the march before the child died. Her powerful autobiographical narrative of her 82-day captivity inspired James Fenimore Cooper to write.

—The Last of the Mohicans

Rowlandson's captors soon turned northward, heading cross-country toward a point on the Connecticut River not far from where it traverses the northern border of Massachusetts. During this "Fourth Remove" she was separated from the other Lancaster captives. Alone and despairing, she saw her journey as a test of her faith in "the Sovereignty and Goodness of God," who had decided whether she would live or die. Her actions, and even those of her captors, were determined—actually predestined—by Him. Calling to mind the words of Psalm 27, she resolved to "Wait on the Lord: be of good courage, and He shall strengthen thine heart: wait, I say, on the Lord."

And wait she did, trusting in the Lord, refusing to contemplate escape, and advising others not to run off. Sustained by her faith, Rowlandson displayed iron strength and firmness of spirit, overcoming the exhaustion and disorientation of long hunger, the wearying strain of constant travel over hard ground, the sleepless grief of Sarah's lingering death, and the plain terror of not knowing what her captors might do. She traveled over mountains and through swamps, often sleeping directly on the frozen earth, at times thinking that "my heart and legs, and all would have broken, and failed me." But she survived.

At the same time, to a degree she did not always realize or later acknowledge, Rowlandson stayed alive due to the actions and restraint of her captors and her own ability to adapt and negotiate. The Indians heaped verbal and physical abuse on her and, having little food for themselves, gave her even less. Still, they had a stake in keeping her and the other captives alive. By taking and keeping these prisoners, the Indians humiliated the seemingly impotent English, and gained valuable pledges that could be bartered for desperately needed gunpowder or, possibly, exchanged for the Nipmuc and other Indians imprisoned by Massachusetts authorities on Deer Isle in Boston Harbor. As the wife of a minister, Rowlandson was particularly valuable, and from the outset received special treatment. Her captors placed her and Sarah on a horse during the first part of their journey, and one of them gave her a stolen Bible, a "wonderful mercy of God to me in those afflictions." Rowlandson was surprised that "not one of them offered the least imaginable miscarriage to me," not realizing that Algonquian customs guarded her from sexual assault. Because she was unaware of these protections, she took seriously every threat that she would "be knockt in [the] head."

Her diet included raw horse liver, boiled horses' hooves, and bear meat.

As she was trekked northwest to the Connecticut River on her fourth through seventh "Removes" in late February and early March, Rowlandson learned, for instance, to eat whatever food came her way. "The first week of my being among them, I hardly ate any thing; the second week, I found my stomach grow very faint for want of something; and yet it was very hard to get down their filthy trash." Her diet included raw horse liver, boiled horses' hooves, raw corn on the cob, peas and groundnuts in broth thickened with bark; and bear meat, the very thought of which at first made her "tremble." By the third week they were all "sweet and savory to my taste."

In some ways, Rowlandson, who was used to being mistress of her own home, found it hard to adjust socially. Soon after being taken prisoner, she had been sold by her captor to Quinnapin, a prominent Narragansett, whom she soon came to regard as "her master," and his three wives as her mistresses. Among the latter was the "severe and proud" Weetamoo, a Wampanoag and a leader in her own right, who was in the opinion of one colonist "next to Philip in respect of the mischief she hath done." Rowlandson studied the women's moods and learned, if not to show them respect, to avoid displaying any disrespect that might bring a blow with fist or stick. By playing one wife against another, she moderated Weetamoo's often abusive behavior. She also knitted stockings for one wife and sewed a shirt for the young child of another. She even made a shirt for the Wampanoag leader Metacom (King Philip); in return, he gave her a shilling that she used to buy "a piece of Horse flesh." Trading upon her skills as a needlewoman, she obtained other things—including a knife—which she presented to Quinnapin and Weetamoo as gifts. Gradually she came to look upon Quinnapin as her protector and "the best friend that I had of an *Indian*," even acknowledging that "glad I was to see him" after one period of separation.

This period of separation ended some days after the Indians reversed course on their "Thirteenth Remove" and headed east from the Connecticut River toward central Massachusetts. Short of food and ammunition, harried by Mohawk raiders in the west, and confronted by colonial militiamen now reinforced by native allies, Rowlandson's captors found themselves back near Lancaster in late April. There the Nipmuc leaders opened negotiations to trade their prisoners. After some hesitation, Rowlandson set the price of her own ransom at 20 pounds and effectively dispensed gifts brought to her by an English negotiator to accelerate the process.

After three anxious days, her captors released her on May 2, 1676. Eventually she was reunited with her husband and children, Mary and Joseph, who had survived their own captivities. Six years later, Rowlandson wrote an account of her captivity, *A True History of the Captivity & Restoration of Mrs. Mary Rowlandson*—part adventure story, part spiritual autobiography, but mostly an extended sermon reminding New Englanders of the power and mercy of Him who had saved one so unworthy.

Mary Rowlandson, who lived to 73, saw her book go through four printings in one year to become the first and perhaps most powerful example of the captivity narrative, an American genre that would influence future generations of American writers and moviemakers, from James Fenimore Cooper to John Ford.

Critical Thinking

1. What was the importance of the "captivity narrative"?
2. How did Rowlandson get her story published at a time when women could generally not publish because of their gender?
3. Why did Native Americans take European settlers as hostages?

Create Central

Internet References

Mary Rowlandson

Mary Rowlandson: The Narrative of Captivity

Article Prepared by: Wendy A. Maier-Sarti, *Oakton Community College*

Blessed and Bedeviled

Tales of remarkable providences in puritan New England.

HELEN MONDLOCH

Learning Outcomes

After reading this article, you will be able to:

- Explain why the Salem Witch Trials occurred.
- Recount the grounds for which someone would be accused.

On October 31, 2001, Massachusetts Gov. Jane Swift signed a bill exonerating the last five souls convicted of witchcraft during the infamous Salem witch trials of 1692. Rectifying a few of history's wrongs on this Halloween day, the governor's conciliatory gesture was arguably ill-timed, given the frivolous revelry associated with this annual celebration of superstition and frights. In the real-life horror of the witch scare, at least 150 people were imprisoned, including a four-year-old girl who was confined for months to a stone dungeon. Twenty-three men and women, all of whom have now been cleared of their crimes, were hanged or died in prison, and one man was pressed (crushed) to death for his refusal to stand trial.

In probing the underpinnings of this tragic and incredible chapter of American history, New England observers past and present have agreed that the nascent Massachusetts Bay Colony provided a fertile ground for the devil's plagues. Among others, folklore scholar Richard Dorson, author of *America in Legend and American Folklore,* has argued that the frenzy culminating in the witch-hunt was fueled by legends that flourished among the Puritans, a populace that imagined itself both blessed and bedeviled. Of key importance was belief in phenomena called "providences" (more commonly called "remarkable providences"). These were visible, often terrifying, signs of God's will that forged themselves onto the fabric of daily life.

As Dorson explains, "Since, in the Puritan and Reformation concept, God willed every event from the black plague to the sparrow's fall, all events held meaning for errant man." The providences brought rewards or protection for the Lord's followers (generally the Puritans themselves) or vengeance upon His enemies. Sprung from European roots and embraced by intellectuals and common folk alike, they became the subject of a passionate story tradition that enlarged and dramatized events in the manner of all oral legends.

The pursuit of providences was greatly reinforced by those who felt compelled to record their occurrence, including John Winthrop, longtime theocratic governor of Massachusetts Bay Colony. Two prominent New England ministers, Increase Mather and his son Cotton, became the most zealous popularizers of such tales. In 1684 the elder Mather set forth guidelines for their documentation in *An Essay for the Recording of Illustrious Providences,* a study that Cotton Mather would later extend in his own works. The Essay defined "illustrious" providences as the most extraordinary of divinely ordained episodes: "tempests, floods, earthquakes, thunders as are unusual, strange apparitions, or whatever else shall happen that is prodigious." The directives for recording the providences—a duty over which the elder Mather would preside in order to preserve the stories for all posterity—are likened by Dorson to methods observed by modern folklore collectors.

The flip side of the providences were the witchcrafts of the devil, who poised himself with a special vengeance against this citadel of God's elect. Where faith and fear converged, the tales of remarkable providences heightened both.

A 'City upon a Hill'

In his *Book of New England Legends and Folklore in Prose and Poetry* (1901), Samuel Adams Drake called New England "the child of a superstitious mother." Dorson acknowledges that folk legends in the colonies were "for the most part carbon copies of the folklore in Tudor and Stuart England." But in grafting themselves onto a New World setting, says Dorson, the old beliefs took on a special intensity in the realm of the Puritans.

Many have credited the Mathers with projecting and magnifying this Puritan zeal. Writing at the turn of the last century, historian Samuel McChord Crothers, quoted in B.A. Botkin's *Treasury of New England Folklore,* captured the fervency of the younger Mather, who became a principal driver of the witch-hunt:

Even Cotton Mather could not avoid a tone of pious boastfulness when he narrated the doings of New England . . .

. . . New England had the most remarkable providences, the most remarkable painful preachers, the most remarkable heresies, the most remarkable witches. Even the local devils were in his judgment more enterprising than those of the old country. They had to be in order to be a match for the New England saints.

Perhaps we can gain the proper perspective on the Puritans' passion when we consider the enormous pains they undertook to escape persecution in England and establish their new covenant across the sea. Upholding that covenant was now critical, as evidenced in the lofty proclamations of a sermon delivered in 1630 by John Winthrop. Excerpted in Frances Hill's *Salem Witch Trials Reader,* the governor's words resound with poignant irony given the events that rocked Salem sixty-two years later: "We shall be as a City upon a Hill, the eyes of all people . . . upon us; so if we shall deal falsely with our God in this work we have undertaken and to cause Him to withdraw His present help from us, we shall be made a story . . . through the world . . . and . . . we shall shame the faces of . . . God's worthy servants, and cause their prayers to be turned into curses upon us."

Clearly, the task of maintaining this sinless "City upon a Hill" wrought insecurity among the Puritans, and so, says Dorson, they "searched the providences for continued evidence of God's favor or wrath." As he reveals, popular legends spurred their confidence: "Marvelous escapes from shipwreck, Indian captivity, or starvation reassured the elect that the Lord was guarding their fortunes under His watchful eye."

Cotton Mather recorded many such episodes in his 1702 chronicle titled *Magnalia Christi Americana: The Ecclesiastical History of New England.* In one renowned tale, a spectral ship appeared to an ecstatic crowd of believers in New Haven harbor in 1647. Six months earlier the heavily freighted vessel was presumed lost, after it had sailed from that harbor and never returned. According to Mather's account, quoted by Botkin, the community lost "the best part of their tradable estates . . . and sundry of their eminent persons." Mather quotes an eyewitness who believed that God had now "condescended" to present the ship's ghostly image as a means of comforting the afflicted souls of the mourners, for whom this remarkable providence affirmed not only their fallen friends' state of grace but also their own.

The Puritans also gleaned affirmation from providences in which the Lord exacted harsh punishments on the enemies of His elect. According to Dorson, the Puritans apparently relished most these tales of divine judgment. Those scourged in the tales included Indians, Quakers, and anyone else deemed blasphemous or profane. In the *Magnalia,* Cotton Mather correlates providential offenses to the Ten Commandments. He cites the destruction of the Narragansett Indian nation by a group of white settlers as retribution for the Indians' foul contempt for the Gospel. Oral legends also relayed the fate of Mary Dyer, a Quaker who was sent to the gallows around 1659; Dyer was said to have given birth to a monster, a common curse meted out to nefarious women. Even members of the elect might be struck down by plague or fatal lightning bolts for lapses ranging from the omission of prayer to adultery and murder. The *Magnalia* narrates the doom suffered by various "heretics" who quarreled with village ministers or voted to cut their salaries.

In addition to these ancient themes of reward and punishment, the providence tales incorporated a host of familiar spectacles from an Old World tradition, including apparitions, wild tempests, and corpses that communicated with blood—all magnanimous instruments of an angry but just Lord. Like the spectral ship, apparitions offered hope and solved mysteries; the apparition of a murder victim often disclosed the identity of his killer, a belief that came into play during the witch trials. The age-old notion that a corpse bleeds at the murderer's touch also surfaced abundantly in the tales.

. . . Mather devoted a whole chapter of his *Essay* to thunder and lightning, perceiving in them signs of God's consternation over the advent of secularism in Massachusetts Bay Colony. Mather declared that thunder and lightning had been observed ever since "the English did first settle these American deserts," but warned that only in recent years had they wrought "fatal and fearful slaughters . . . among us." In the *Magnalia,* Cotton Mather, too, expounded on thunder, a phenomenon that the Harvard scholar and scientist, quoted in Dorson, astutely attributed to the "laws of matter and motion [and] . . . divers weighty clouds" in collision; lightning, he postulated, derived from "subtil and sulphureos vapours." Like his erudite father, however, Cotton maintained that God was the omnipotent "first mover" of these and other natural forces.

Tales of Witchcraft

Dorson explains that "providences issued from God and witchcrafts from the devil, and they marked the tide of battle between the forces of Christ and the minions of Satan." Tales of witchery had their own illustrious elements, including menacing poltergeists, enchantments, and innocent creatures who became possessed and tormented by wicked sorcerers.

He and others have argued that the widely circulated tales of remarkable providences, wherein the Puritans sealed their identity of chosenness, created a fertile climate for witch tales and the witch-hunt. According to Dorson, "Other Protestants in New York and Virginia, and the Roman Catholics in Maryland, spoke of witchery, but the neurotic intensity of the New England witch scare . . . grew from the providential aura the Puritans gave their colonial enterprise."

Cotton Mather himself, quoted in Dorson, described the devil's vengeful plot to "destroy the kingdom of our Lord Jesus Christ" in this region that had once been "the Devil's territories" (that is, inhabited by Indians). Both Mathers were implicated as early as the mid-eighteenth-century for promoting bloodlust over witchcraft with their recordings of providence tales. Thomas Hutchinson, governor of Massachusetts Bay in 1771–74, lamented the witch debacle in his *History of the Colony of Massachusetts Bay* (1765). According to Hill, who refers to the governor as a "man of the Enlightenment," Hutchinson's chronicle suggests "that there was widespread disapproval of hanging witches until the *Illustrious Providences and Memorable Providences* [Cotton's later work] . . . changed the climate of opinion."

Providence lore undoubtedly played a part in the actions of those who spearheaded the witch scare with their clamorous cries of demonic possession. The trouble began in January 1692 when two girls, Betty Parris, the nine-year-old daughter of Salem

Article   Prepared by: Wendy A. Maier-Sarti, *Oakton Community College*

Pontiac's War

A Great Lakes Indian rebellion against the British changed the balance forever between Indian and colonist.

ALAN TAYLOR

Learning Outcomes

After reading this article, you will be able to:

- Explain what caused Pontiac's War

- Analyze the outcome of Pontiac's War

The dead woman was one of the lowly Indian slaves known as Panis. Near Detroit in August 1762, she had helped another Pani to murder their master, a British trader. The outraged British commander in North America, Baron Jeffery Amherst, ordered them executed "with the utmost rigor and in the most publick manner." By putting them publicly to death, Amherst meant to demonstrate that the Indians had become colonial subjects answerable to British law. Earlier in the year, the French provincial authorities had surrendered their forts around the Great Lakes to the British under the Treaty of Paris that ended the Seven Years' War. Emboldened by victory, Amherst vowed to impose a harsh peace on the Indians who had so long and ably supported their French allies. The Pani man broke his leg irons and escaped, leaving the woman to hang in late April 1763.

Amherst had no idea that her execution would set off a bloody and widespread rebellion two weeks later, which would remake the continent and lead to revolution. The nearby Ottawa dreaded the British execution of an Indian as an implicit assertion that they were now subordinate. They already felt insulted by Amherst's cutting off the flood of trade goods customarily paid by the French for permission to occupy the forts. No longer could the Indians play one European nation off the other to maintain their own independence, maximize their presents, and ensure trade competition. Meanwhile British colonists poured across the frontier to take lands from them.

Amherst had no idea that his execution order would set off a bloody and widespread rebellion two weeks later.

Setting aside old rivalries, the chiefs of many nations developed a new cooperation by exchanging covert messages from Illinois to Niagara and from Pennsylvania to Lake Superior. But someone had to act first; it was to be the Ottawa, led by their chief, Pontiac, who were pressed to the point of violence by the hanging.

During the spring of 1763, the tribes surprised and captured most of the British forts around the Great Lakes and in the Ohio Valley. In June a band of Ojibwa playing lacrosse outside of Fort Michilimackinac pursued the ball into the surprised fort and slaughtered most of the garrison. Through the summer and fall, the rebels raided the Pennsylvania, Maryland, and Virginia frontiers, killing or capturing about two thousand colonists, but failing to take the three strongest British forts: Detroit, Niagara, and Fort Pitt.

Embarrassed by the expensive war, the British sought peace by making concessions. Blaming Amherst for the crisis, the crown recalled him in disgrace. The new commander, Thomas Gage, followed the conciliatory advice of the crown's northern superintendent for Indian affairs, Sir William Johnson, who understood that diplomacy was cheaper than war. By lavishing presents and deference upon the Indians, Johnson enticed them to sign several peace treaties between 1764 and 1766.

The British rebuilt their forts but had to adopt a new, more generous policy, treating the Indians as allies rather than foes. In 1766 Pontiac assured Johnson that "if you expect to keep these Posts, we will expect to have proper returns from you." Johnson and Gage covertly agreed to exempt the Great Lakes Indians from British law. During the next decade, an Indian who murdered a colonist could settle the matter by customary tribal procedure—by giving presents to the victim's kin. And the British crown laid out comparable goods to cover the Indians whom the settlers had killed.

To further mollify the Indians, the crown mandated a new boundary line along the crest of the Appalachian Mountains, in the hope that holding settlers to the east would avert conflict. The policy failed. It proved unenforceable because the British lacked the troops to patrol thousands of square miles of forest; it also angered the colonists, already less bound to the empire by the elimination of the French threat. While drawing the British and the Indians closer together, the resolution of Pontiac's Rebellion deepened the clash between the Indians and the colonists. In 1775–76, when the colonists launched their own rebellion, most of the tribes defended the British forts that they had tried to destroy under Pontiac's leadership a mere half-generation before.

Critical Thinking

1. What led to the murder of the slave master?
2. Why did the Ottawa revolt?
3. Why did this war have an impact on the Americans?

Create Central

www.mhhe.com/createcentral

Internet References

Pontiac
www.ohiohistorycentral.org/w/Pontiac
Pontiac's Rebellion Begins
www.history.com/this-day-in-history/pontiacs-rebellion-begins
Pontiac's Rebellion
www.u-s-history.com/pages/h598.html

ALAN TAYLOR, winner of the 1996 Pulitzer Prize for *William Cooper's Town: Power and Persuasion on the Frontier of the Early American Republic* (Vintage Books 1995), is a professor of history at the University of California at Davis.

Unit 2

UNIT

Prepared by: Wendy A. Maier-Sarti, *Oakton Community College*

Revolutionary America

In the eighteenth century, it took weeks for a message to be delivered from London to one of the colonies, and weeks more to receive a reply. Under such circumstances the British understandably gave wide latitude to royal governors who were on the scene and who knew more about local conditions than could the bureaucrats at home. The fact that the American colonies were but part of the British world empire also discouraged attempts to micromanage their affairs.

According to economic theory at the time, an empire could be likened to an organism with each part functioning in such a way as to benefit the whole. The ideal role of a colony, aside from helping to defend the empire when the need arose, was to serve as a protected market for the mother country's manufactured goods and as a provider of raw material for its mills and factories. Because imperial rivalries often led to war, particular emphasis was placed on achieving self-sufficiency. An imperial power did not wish to be dependent on another empire for materials, especially those of strategic value such as shipbuilding materials that might be cut off if the two came into conflict.

With regard to the American colonies, those in the south most nearly fit the imperial model. Southern colonies produced goods such as cotton and tobacco that could not be grown in Great Britain, and southerners were disinclined to become involved in activities that would compete with British manufacturers. The New England and the middle colonies were another matter. Individuals in both areas often chafed at imperial restrictions that prevented them from purchasing products more cheaply from other countries or from engaging in manufacturing their own. What served to temper discontent among these colonists was the knowledge that they depended on the British army and navy against threats by other powers, most notably the French.

During the middle decades of the 1700s, London permitted the colonists to exercise a great deal of control over their own internal affairs so long as they played their designated economic role within the empire. This attitude, which came to be known as "benign neglect," meant that colonies, for all practical purposes, became nearly autonomous. The passage of time and the great distances involved combined to make British rule more of an abstraction than a day-to-day relationship. Most colonists never visited the mother country, and they might go months or years without seeing any overt signs of British authority. They came to regard this as the normal order of things.

This casual relationship was altered in 1763 when what the colonists called the French and Indian War came to an end after seven years of fighting. The peace brought two results that had enormous consequences. First, British acquisition of French possessions in North America meant that the military threat to the colonists had ended. Second, the war had been enormously costly to the British people who were suffering under staggering tax burdens. The government in London, taking the understandable view that the colonists ought to pay their fair share of the costs, began levying a variety of new taxes and enforcing shipping regulations that previously had been ignored.

The new British crackdown represented to the colonists an unwarranted assault on the rights and privileges they had long enjoyed. Disputes over economic matters escalated into larger concerns about rights and freedoms in other areas. Many colonists who regarded themselves as loyal subjects of the crown at first looked upon the situation as a family quarrel that could be smoothed over provided that there was goodwill on both sides. Most accounts of the Revolutionary War, for good reason, focus on those "patriots" who fought against the British, but there were also "Loyalists" who remained faithful to the crown. Most, though, were moving with the tide which demanded freedom from monarchical rule. When clashes escalated, more people who now regarded themselves as "Americans" began calling for independence from the motherland, whereas the British, of course, did not intend to hand over portions of their hard-won empire to the upstarts. War became inevitable.

Even after the early battles of the Revolutionary War, many colonists sought a negotiated settlement with Great Britain rather than to embark on the uncertain quest for independence. Those who wished to sever all ties with Great Britain defeated them. The Declaration of Independence emerged in its final form from the second Continental Congress. The Declaration listed the many grievances against the king and declared the states united. Some opposed the Declaration, like John Dickenson, a man who had opposed the British on numerous occasions in the past, and who argued for a governing document to serve the states; Dickenson shortly prepared a draft of the Articles of Confederation, which established the legitimacy of United States of America. The Constitution eventually replaced the Articles, but not without much disagreement. States rights and the power of the federal government was an oft-debated topic, with the struggle over state sovereignty and federal power remaining a topic debated for decades to come.

Winning the war came at a high price, and, for a time, it was not clear if the fledgling United States could arrive at a peace plan, let alone survive fiscally. Benjamin Franklin successfully negotiated a settlement with the British and with loans from France, the United States was on its way to becoming a force with which to be reckoned.

Article   Prepared by: Wendy A. Maier-Sarti, *Oakton Community College*

"The Sparck of Rebellion"

Badly disguised as Indians, a rowdy group of patriotic vandals kicked a revolution into motion.

DOUGLAS BRINKLEY

Learning Outcomes

After reading this article, you will be able to:

• Recount the factors that led to the Boston Tea Party.

• Explain the events of the Boston Tea Party.

• Analyze the impact of the Boston Tea Party.

On the evening of December 16, 1773, in Boston, several score Americans, some badly disguised as Mohawk Indians, their faces smudged with blacksmith's coal dust, ran down to Griffin's Wharf, where they boarded three British vessels. Within three hours, the men—members of the Sons of Liberty, an intercolonial association bent on resisting British law—had cracked open more than 300 crates of English tea with hatchets and clubs, then poured the contents into Boston Harbor.

News of the "Boston Tea Party" quickly spread throughout the colonies, and other seaports soon staged their own tea parties. While tensions between the Americans and the British had simmered for the past several years, there had been few acts of outright rebellion. The tea party lit the smoldering coals of discontent and ignited events that would lead to rebellion, war, and, finally, independence.

The first bloodshed of the Revolution had occurred nearly three years earlier, on March 5, 1770. A continual source of tension was the taxes levied by the British government on the colonists. Although British Prime Minister Lord North tried to placate the colonists with a pledge of no new taxes from London, on March 5 a mob of radical Americans, unaware of the announcement, had attacked the customhouse in Boston, prompting a confrontation with British redcoats. The crowd had begun to throw hard-packed snowballs at the British sentries guarding the customhouse. Goaded beyond endurance, the soldiers began to fire, killing five people and wounding several others in what came to be known as the Boston Massacre.

But North's concessions had dampened the rebellious attitude that had been spreading through the colonies, causing a backlash among moderates who believed that the Sons of Liberty presented a greater danger to America than did British taxes and troops. By October 1770 Boston's merchants announced that they would no longer honor the patriots' boycott of British imports, and it looked as though the flames of rebellion had been snuffed out. Although some of the more ardent revolutionaries kept in contact through committees of correspondence that issued statements of colonial rights and grievances—Samuel Adams pledging that "Where there is a Spark of patriotic fire, we will enkindle it"—no more significant incidents of violence would occur until late 1773.

During this reprieve North became more concerned with Britain's economic policies than with colonial discontent. The behemoth of British international trade, the East India Company, teetered on the verge of insolvency. Because many leading British politicians were company shareholders, saving it was of particular concern to Parliament. One potential solution seemed at hand: the company's London warehouse held more than 17 million pounds of tea. If these stores could be sold, the East India Company might survive. North concocted an ingenious plan to sell the tea in America at much lower prices than those offered by smugglers such as John Hancock, who brought in goods from Dutch possessions in the West Indies. Even with the British tax, the company's tea would still be cheaper than any imported from the Dutch. If everything went according to plan, the Americans would concede England's right to tax them in order to get inexpensive tea, and the East India Company would be saved in the bargain.

But things did not go according to North's plan. The Sons of Liberty believed it reeked of subterfuge, an underhanded attempt to force the colonists to continue to pay taxes. Hancock, who hated the British as much as he loved his profits, finally saw a chance to strike at the former while preserving the latter. On December 16, 1773, he and Samuel Adams directed a group, most of whom were members of the Sons of Liberty, to board the British tea ships and destroy their cargoes.

London was shocked and angered. Parliament bristled with loose, vengeful talk of sending a large expeditionary force to America to hang the rebels, level the settlements, and erect a blockade in the Atlantic to starve the ungrateful colonists. A few voices of reason, such as Charles James Fox and Edmund Burke, rose in the House of Commons to endorse punishing those directly involved but warning against a blanket indictment of all Americans.

In March 1774 Parliament passed the Boston Port Act, mandating that the city's harbor be closed until the colony paid Britain 9,570 pounds for the lost tea. (The bill was not paid.) A firestorm of protest exploded in the colonies, where radical leaders sneered at the new laws as "the Intolerable Acts" or "the Coercive Acts." Sympathetic demonstrations took place in many cities. Samuel Adams demanded action from the committees of correspondence in the form of a complete embargo on British goods. In Virginia Thomas Jefferson burst upon the revolutionary scene when he published his *Summary View of the Rights of British America,* which took issue with Parliament's right to legislate colonial matters on the grounds that "The God who gave us life, gave us liberty at the same time."

On September 5 representatives from every colony except Georgia met in Philadelphia at what came to be known as the first Continental Congress. Radicals called for Samuel Adams's trade embargo, while moderates led by John Jay of New York and Joseph Galloway of Pennsylvania supported a strongly worded protest. All agreed that some form of action had to be taken. On behalf of the radicals, Joseph Warren of Massachusetts introduced the Suffolk Resolves, declaring the Intolerable Acts to be in violation of the colonists' rights as English citizens and urging the creation of a revolutionary colonial government. Much to his surprise, the resolves passed, if just barely. George III was infuriated at the whole business. To him, the very calling of the Continental Congress was proof of perfidy. "The New England governments are in a state of rebellion," he told North.

Gen. Thomas Gage, the British commander and now Massachusetts governor, received orders to strike a blow at the New England rebels. Gage learned of their whereabouts and sent troops to seize them and then destroy the supply facility at Concord. But that night Boston silversmith Paul Revere rode the 20 miles to Lexington to warn the radical leaders and everyone else along the way that the British were coming. When British troops reached the town on April 19, 1775, they encountered an armed force of 70, some of them "minutemen," a local militia formed by an act of the provincial congress the previous year. Tensions were high and tempers short on both sides, but as the Lexington militia's leader, Capt. John Parker, would state after the battle, he had not intended to "make or meddle" with the British troops. In fact it was the British who were advancing to form a battle line when a shot rang out—whether it was from a British or colonial musket, no one knows to this day. At the time neither side realized it was the first blast of the American Revolution.

The lone shot was followed by volleys of bullets that killed eight and wounded 10 minutemen before the British troops marched on to Concord and burned the few supplies the Americans had left there. But on their march back to Boston, the British faced the ire of local farmers organized into a well-trained embryo army, which outnumbered the British five to one and shot at them from every house, barn, and tree. By nightfall total casualties numbered 93 colonists and 273 British soldiers, putting a grim twist on Samuel Adams's earlier exclamation to John Hancock, "What a glorious morning for America is this!"

A declaration of independence was no longer a pipe dream but a revolutionary plan in the making. From the Tea Party to the bloody fields of Concord, the thirteen colonies had proved that direct action was the surest way to free themselves from British tyranny.

Critical Thinking

1. Did the dumping of tea really lead to the American Revolution or was it merely another trigger factor that led to war?

2. What was the English government's response to the tea dumping?

3. What economic impact did the tea rebellion have on the English colonies?

Create Central

www.mhhe.com/createcentral

Internet References

The Boston Tea Party
www.masshist.org/revolution/teaparty.php

The American War of Independence: The Rebels and the Redcoats
www.bbc.co.uk/history/british/empire_seapower/rebels_redcoats_01.shtml

Ten Things You May Not Know about the Boston Tea Party
www.history.com/news/10-things-you-may-not-know-about-the-boston-tea-party

---

DOUGLAS BRINKLEY, author of *The American Heritage History of the United States* (Viking 1998), is a professor of history at Rice University and recently wrote *The Wilderness Warrior: Theodore Roosevelt and the Crusade for America* (Harper 2009).

Brinkley, Douglas. From *American Heritage*, Winter 2010, pp. 33–34. Copyright © 2010 by American Heritage, Inc. Reprinted by permission of American Heritage Publishing and Douglas Brinkley.

Article   Prepared by: Wendy A. Maier-Sarti, *Oakton Community College*

The Gain from Thomas Paine

Thomas Paine, who died 200 years ago, inspired and witnessed the revolutions that gave birth to the United States and destroyed the French monarchy. A genuinely global figure, he anticipated modern ideas on human rights, atheism, and rationalism. David Nash looks at his enduring impact.

DAVID NASH

Learning Outcomes

After reading this article, you will be able to:

• Explain three basic concepts from *Common Sense*.

• Analyze why *Common Sense* was so popular.

• Describe the political views of Thomas Paine.

At the end of President Obama's inaugural address in January 2009, he alluded to a small passage that appeared in Thomas Paine's pamphlet *Common Sense*. Faced with an American economy wracked by nervousness and self-doubt Obama noted Paine's rallying cry that galvanised and gave hope to the despairing:

> "Let it be told to the future world . . . that in the depth of winter, when nothing but hope and virtue could survive . . . that the city and the country, alarmed at one common danger, came forth to meet [this danger]."

Unique among radicals, the 200th anniversary of the death of Thomas Paine will be marked in England, in France and across the Atlantic. This is a measure of the impact of Paine's ideas both in his own country and in parts of the world that became the centre of revolutionary political change at the end of the 18th century. Paine was perhaps fortunate to live in such invigorating times and to be able to think about them so constructively. Yet what is remarkable is that his message has been capable of speaking with immediacy to each successive generation, providing radical inspiration and comfort in troubled times. This is because Paine was a persuasive author with a gift for penetrating, lucid and memorable language. However, he was also actively participating in the revolutions he wished to inspire. Both through word and deed he could justly claim "the world is my country and my religion to do good."

Thomas Paine's origins were anything but promising. He was born in Thetford in Norfolk in 1737 and was apprenticed to his father as a corset- and stay-maker, a trade that he followed intermittently. Some commentators would not let him forget this and later a number of cartoons portrayed his

radicalism as an attempt forcibly to lace the English constitution in the shape of Britannia into an uncomfortable corset. After a spell in the capital, Paine embarked on a similarly lacklustre career as an excise officer. In 1768 he moved to Lewes, but debt and disillusion with this career led to his emigration to America in 1774.

Arriving in Philadelphia with a letter of introduction from Benjamin Franklin, Paine immediately began to mix with radical journalists and to make his mark. His first venture into radical journalism, as the editor of the *Pennsylvania Magazine,* was a success. The magazine focused on American colonial opposition to high-handed British policies and it flourished. From this success, Paine distilled his arguments for American independence into one of his most important pamphlets, *Common Sense:*

> . . . many strong and striking reasons may be given, to shew, that nothing can settle our affairs so expeditiously as an open and determined declaration of independence.

The pamphlet appeared in the first month of 1776 and by the end of the year had sold 150,000 copies in 56 separate editions. So impassioned was Paine that he enlisted himself in the colonists' fight for freedom, serving as aide-de-camp to an American general. He became a trusted adviser to Washington, coming to the practical and ideological defence of the colonists with a series of pamphlets under the umbrella title of *The Crisis.* These galvanised resistance and were responsible for stabilising the army's morale when it was on the point of collapse. Paine received the gratitude of the American nation and a number of states granted him pensions or gave him gifts in kind.

In the 1780s, after the defeat of the British forces and the gaining of American independence, Paine returned to England where he briefly switched his attention to scientific and engineering projects, in particular the construction of a single-span iron bridge. The movement between political science and pure science was not uncommon among Enlightenment thinkers. Just as mechanics and magnetism were mysteries of the natural world, the study of which would yield their significance, so too could similar analysis be applied to man's political instincts and relationships.

When the French Revolution ignited in 1789 Paine, though still a political animal, was initially preoccupied with other business. However, when in November 1790 Edmund Burke published *Reflections on the Revolution in France,* his shocked reaction to the violence in Paris, a response from Paine was guaranteed. Paine must have been surprised at Burke's apparent change of heart since Burke had also supported the American colonists. The two had met in 1788 and corresponded. Paine swiftly replied with what was to be his most famous and widely read work *Rights of Man,* published in early 1791. Written in an immediate and engaging style, it was spectacularly popular, selling in the region of 250,000 copies within the space of two years. Although Paine hoped for open debate, he found himself a wanted man for views that incited revolution and unrest and which threatened the established monarchical order in England. While he continued to lecture on constitutional change, government reaction was rising against him and in September 1792 he eventually fled to France, where he had been made an honorary citizen the previous month, missing the order for his arrest at Dover by some 20 minutes. In France he was feted as a defender and promoter of liberty.

"Government by kings was first introduced into the world by the Heathens . . . It was the most prosperous invention the Devil ever set foot for the promotion of idolatry"

Thomas Paine, *Common Sense*

Paine now took a role in the revolutionary government of France and was one of only two foreigners to be elected to the country's National Convention. He was instrumental in ensuring Louis XVI was tried but also argued against his execution. Meanwhile, in England Paine had been convicted in his absence of seditious libel and this effectively ended his relationship with the land of his birth. He also fell out of favour in his adopted country, falling victim to the factionalism and political upheavals that wracked France. He was imprisoned at the end of 1793, possibly on the fabricated grounds that he was an enemy alien. Indeed, several Americans in post-revolutionary Paris petitioned for Paine's release on the grounds that he was an American citizen and was deserving of that country's protection. Narrowly escaping execution when others imprisoned with him went to the guillotine, his American connections eventually saved him and he was freed with the help of the American ambassador James Monroe on November 4th, 1794. Within a few years Paine was rehabilitated by the Convention and was voted a pension.

During the troubled early years of the 1790s Paine wrote another of his most enduring works, *The Age of Reason.* This was intended to undermine the pretensions of established religion and the structures associated with it.

Paine eventually returned to America in 1802 to discover that he was no longer a hero. He had quarrelled with Washington and this was remembered by those who revered the country's first president after his death in 1799. Paine's anti-Christian views were also extremely unpopular and were more readily recalled than his earlier exertions for the young republic. His last years were characterised by ill-health exacerbated by his periods of imprisonment. His mood was not helped by a series of small slights and the refusal of financial support which he took to be poor recompense for all he had done for the cause of American freedom. He died in 1809 a somewhat bitter man. Even his dying wish to be interred in a Quaker cemetery was refused. His funeral was a miserable affair and he was mourned by a tiny group of friends and two African-Americans who wanted to pay tribute to one of the few founding fathers of the United States who had argued against slavery.

Paine's story might have belonged solely to the 18th century were it not for the importance of his ideas, the captivating nature of his writing and its dramatic appeal. Paine's skill at producing political tracts for specific purposes was aided by his ability to write quickly when the mood took him. He was also adept at creating memorable phrases that enlivened his major works, ensuring them a wide audience. Paine's fame and legacy largely rests on the ideas and concepts conveyed in his three central works, *Common Sense, Rights of Man* and *The Age of Reason.* In a sense these represent a fitting trio since each was written in one of the three countries whose welfare preoccupied his life: America, Britain and France, and each addressed the particular problems those countries faced at a historic moment in time.

Common Sense conveys a breathless energy and appetite for change. In its first few pages Paine urges the American people to form a government from scratch, a chance almost without precedent, which the colonists should grasp with both hands since it was likely this would be their best opportunity. The fact that this would lead to conflict and a swift call to arms was a dramatic consequence that should be recognised:

> By referring the matter from argument to arms, a new era for politics is struck; a new method of thinking hath arisen. All plans, proposals . . . are like the almanacks of the last year, which though proper then, are superseded and useless now.

Paine argued that the American colonists had right and justice on their side in their struggle for independence. He also suggested that the colonies could afford such a break with Britain since they were prosperous and economically independent. However, he did not simply offer these as arguments for freedom, but went further to ask Americans to think about what they wished to do with their independence once they had gained it. Paine demonstrated that American freedom was wholly justified since the ancient, corrupt and privilege-ridden British monarchy had dispensed with fairness and justice in favour of coercing the colonies into submission.

By seeking independence the colonies could cast off such tyranny and look forward to the creation of a new society that would be governed by properly elected and accountable representatives of the people. Paine sketched the form this government might take and also suggested crucial social reforms to promote and sustain the common good. This blend of radical right to independence, ask americans to think about what they'd do w/ their freedom, and showed how a break from the organization of the old world

Edmund Burke before Marie Antoinette, 1790 satire (Library of Congress)

political ideals with concrete schemes for reforms of everyday life was a theme he would return to. Nonetheless, his immediate intention in *Common Sense* was to show how a break with the forms of organisation of the old world was essential. In so doing he unashamedly urged republican thinking: "Government by kings was first introduced into the world by Heathens", he wrote, "from whom the children of Israel copied the custom. It was the most prosperous invention the Devil ever set on foot for the promotion of idolatry." Individuals were not protected or privileged by birth or position in the society he envisaged. He answered those who wondered where America might find its future monarch with the telling phrase "the Law is King". The accountability of people for their actions was seen as a central core of the new society, a reflection of wider Enlightenment thinking that increasingly viewed humankind in terms of the individual.

Having given the American colonists the reason to fight, *The American Crisis* offered support when their backs were against the wall:

These are times that try men's souls. The summer soldier and the sunshine patriot will shrink from the service of

their country; but he that stands now, deserves the love and thanks of man and woman . . . What we obtain too cheap, we esteem too lightly; it is dearness only that gives everything its value. Heaven knows how to put a proper price upon its goods; and it would be strange indeed if so celestial an article as freedom should not be highly rated.

When Paine came to write in defence of English liberty his thoughts upon the subject were able to be couched as replies and refutations to the arguments presented in Burke's *Reflections*. Outraged and alarmed by the consequences of the French Revolution, Burke argued for a retention of what was antique, tried and tested. The destruction of the apparatus of the *ancien régime* clearly alarmed those who felt civilisation itself would be compromised in France and beyond. Burke argued that the English constitution was robust and should be defended because it had stood the test of time and had conveyed benefits upon its citizens. It operated through a system of checks and balances that always represented a control on each area of government, ensuring against overmighty subjects or tyrannical kings.

Burke argued this system had evolved organically and had thus been able to incorporate gradual change and newly developing interests. Moreover, it was capable of recognising that those who had a stake in the welfare of society were those best able to govern and those most likely to govern justly and for the benefit of the community. Burke focused upon the Glorious Revolution of 1688 as a dramatic illustration of his case. The tyrannical James II had been persuaded to abdicate in favour of the reforming William of Orange. Not surprisingly, many have seen this as a blueprint for more modern forms of conservatism that see society protected by property ownership and trust in governing institutions.

Paine challenged Burke's arguments, suggesting that they were an overblown defence of vested interests and privileges. His anger towards Burke's position played out in a carping personal attack on his writing style in the opening sections of *Rights of Man*. Paine noted that the so-called legitimate monarchy Burke was so fond of rested on the actions of an "armed banditti" led by someone who in his own land had been known as "William the Bastard". In this Paine was stoking the radical idea of the "Norman Yoke" which posited that freeborn Englishmen had been dispossessed by the Anglo-French interlopers who had taken control of the country after the Conquest of 1066.

Rejecting Burke's view that a country's government was organic and preordained by providence, Paine saw this tradition as an intolerable burden, one which fostered what he called "Old Corruption", a conspiracy in which those who produced little or nothing defrauded those who created the nation's wealth. Paine argued instead that individuals were not born to their position in life but came into the world with certain basic, indestructible rights. These gave individuals freedom to make choices about everything, including the type of government they wished for themselves. No previous generation had any right to predetermine the nature of this government or to commit subsequent generations to its will. "Man has no property in man, neither has one generation a property in the generations that are to follow", Paine wrote.

Age of Reason has attracted attention from some rather different quarters. Paine was a vociferous opponent of organised religion, writing that "All national institutions of churches, whether Jewish, Christian or Turkish [Islamic], appear to me no other than human inventions, set up to terrify and enslave mankind, and monopolise power and profit." But he was anxious to save the French nation from its collapse into destructive anti-clericalism and atheism. Paine stopped short of holding this extreme position, seeing instead the hand of a creator at work in the universe. Much of the *Age of Reason* explored the effect of applying rational thought to the stories and accounts of the Old and New Testaments. Paine subjected these texts to the test of reason and concluded that their claim to ultimate truth was suspect. Facts appeared implausible and the textual consistency they would require if they were the truthful word of God was lacking, inviting not belief and reverence but ridicule. Importantly for his own deism Paine's *Age of Reason* pushed God and established religion further and further apart. This was apparent in his suggestion that a moral God who had created the universe as it was bore no relation to the God portrayed in the Bible, who was by turns jealous, devious and tyrannical.

Paine's ideas did not melt away after his death. For generations, his analysis made sense and inspired confidence in those whose Christian faith was wavering. *Age of Reason* has been regularly republished in cheap editions in both Britain and the United States up until the present day.

In the first years of the 19th century political radicals latched onto Paine's attacks on "Old Corruption" and how they might dismantle the privileged aristocratic rule inherited from the 18th century. These ideas spoke to artisans and small producers and laid the foundations for 19th-century examinations of wealth and its distribution, even if Paine's analysis which attacked the landed aristocrat would later be replaced by an indictment of the capitalist.

Although Paine's critique did not fit the analysis of later Marxist socialism he had an influence on social democratic ideals. With the collapse and discredit of Marxism in the years after 1989 interest in Paine, with his undiluted focus upon individual rights surrounded by a network of enabling social mechanisms, was to some extent revived. Yet some socialists never lost sight of Paine's meritocratic messages. E.P. Thompson saw him as a great publicist of the issues associated with freedom and wove him centrally into the narrative of his 1963 classic, *The Making of the English Working Class*. Thompson also acknowledged a debt to Paine for lessons about activism and writing for a purpose. Thompson's involvement in the Campaign for Nuclear Disarmament (CND) echoed Paine's desire to get actively involved in the politics he wrote about. Similarly Thompson's *Writing by Candlelight* (1980), in which he despaired about the superpowers' relentless arms race and diplomatic posturing, was written for a purpose. Thompson may equally have concluded that, like Paine, he was living through a "time to try men's souls".

Similarly Tony Benn throughout his parliamentary career as a radical socialist has often referred to Paine's punchy political language and his inspirational quest for accountable government. When Benn met world leaders he would ask them three questions: Who had elected them? Were such elections fair? And, finally, did the people have a chance of getting rid of them? All these sentiments echo Paine and reflect the influence of a voice that speaks across the centuries. It might even be argued that Paine created the idea of the global village where individuals co-exist as citizens; certainly he was the first to make the message of individual and natural rights traverse boundaries in what, for the 18th century, was the blink of an eye.

Further Readings

G. Claeys, *Thomas Paine: Social and Political Thought* (Unwin Hyman, 1989)

I. Dyck, *Citizen of the World: Essays on Thomas Paine* (St Martin's Press, 1988)

J. Fruchtman, *Thomas Paine: Apostle of Freedom* (Four Walls Eight Windows, 1994)

J. Keane, *Tom Paine: A Political Life* (Little, Brown, 1995)

B. Kuklick, *Thomas Paine* (Ashgate, 2006)

T. Paine and J. Dos Passos, *The Essential Thomas Paine* (David & Charles, 2008)

M. Philip, *Thomas Paine* (OUP, 2007)

B. Vincent, *The Transatlantic Republican: Thomas Paine and the Age of Revolutions* (Penguin, 2005)

Critical Thinking

1. What was the impact of *Common Sense* on the founding fathers?

2. How did George Washington come to appoint Paine as an advisor?

3. What was the danger in publishing a pamphlet like *Common Sense*?

Create Central

www.mhhe.com/createcentral

Internet References

Common Sense by Thomas Paine
www.ushistory.org/paine/commonsense/

Thomas Paine
www.history.com/topics/thomas-paine

Thomas Paine Biography
www.biography.com/people/thomas-paine-9431951

DAVID NASH is Professor of History at Oxford Brookes University and the author of *Blasphemy in the Christian World: A History* (Oxford University Press, 2007).

Nash, David. From *History Today*, June 2009, pp. 12–18. Copyright © 2009 by History Today, Ltd. Reprinted by permission.

Article   Prepared by: Wendy A. Maier-Sarti, *Oakton Community College*

One Revolution Two Wars

Redcoats were not the only enemies of American Independence.

THOMAS B. ALLEN

Learning Outcomes

After reading this article, you will be able to:

• Explain the Loyalists and their role in the war.

• Analyze why the lines between the British and the revolutionaries were not readily apparent.

The Declaration of Independence said that by July 1776 the time had come "for one people to dissolve the political bands which have connected them with another." But the signers knew they did not speak for "one people" but for a people including Americans who opposed the Revolution. The latter called themselves Loyalists; the Patriots called them Tories. Thousands of them armed themselves and began a civil war whose savagery shocked even battle-hardened Redcoats and Hessians. That war all but vanished in the glory that enfolds the grand story of the American Revolution. But those men and women who fought for the king were Americans, and they live on as reminders that within the tapestry known as "We the People," there will always be strands of a defiant, fervent minority.

There were truly and clearly two Americas—one governed by the British military operating from New York and the other a group of colonies in rebellion but not quite governed. Every American now had a choice: to remain a subject of King George III and thus a traitor to a new regime called the United States of America or to support the rebellion and become a traitor to the Crown.

Loyalists by the thousands signed oaths administered by Royal Governor of New York William Tryon, who traveled to territory occupied by British troops. Few refused to swear allegiance to the Crown.

And those who chose the king had another way to show their choice. In taverns and meeting halls throughout New York City, Tryon's recruiters signed up wealthy, well-connected young men for commissions in Loyalist regiments. The Loyalist recruits were issued weapons and uniforms, usually designed by their regimental commanders. Ultimately, New York would send more men into Loyalist regiments than into the Continental Army.

As soon as the British army took root on Long Island, scores of young Connecticut men sailed across the sound to enlist. Many described themselves as churchmen, Anglicans who equated service to the king with their religious beliefs. Their names appeared on the musters of the Queens Rangers, the King's American Regiment and the Prince of Wales' American Volunteers.

The latter unit was the creation of Montfort Browne, former governor of His Majesty's Bahamas. Browne fell into enemy hands in March 1776 at Nassau, New Providence, when Esek Hopkins, commander in chief of the fledgling Continental Navy, led its first amphibious operation, landing some 270 Marines and sailors from whaleboats. No one offered resistance when the Continentals cleared the island's fort of military stores—including dozens of cannon and a ton of gunpowder—and took Browne prisoner.

Despite being placed under house arrest in Middletown, Conn., Browne managed to raise the Prince of Wales' Volunteers by smuggling out invitations to Tory friends, much as he might have arranged a dinner party on New Providence. Freed in a prisoner exchange that September, Browne set up his headquarters in Flushing, Long Island, and began issuing warrants to recruiters.

In New Jersey, Cortlandt Skinner, a member of one of the state's oldest and wealthiest families and a longtime spy for the British, accepted a brigadier general's commission from British Commander in Chief William Howe. Skinner raised four 400-man battalions of volunteers. Outfitted in green—a common color choice for Loyalist units—his men became known as Skinner's Greens. They would fight battles from New Jersey to Virginia.

In Hackensack, N.J., Continental Commander in Chief General George Washington was racing time as well as British Lt. Gen. Charles Cornwallis, for the enlistments of many Continentals would soon expire. With the addition of Maj. Gen. Nathanael Greene's men—who had abandoned Fort Lee and moved down to Hackensack—Washington had a force of about 3,000 troops. But they were "much broken and dispirited men."

Washington bid farewell to Peter Zabriskie, a Patriot in whose mansion the American general had been staying. According to family tradition, Zabriskie asked the general where he was heading. And, the story goes, Washington leaned down from his saddle and whispered, "Can you keep a secret?" Zabriskie assured him that he could, and Washington replied, "I can, too."

The story underlined the Patriots' distrust of New Jersey people. "A large part of the Jerseys," Washington bitterly observed, "have given every proof of disaffection that a people can do."

As soon as Washington's troops left Hackensack, young men from local homes and outlying areas began to converge on the village green. They were Loyalists, who had secretly enlisted in the 4th Battalion of New Jersey Volunteers. Formed in 1776, it was the state's first Loyalist regiment and one of New Jersey's three major Loyalist units. Most enlisted men were Scotch-Irish; the officers scions of old Dutch families, known as the Tory Dutch.

Local Patriots, especially farmers, led worrisome lives, trying to earn a living while wondering where and when Tory raiders might strike. Sometimes the latter staged small-scale raids, picking up some cattle here, a few horses there. Or they might launch a major foraging expedition, with several hundred British troops and members of the 4th Battalion, who would first jail the Patriots and then plunder their homes and farms. The Patriots retaliated by ambushing the smaller foraging parties. Each side lost men to sudden skirmishes on this strange, unexpected battlefield called the "Neutral Ground."

As Washington retreated into New Jersey, taking the war westward, citizens' allegiance also began to turn. In parts of New Jersey, as Washington would learn, Tories were in the majority and in control. Back in New York, there were so many Loyalists in some areas that they pinned down Patriot militiamen who otherwise might be aiding Washington in New Jersey. New Jersey's government was under Patriot control, but its population included thousands of Tories.

In flight with Washington's army across New Jersey was Tom Paine, whose *Common Sense* had stirred the Rebels and thrust them toward independence. Now, in a dark December of defeats, in "times that try men's souls," when the "summer soldier and the sunshine patriot . . . shrink from the service of their country," he looked around and began to envision what he soon would write in *The Crisis*. He noted an infestation of Tories and realized the time had come when Rebels and Tories would fight each other, regardless of whether the British army was present.

L oyalists in Bergen County, New Jersey, provided the British in New York City with not only food but also spies and recruits, many of whom Tryon secretly signed up aboard the ship of the line HMS *Duchess of Gordon,* where he sought refuge in the fall of 1775 when Rebels controlled the city. Those shipboard enlistees were instructed to return home and tell no one about their enlistments until British troops arrived in New Jersey. This was an unprecedented move, going beyond usual British military doctrine by setting up advance Loyalist units in places the British army had yet to invade.

Volunteers for Loyalist regiments were given equipment and paid in British money, not in the ever-declining currency printed by the Continental Congress. Some Loyalist recruiters promised prospective soldiers a 5 guinea signing bonus, rather than the advertised 40 guineas, but added the lure of 200 acres of land, with an extra 100 acres for his wife and 50 for each child. A Patriot enlisting in a Rebel militia typically had to provide his own musket and bayonet, a sword or tomahawk, cartridge box and belt, 23 cartridges, 12 flints, a knapsack, 1 pound of gunpowder and 3 pounds of bullets in reserve. All this was an expensive outlay for a poor farmer.

Each Tory battalion had, in addition to its commissioned officers, a surgeon and a chaplain, all drawn from New York and New Jersey. The most distinguished of the chaplains was the Rev. Charles Inglis, assistant minister at Trinity Church, New York City's most esteemed Anglican congregation. Inglis was a passionate Loyalist who, after the occupation of the city, became an eloquent propagandist.

Loyalists who enlisted or were commissioned in areas under Patriot control had to make their way to safe ground in New York City or Long Island. Patriots regarded these traveling new soldiers of the Provincial Corps (as the British army collectively termed the Loyalist units) as either spies or armed foes.

New York's Ulster County fielded one of the largest Loyalist units, numbering about 50 men. In April 1777, Patriots spotted this group at Wallkill, about 85 miles north of New York City. In the brief firefight that followed, the Loyalists wounded three Rebels before slipping away. Patriots spread the alarm through the countryside, so the recruits, aided by local Loyalists, hid out in the woods or in the cellars or barns of sympathizers by day and traveled by night. They had not gone far before a militia patrol caught up to them and captured about 30. Eleven were charged with "levying war against the United States of America," five for "aiding and assisting [and] giving comfort" to the enemy. They were brought before a court-martial ordered by Brig. Gen. George Clinton, a former member of the Continental Congress and soon to become governor of New York.

The court-martial, after listening to Patriots who told of encounters with the armed Tories, resolved that "an immediate example was necessary and requisite to deter intestine enemys [*sic*] from continuing treasonable practices against the state." Fourteen men "were adjudged to suffer the pains and penalties of death by being hanged by the neck until they are dead." After hearing petitions and statements, the Convention of the Representatives of the State of New York, the provisional state government, ruled that only the leader and his assistant were to be executed. The others received various sentences, ranging from parole to confinement through war's end.

In October 1775, the New York Provincial Congress had described widespread Tory recruiting as a "conspiracy from Haverstraw [New York] to Hackensack [New Jersey]," roughly encompassing what became known as the "Neutral Ground." It stretched along both banks of the Hudson River from above the New York–New Jersey border south to Sandy Hook. In Westchester County, the term referred to the land between the British-held Bronx and American-held Peekskill. The label was ironic, for on this so-called Neutral Ground both sides would fight, not to gain territory but to forage for food and firewood, demand loyalty oaths, kill each other in skirmishes—and spy.

On this so-called Neutral Ground both sides would fight, not to gain territory but to forage for food and firewood, demand loyalty oaths, kill each other in skirmishes—and spy.

James Fenimore Cooper made famous the label "spy" in his Revolutionary War novel *The Spy,* published in 1821 with the subtitle *A Tale of the Neutral Ground.* Cooper wrote the book while living in Scarsdale, a Westchester County town that had been part of the Neutral Ground. Cooper's hero, Harvey Birch, was based in part on Enoch Crosby, a true spy of the Neutral Ground. Crosby, masquerading as a Tory recruiter, secretly worked for John Jay, chairman of the New York State Committee and Commission for Detecting and Defeating Conspiracies. Jay had the power to send Tories to the notorious "fleet prison," a string of former privateer ships anchored off Kingston, N.Y.

Cooper never publicly linked the real Crosby and the fictional Birch. But he did say that Jay had told him spy stories, and presumably Cooper learned about Loyalist activities from his wife and in-laws, descendants of a powerful Tory family. In his petition for a federal pension, Crosby told his own story, which began in the summer of 1776, when his eight-month enlistment in a Connecticut regiment ended and he found himself in the Neutral Ground. On his way to join another regiment, he met a stranger who took him to be a Tory. Realizing the stranger "intended to go to the British," Crosby instantly decided to string along the Tory. The talkative stranger told Crosby where and by whom a Loyalist regiment was secretly being raised.

Crosby took his information to a member of the Westchester County Committee of Safety. Once vetted by the committee, Crosby became an agent. Among the Tories he exposed were some 30 men recruited by Lt. Col. Beverley Robinson, son of the Tory commander of the Loyal American Regiment.

Patriot officials withheld Crosby's true status from Captain Micah Townsend of Westchester, commander of Townsend's Rangers and the principal hunter of Tory spies in the area. Townsend later detained Crosby on suspicion of spying, and Crosby genuinely escaped, risking his life to preserve his secret identity. The escape helped secure his reputation among Tories.

Crosby's real and staged escapes, under various names and in various Neutral Ground locales, did not raise suspicion. In the Neutral Ground war, many real Tories were captured and later able to escape from inept Rebel guards. But the ruse could not last forever, and after nine months as a secret agent, Crosby enlisted in a new regiment and served as a sergeant on regular service.

While Crosby was hunting Tories in the Neutral Ground, a small but brutal civil war was heating up between New Jersey's Dutch Tories and Dutch Rebels. British forces, Loyalist volunteers and Patriot militiamen took turns at hit-and-run raids, keeping residents jittery. No one knew when a Tory or a Rebel might shatter the night. Bergen County was particularly divided due to a schism in the Dutch Reformed Church—some congregations supporting American-trained clergy and the Rebels, others backing more conservative factions and the Loyalists.

In New York's Orange County, which bordered New Jersey on the north, a militia leader reported that "matters are come to such a height that they who are friends of the American cause must (for their own safety) be cautious how they speak in public" and that some of those "who have been active in favor of our cause, will soon (if an opportunity offers) be carried down to New York." Patriots carried down to New York City faced confinement in a prison ship or in the Sugar House, a sugar refinery turned dank stone prison.

Matters are come to such a height that they who are friends of the American cause must . . . be cautious how they speak in public, for I make no doubt but we have often spies amongst us

At anchor in a small Brooklyn bay rode several British prison ships—dreaded dungeons for thousands of captured Continental Army soldiers, Rebel militiamen and Patriot civilians. Joshua Loring, commissary of American prisoners, showed little interest in his captives, except as a source of income from contractors' kickbacks. Prisoners were jammed into holds, where so many died of disease or starvation that each day guards would open the hatches and yell down, "Turn out your dead!" The British either tossed the bodies into the sea or buried them ashore in shallow graves. Estimates of the total death toll ran as high as 11,500.

The Sugar House, although less notorious than the prison ships, was as horrifying. "Cold and famine were now our destiny," a survivor wrote. "Not a pane of glass, nor even a board to a single window in the house, and no fire but once in three days to cook our small allowance of provision. There was a scene that truly tried body and soul. Old shoes were bought and eaten with as much relish as a pig or a turkey; a beef bone of 4 or 5 ounces, after it was picked clean, was sold by the British guard for as many coppers."

Thomas Jones, who lived in New York and knew Loring, wrote that "[he] was determined to make the most of his commission and, by appropriating to his own use nearly two-thirds of the rations allowed the prisoners, he actually starved to death about 300 of the poor wretches before an exchange took place." Noting General Howe's fondness for Mrs. Loring, Jones wrote, "Joshua made no objections. He fingered the cash; the general enjoyed Madam."

As Cornwallis pursued Washington across New Jersey, guerrilla war was declared. In a special order, Howe empowered his own troops, including Loyalist forces, to treat their retreating foes as outlaws: "Small straggling parties, not dressed like soldiers and without officers, not being admissible in war, who presume to molest or fire upon soldiers, or peaceable inhabitants of the country, will be immediately hanged without tryal [*sic*] as assassins."

Vicious little actions, hardly noticed in the chronicles of the Washington–Cornwallis saga, took uncounted lives. Kidnappings were all too common. One claimed a famous Patriot as its victim: Richard Stockton, a member of Congress and a signer of the Declaration of Independence.

As the British set their sights on Princeton in late 1776, Stockton fled with his family to a friend's house in Monmouth County, N.J., where Loyalists soon betrayed him to the British. A descendant of an old and distinguished Quaker family and a member of Princeton's first graduating class, Stockton was a prize catch. The British jailed him as a criminal, mistreating him until he broke under duress and signed an oath of allegiance to the king—an act that disavowed his signature on the Declaration.

Sometime around mid-March, 1777, Stockton was released without any public explanation and returned to his magnificent Princeton home. The mansion—Cornwallis' headquarters during his occupation of Princeton—lay in ruin. Tories blamed Hessians for making firewood of fine furniture, drinking their way through the wine cellar, bayoneting family portraits and stealing Stockton's horses and livestock. But the Tories had led looters to hastily buried silver plate and other treasures. Stockton had returned from captivity under a cloud, as congressmen possessed unpublicized knowledge that he had foresworn the Declaration. Later, an ailing Stockton tried to recant his oath to the king by signing oaths of adjuration and allegiance prescribed by the New Jersey legislature as a way to redeem tainted citizens.

Tryon, New York's provincial governor, participated in the Neutral Ground guerrilla conflict by organizing a troop of Westchester County cavalry raiders under the command of Colonel James De Lancey. The cavalry soon became known as De Lancey's Cowboys, a dubious term with origins in cattle and horse rustling.

A typical raid, as reported in an October 1777 edition of the Loyalist *New-York Gazette:* "Last Sunday Colonel James De Lancey, with 60 of his Westchester Light Horse, went from Kingsbridge to the White Plains, where they took from the Rebels 44 barrels of flour, two ox teams, near 100 head of black cattle and 300 fat sheep and hogs."

The following month Patriots savagely retaliated against De Lancey's Cow-boys by attacking Oliver De Lancey's country home at Blooming dale, about seven miles up the Hudson from New York City. As victims later recounted, strange noises awakened De Lancey's teenage daughter Charlotte and her friend Elizabeth Floyd, daughter of a Long Island Loyalist. They ran to a window, opened it and shouted, "Who is there?" From below a gruff voice answered, "Put in your heads, you bitches!"

Men entered the house from front and rear and, prodding the teenagers with muskets, ordered them out of the house. The girls fled to a swampy wood and spent the night "sitting upon their feet to keep a little warmth in them" and watching the house burn to the ground. The elder Mrs. De Lancey managed to hobble from the house and hid in a dog kennel beneath the stoop.

De Lancey's horsemen also foraged on Long Island, the site of frequent clashes between mounted Tories and amphibious Rebels. Earlier that year, in one of the biggest whaleboat attacks, Colonel Return Jonathan Meigs led 170 Patriots across the Sound to Sag Harbor and pounced on the foragers, killing six of them. After burning the Tory boats and forage, Meigs returned to Connecticut with 90 prisoners. The entire operation took 25 hours. Congress rewarded Meigs with a commendation and a sword.

Governor Tryon, commissioned a major general of provincials, waged what he called "desolation warfare," sending the Cow-boys and Emmerich's Chasseurs, another mounted Loyalist unit, to torch the homes of leading Patriots. In the fall of 1777, during one of the horsemen's harshest raids, they burned down sections of Tarrytown, a Hudson River community split between Loyalists and Patriots.

German native Andreas Emmerich's Chasseurs unit added a European element to Loyalist guerrilla forces. Emmerich had emigrated to England, then to America, where he secured a lieutenant colonel's commission and raised the corps of light troops named after himself. About half of his officers were Europeans and did not get along with their American counterparts.

Mutinous American officers asked Lt. Gen. Sir Henry Clinton (brother of Governor George Clinton) to court-martial Emmerich "for employing soldiers, negroes, and [Tory] refugees, to robb [*sic*] and plunder the inhabitants of Westchester County" and for taking a cut of the loot from the looters. The officers also accused him of "imprisoning, whipping and cruelly beating the inhabitants without cause or tryal [*sic*]," selling British army horses and stealing from the army payroll. Clinton sidestepped the court-martial by transferring the officers into other regiments. Emmerich somehow managed to keep his colonelcy.

For a time Continental Army Maj. Gen. Israel Putnam kept his headquarters at Peekskill, N.Y. Putnam tried to rein in Tory raiders by sending Colonel Meigs down the Hudson to attack the pillagers. Rumors circulated that, in retaliation, Tryon planned to kidnap Putnam. Coincidentally, Patriots reported a sudden surge of Tory spies in the area. One of them, a Loyalist lieutenant named Nathan Palmer, managed to infiltrate the headquarters encampment. Soldiers discovered him, and Putnam brought him before a court-martial to be tried as a spy. Tryon tried to intercede, threatening Putnam personally if he did not release Palmer.

Putnam replied:

Sir—Nathan Palmer, a lieutenant in your king's service, was taken in my camp as a spy, he was tried as a spy, he was condemned as a spy, and you may rest assured, sir, that he shall be hanged as a spy.

I have the honor to be, &c,

Israel Putnam

PS. Afternoon. He is hanged.

Critical Thinking

1. Why did so many Americans stay loyal to the English government?

2. How were the loyalists dealt with after American victory in war?

Create Central

www.mhhe.com/createcentral

Internet References

The Loyalists

www.ushistory.org/us/13c.asp

Simple List of Important People

www.theamericanrevolution.org/peopledetails.aspx

The Changing Roles of Printers and Newspapers in the Era of Revolution

www1.assumption.edu/ahc/1770s/pprinttoryloyal.html

Article　　　　　　　　　　　Prepared by: Wendy A. Maier-Sarti, *Oakton Community College*

Equality and Schooling: Laggards, Percentiles and the U.S. Constitution

BENJAMIN H. WELSH

Learning Outcomes

After reading this article, you will be able to:

- Explain why the founding fathers did not address formal education requirements.

- Explain how the founding fathers created a "power vacuum" as stated in the article.

- Explain the impact of uneducated people in a democratic society.

. . . I assumed that the following passage appeared in the Constitution when, in fact, it appears in the Declaration of Independence: "We hold these truths to be self-evident, that all men are created equal, that they are endowed by their Creator with certain unalienable rights, that among these are life, liberty and the pursuit of happiness."[1] Not only did I discover that the passage does not appear in the Constitution, the Constitution makes no reference to the passage *or* the Declaration of Independence. To my surprise, this famous passage that is said to link the founding fathers such as Thomas Jefferson (together with the political ideology of the United States) to Enlightenment thinkers such as Montesquieu and John Locke exists only in a document that was never formally adopted by the United States of America and that was, for all intents and purposes, a declaration of war.[2]

Investigation of the Constitution reveals another remarkable fact: the Constitution distances itself from the central idea expressed in the famous passage above—namely the idea of unconditional equality for all male citizens. Where the Declaration of Independence states unequivocally that "all men are created equal," the Constitution states with equal clarity that representation and taxation were to be determined by "... adding to the whole Number of free Persons, including those bound to Service for a Term of Years, and excluding Indians not taxed, three fifths of all other Persons (sic)."[3] The definition of equality in the Constitution clearly contradicts the definition of equality in the Declaration of Independence. On numeric grounds alone, "all men" could not be "created equal"

if "Indian" (i.e. Native American or indigenous) men were *not* counted as "persons" and "all other" (usually interpreted as enslaved Africans or their descendents) men were counted as "three fifths" of, or less than, a whole person. While this contradiction may never be adequately explained, highlighting it demonstrates that confusion around the concept was present from the country's inception. It also offers explanation as to why the confusion continues unabated.

The contradiction between the concept of equality found in the Declaration of Independence and that found in the U.S. Constitution led me to question what the Constitution had to say about education. After all, Montesquieu (1689–1755), a French *philosophe* whose work heavily influenced Thomas Jefferson, James Madison and the U.S. Constitution, understood that education was a prerequisite for equality. Specifically, Montesquieu believed that the principle of equality had to be "inculcated through a 'general education' by 'raising the whole people as a family.'"[4] Thus, one would suppose that if the concept of equality was going to be addressed anywhere in the Constitution, it would be where education was also discussed.

Surprisingly, the U.S. Constitution is found to make no mention of education. No article or section established education as a states' right either. The silence is made all the more deafening by the fact that the colony of Massachusetts had legislated a tax-funded school system one hundred and forty years before the Constitution was signed.[5] Thomas Jefferson had also argued that "... it is highly interesting to our country ... to provide that every citizen in it should receive an education proportioned to the condition and pursuits of his life," putting Jefferson's thinking on the topic in line with Montesquieu's.[6] What happened to the ideological orientation of the colonial leadership in the eleven years between July 4, 1776 and September 17, 1787? Could there have been a relationship between the decision to back away from the Declaration's unconditional concept of equality and the Constitution's omission of universal education? More specifically, could political wrangling, disagreement, and expediency have led to *both* the abandonment of unconditional equality as an ideal *and* the abandonment of universal education?

Through the omission of universal education on one hand and the failure to clarify the meaning of equality on the other, the U.S. Constitution created a power vacuum with both institutional and conceptual dimensions. Thus, the educational leadership that emerged over the next two hundred years can be viewed as attempts to fill those dimensions of the power vacuum in various ways. Whether in the form of individual luminaries such as Horace Mann, influential organizations such as The Russell Sage Foundation or more recently The Carnegie Foundation or even the federal government, American educational leadership addressed the power vacuum in unique ways that were determined in part by the cultural, historical and political forces at play at any given point in time.

But, unlike the students of Ayres's day, each of today's students receives his or her own individual ranking. What is more, entire schools are now being ranked and stigmatized in a similar manner using the very same scores. Finally, no school of students is safe from either the stigma or the economic punishment meted out by NCLB. Thus, student test scores are transformed from one potential tool among many that might help with school improvement to a single blunt instrument inspiring fear and paranoia, against which a school lives or dies.

With the passage of NCLB, not only did the Bush administration put the 'old wine' of Gulick and Ayres into new bottles, it created new labels covered with the 'rhetoric of diversity' that suggested the wine was new. Finally, it added a strong hallucinogen to the old wine to create fear and paranoia in those who partake of it. The result: a system that lives in fear of losing resources, that 'measures' each individual student in terms of what they are not, and that can blame the lowest performing students, i.e. the 'defective 2%', for a school's apparent shortcomings.

Conclusions

Although the definition of equality may have changed in the hundred years since Ayres's *Laggards in our schools,* it does not appear to have changed much where it should matter most: the public schools. The Constitution created a power vacuum around equality and education when the founding fathers failed to address it. In response, people with strong opinions about education such as Ayres and philanthropic organizations such as the Russell Sage Foundation stepped in to fill that vacuum. Consequently, *their* competing ideas about equality and education, interacting with changing ideas about equality and other historical factors, shaped and continue to shape an ever-changing educational agenda, contributing to never-ending 'policy churn'.[7]

Most recently, the executive branch of the government entered directly into the on-going quagmire, setting an extremely conditioned, hegemonic view of equality and education into

law. Is there any real chance at substantive change as long as students and now schools are being sorted into categories that are defined according to what they are not? Unfortunately, history suggests not. The American public schools appear to have inherited a hegemonic understanding of equality and do little but repackage it. Meanwhile, universal education as the means to Jeffersonian equality remains more elusive than ever.

Notes

1. Declaration of Independence (adopted in Congress July 4, 1776).
2. To Jefferson and his circle "equality was first and foremost a biological fact." Daniel J. Boorstin, *The Lost World of Thomas Jefferson.* (Boston: Beacon Press, 1948), 105.
3. U.S. Constitution (signed September 17, 1897), art. 1, sec. 2.
4. Christopher Wolfe, "The Confederate Republic in Montesquieu," *Polity* 9, no. 4 (summer 1977): 430.
5. L. Dean Webb, *The History of American Education: A Great American Experiment.* (Upper Saddle River, NJ: Pearson Education, Inc, 2006), 69.
6. Boorstin, *The Lost World of Thomas Jefferson*, 223.
7. See Kenneth K. Wong, *Funding Public Schools: Politics and Policies.* (Lawrence, KS: University of Kansas Press, 1999).

Critical Thinking

1. How well does the educational system work in America?
2. In America, citizens have the right to a public education. Should that opportunity be extended to everyone who resides in the United States?
3. Is the responsibility for guiding education best held at the federal, state, or local level?

Create Central

www.mhhe.com/createcentral

Internet References

The Role of Higher Education in Social Mobility
    www.princeton.edu/futureofchildren/publications/journals/article/index
    .xml?journalid=35&articleid=90

Great Expectations: The Impact of Education on Women's Roles in Society
    www.dean.sbc.edu/pegues.html

The Role of Education
    www.unesco.org/new/en/social-and-human-sciences/themes/fight-against
    -discrimination/role-of-education/

Article   Prepared by: Wendy A. Maier-Sarti, *Oakton Community College*

A Day to Remember: July 4, 1776

CHARLES PHILLIPS

Learning Outcomes

After reading this article, you will be able to:

- Explain the process by which the Declaration of Independence was approved.

- Analyze three main causes behind the Declaration.

On Independence Day every year, millions of Americans turn out for myriad parades, public and backyard barbecues, concerts of patriotically stirring music and spectacular pyrotechnic displays, and they do so to celebrate the day on which we declared our independence from Great Britain.

But America did not declare its independence on July 4, 1776. That happened two days earlier, when the second Continental Congress approved a resolution stating that "these United Colonies are, and of a right ought to be, free and independent States." The resolution itself had first been introduced back on June 7, when Virginia's Richard Henry Lee rose in the sweltering heat of the Congress' Philadelphia meeting house to propose an action many delegates had been anticipating—and not a few dreading—since the opening shots of the American Revolution at Lexington and Concord.

Lee asked for a newly declared independent government, one that could form alliances and draw up a plan for confederation of the separate Colonies. The need for some such move had become increasingly clear during the last year, especially to George Washington, if for no other reason than as a rallying cry for his troops. The Virginia soldier chosen by Congress to general its Continental Army languished in New York, short of supplies, short of men and short of morale while facing the threat of a massive British offensive.

But many in Congress, some sent with express instructions against independence, were leery of Lee's proposal despite the growing sentiment for independence stirred up by such rebel rousers as Boston's Samuel Adams and the recent émigré Thomas Paine. Paine's political pamphlet, *Common Sense,* openly attacked King George III and quickly became a bestseller in the Colonies; Paine donated the proceeds to the Continental Congress. Lee was so closely associated with Adams that critics charged Lee with representing Massachusetts better than he did Virginia. On the night before Lee offered up his resolution, Adams boasted to friends that Lee's resolution would decide the most important issue Americans ever had faced.

Little wonder that the more conservative delegates, men such as Pennsylvania's John Dickinson and South Carolina's Edward Rutledge, balked. Treaty with France? Surely. Draw up articles of confederation? Fine. But why declare independence? The Colonies, they argued, were not even sure they could achieve it. To declare their intent now would serve merely to warn the British, and hence forearm them. Dickinson wanted to postpone the discussion—forever if he could—and he managed to muster support for three weeks of delay. At the same time, Lee's faction won approval to appoint committees to spend the three weeks preparing drafts on each point of the resolution.

Sam Adams was named to the committee writing articles of confederation. His cousin, John Adams, a great talker, headed the committee drawing up a treaty with France. John Adams also was appointed to help draft a declaration of independence along with the inevitable choice, the celebrated author and internationally renowned philosopher Benjamin Franklin. Congress also assigned New York conservative Robert Livingston and Connecticut Yankee Roger Sherman to the committee but fell to arguing over a fifth member.

Southern delegates wanted one of their own to achieve balance. But many in Congress disfavored the two obvious candidates, considering Lee too radical and his fellow Virginian Benjamin Harrison too conservative. There was another Virginian, however, a 32-year-old lanky, red-haired newcomer named Thomas Jefferson, who had a reputation for learning in both literature and science. Though he seemed to shrink from public speaking, the Adamses liked him, and John pushed so effectively for Jefferson to join the committee that, when the votes were counted, he tallied more than anyone else.

Franklin's health was clearly failing, and he wouldn't be able to draft the declaration. Adams was busy with what he probably considered at the time the more important work of drafting an alliance with France (though he would live to regret such an opinion). Neither Livingston nor Sherman evidently had the desire nor, most probably, the talent to pen the kind of document needed. To Jefferson, then, with his reputation as a fine writer, fell the task of drafting a resolution whose language, edited and approved by the committee, would be acceptable to all the delegates.

Jefferson worried about his sick wife, Martha, back home and longed to be in Virginia working on the colony's new constitution, then under debate in Williamsburg. Nevertheless, he set to work and quickly produced what, given the time constraints, was a remarkable document. A justification to the world of the action being taken by Britain's American Colonies assembled in Congress, the declaration was part bill of indictment and part philosophical assertion, the latter an incisive summary of Whig political thought.

With the document's key sentiments much inspired, say some, by such Scottish Enlightenment figures as Francis Hutcheson, and its thinking much influenced, say many, by John Locke's *Two Treatises of Government,* the declaration summarized common notions expressed everywhere in the Colonies in those days. Many such notions could be found in numerous local proclamations. Especially relevant, because it was on Jefferson's mind, was the language of the new Virginia constitution with its elaborate Bill of Rights penned by his cohort, George Mason. Indeed, Jefferson's assignment was to capture the sense of the current rebellion in the 13 Colonies and distill its essence into a single document.

In this, as everyone recognized, he greatly succeeded, though he did not do it alone. Despite what Jefferson himself later wrote, and John Adams, too, when age and the glory of the Revolution led them both to embroider their accounts, the committee reviewed Jefferson's work, and then he ran it past both senior members, Adams and Franklin. He incorporated suggested changes before writing a clean copy. Still, Jefferson personally was quite proud of the draft he laid before Congress on June 28, 1776.

On the first day of July, with Jefferson's manuscript at the ready, the delegates once more took up Richard Henry Lee's resolution to openly declare independence. Lee was off in Virginia, where Jefferson wished to be, so he was not there to see John Dickinson's last protest seemingly cow the Congress, before an eloquent rebuttal by a determined John Adams carried the motion. Congress on July 2 without dissent voted that the American Colonies were from that day forward free and independent states.

That evening an exultant John Adams wrote home to his wife that July 2, 1776, would "be celebrated by succeeding generations as the great anniversary festival." It was his day of triumph, as well he knew, and he imagined it "commemorated as the day of deliverance by acts of devotion to God Almighty. It ought to be solemnized with pomp and parade, with shows, games, sports, guns, bells, bonfires and illuminations from one end of the continent to the other, from this time forward forever more."

Congress immediately turned to consider Jefferson's document. It would have to serve as a sort of early version of a press release—an explanation that could be disseminated at home and around the globe by broadside and to be read aloud at gatherings. Its statements had to inspire the troops and garner public support for the action Congress had just taken. Not surprisingly, Congress paid close attention to the document's language.

The delegates took the time to spruce it up a little and edit out what they found objectionable. In general the Congress

was fine with the vague sentiments of the early paragraphs that have since become the cornerstone of American democracy: "We hold these truths to be self-evident: that all men are created equal, that they are endowed by their Creator with certain unalienable rights; that among these are life, liberty, and the pursuit of happiness; that to secure these rights, governments are instituted among men, deriving their just powers from the consent of the governed" and so on.

What the delegates were more interested in, however, and what they saw as the meat of the document, were the more concrete declarations. For years, they had based their resistance to England on the belief they were not fighting a divinely chosen king, but his ministers and parliament. But during the previous 14 months the Crown had waged war on them, and King George had declared the Colonials in rebellion, that is, outside his protection. *Common Sense* had gotten them used to thinking of the king as that "royal brute" and this document was supposed to explain why he should be so considered. Thus Jefferson had produced a catalog of George III's tyrannies as its heart and soul.

Congress at length struck out some sentimental language in which Jefferson tried to paint the British people as brothers indifferent to American suffering and a paragraph where he ran on about the glories the two people might otherwise have realized together. But more substantive changes were especially telling. Among George's crimes, Jefferson had listed the slave trade, contending that the king had "waged a cruel war against human nature" by assaulting a "distant people" and carrying them into slavery in "another hemisphere." This was too much for Jefferson's fellow slaveholders in the South, especially South Carolina, and certain Yankee traders who had made fortunes from what Jefferson called the "execrable commerce." Together, representatives of these Southern and Yankee interests deleted the section.

For the rest, the delegates also changed a word here and there, usually improving some of the hasty writing. They worked the language of Lee's resolution into the conclusion and added a reference to the Almighty, which Jefferson would have been happier without. "And," the document now concluded, "for support of this Declaration, with a firm reliance on the protection of divine Providence, we mutually pledge to each other our lives, our fortunes, and our sacred honor."

None of this sat well with the young author. He made a copy of the declaration as he submitted it and the "mutilated" version Congress approved, and sent both to his friends and colleagues, including Richard Henry Lee, who agreed the original was superior, though most historians since have concluded otherwise.

In any case, after more than two days of sometimes-heated debate, on July 4, 1776, the Continental Congress approved the revised document that explained its declaration of independence of July 2. The approval was not immediately unanimous, since the New York delegates had to await instructions from home and did not assent until July 9. At the time of approval, Congress ordered the document "authenticated and printed," and that copies "be sent to several assemblies, conventions and committees, or councils of safety, and to the several commanding officers of the Continental troops; that it be proclaimed in each of the United States, and at the head of the army." If any delegates officially signed the approved document on the glorious Fourth, they were President John Hancock and Secretary Charles Thomson.

Within days the printed document was circulated across the land. The declaration was read aloud in the yard of the Philadelphia State House to much loud cheering. When New York formally accepted the declaration, the state celebrated by releasing its debtors from prison; Baltimoreans burned George III in effigy; the citizens of Savannah, Ga., gave him an official funeral.

The carefully engrossed copy we see reproduced everywhere today, with its large handwritten calligraphy, was not ordered prepared until July 19, and it was not ready for signing until August 2. Delegates probably dropped in throughout the summer to add their names to the bottom of the document. In any event, since the proceedings were secret and the signers all in danger of their lives, the names were not broadcast.

Even before the engrossed copy was ready, and long before it was signed by all, the legends were growing—how Hancock signed the parchment so boldly that John Bull could read his name without spectacles. How Hancock remarked to Benjamin Franklin: "We must be unanimous. There must be no pulling in different ways. We must all hang together." And how Franklin replied, "Yes, we must indeed all hang together, or most assuredly we shall hang separately."

Almost from the start, confusion blurred the distinctions between the July 2 act of declaring independence, the July 4 approval of the document explaining that declaration, and the actual signing of the Declaration. That confusion might best be represented by John Trumbull's famous 1819 painting, which now hangs in the Capitol Rotunda and appears on the back of the $2 bill. Thought by most Americans to represent the signing of the Declaration of Independence, it was intended by Trumbull "to preserve the resemblance of the men who were the authors of this memorable act," not to portray a specific day or moment in our history.

The Fourth of July was not as widely celebrated during the heat of the Revolutionary War or during the period of confederation as it was afterward. It became much more popular as a national holiday in the wake of the War of 1812 and with the passing of the Revolutionary generation.

And then four score and seven years after that July 4, 1776, President Abraham Lincoln used the lofty ideas and flowing words of the Declaration as the basis for his famous Gettysburg Address to sanctify the country's sacrifices in the Civil War and, in so doing, he redefined the nation as a land of equality for all. Ever since, those early paragraphs of the Declaration, with their beautifully phrased abstractions and sentiments, have served virtually to define the American faith in secular democracy. His well-chosen remarks and our July 4 Independence Day celebrations, like Trumbull's painting, honor not a single event but, rather, the democratic process, the ideas proposed back then and the men who directly made them possible.

Critical Thinking

1. Why was the Declaration such an important step toward autonomy for the English colonies?

2. How big of a risk did the founding fathers take in issuing the Declaration, which was primarily written against George III?

3. What was the expected outcome of the Declaration? Was a truce to the war expected?

Create Central

www.mhhe.com/createcentral

Internet References

The Declaration of Independence
www.archives.gov/exhibits/charters/declaration_transcript.html
Declaration of Independence
www.loc.gov/rr/program/bib/ourdocs/DeclarInd.html
The Dark Side of Thomas Jefferson
www.smithsonianmag.com/history-archaeology/The-Little-Known-Dark-Side-of-Thomas-Jefferson-169780996.html

CHARLES PHILLIPS is the author and co-author of numerous works of history and biography. These include *What Every American Should Know About American History, The Macmillan Dictionary of Military Biography; Cops, Crooks, and Criminologists; What Everyone Should Know About the Twentieth Century, Tyrants, Dictators, and Despots;* and *The Wages of History.* Phillips has edited several multivolume historical reference works, including the *Encyclopedia of the American West, the Encyclopedia of War* and *the Encyclopedia of Historical Treaties.*

Article   Prepared by: Wendy A. Maier-Sarti, *Oakton Community College*

Building a Nation from Thirteen States: The Constitutional Convention and Preemption

EDWARD J. LARSON

Learning Outcomes

After reading this article, you will be able to:

- Explain why the states rights advocates prevailed in framing the Consitution.

- Explain why so much of the language in the Constitution was intentionally left open to interpretation.

Mr. [John] Dickinson. The preservation of the States in a certain degree of agency is indispensable. It will produce that collision between the different authorities which should be wished for in order to check each other. To attempt to abolish the States altogether, would degrade the Councils of our Country, would be impracticable, would be ruinous. He compared the proposed National System to the Solar System, in which the States were the planets, and ought to be left to move freely in their proper orbits.[1]

Col. [George] Mason. [W]hatever power may be necessary for the Nat[iona]l Gov[ernmen]t a certain portion must necessarily be left in the States. It is impossible for one power to pervade the extreme parts of the U. S. [sic] so as to carry equal justice to them. The State Legislatures also ought to have some means of defending themselves ag[ain]st encroachments of the Nat[iona]l Gov[ernmen]t. In every other department we have studiously endeavored to provide for its self-defense. Shall we leave the States alone unprovided with the means for this purpose? And what better means can we provide than the giving them some share in, or rather to make them a constituent part of, the Nat[iona]l Establishment[?][2]

On Mr. Dickinson's motion for an appointment of the Senate by the State-Legislatures.[3]

MA, CT, NY, PA, DL, MD, VA, NC, SC, GA, aye 10.[4]

On Friday, June 8, the delegates debated whether the national legislature should have the power to veto state laws.[5] Madison strongly supported the proposal, but this effort to radically curtail the power of the states was decisively rejected, just as his effort to prevent the state legislatures from electing senators was defeated the day before.[6]

As debate on Governor Randoph's Virginia Plan for a strong national government continued, some delegates (particularly those from smaller states) began to worry that the emerging document was giving too much power to the central government at the expense of the states. On Friday, June 15, William Patterson of New Jersey, acting on behalf of his state's delegation and with the support of other delegates, introduced an alternative plan that would strengthen the confederation while retaining significant power in the state.[7] His plan became know as the New Jersey Plan. Debate on the two plans began in earnest on June 16.[8] That debate reveals the extent of national power assumed under the Virginia Plan, which ultimately prevailed over the New Jersey Plan as the basis for the Constitution.

Mr. [Stephen] Lansing called for the reading of the [first] resolution of each plan, which he considered as involving principles directly in contrast; that of Mr. Patterson says he sustains the sovereignty of the respective States, that of Mr. Randolph destroys it: the latter requires a negative on all the laws of the particular States; the former, only certain general powers for the general good. The plan of Mr. R[andolph] in short absorbs all power except what may be exercised in the little local matters of the States which are not objects worthy of the supreme cognizance. He grounded his preference of Mr. P[atterson]'s plan, chiefly on two objections ag[ain]st that of Mr. R[andolph] 1. want of power in the Convention to discuss [and] propose it. 2[.] the improbability of its being adopted.[9]

Although the convention voted to proceed with framing a constitution using the Virginia Plan as its basis, the delegates repeatedly returned to the issue of the status of the states within the proposed constitutional union. Some of their comments follow.

Mr. [Alexander] Hamilton.... But as States are a collection of individual men which ought we to respect most, the rights of the people composing them, or of the artificial beings resulting from the composition[?] Nothing could be more preposterous or absurd than to sacrifice the former to the latter. It has been s[ai]d that if the smaller States renounce their *equality,* they renounce at the same time their liberty. The truth is it is a contest for power, not for *liberty*.[10]

Some of the consequences of a dissolution of the Union, and the establishment of partial confederacies, had been pointed out. He would add another of a most serious nature. Alliances will immediately be formed with different rival [and] hostile nations of Europe[], who will foment disturbances among ourselves and make us parties to all their own quarrels. Foreign nations having American dominions are [and] must be jealous of us. Their representatives betray the utmost anxiety for our fate, [and] for the result of this meeting, which must have an essential influence on it.—It had been said that respectability in the eyes of foreign Nations was not the object at which we aimed; that the proper object of republican Government was domestic tranquillity [and] happiness. This was an ideal distinction. No Governm[en]t could give us tranquillity [and] happiness at home, which did not possess sufficient stability and strength to make us respectable abroad. This was the critical moment for forming such a government.[11]

Mr. [William] Pierce. The great difficulty in [the Confederation] congress arose from the mode of voting. Members spoke on the floor as state advocates, and were bias[]ed by local advantages.—What is federal? No more than a compact between states; and the one heretofore formed is insufficient. We are now met to remedy its defects, and our difficulties are great, but not, I hope, insurmountable. State distinctions must be sacrificed so far as the general government shall render it necessary—without, however, destroying them altogether. Although I am here as a representative from a small state, I consider myself as a citizen of the United States, whose general interest I will always support.[12]

Mr. [Elbridge] Gerry, urged that we never were independent States, were not such now, [and] never could be even on the principles of the Confederation. The States [and] the advocates for them were intoxicated with the idea of their *sovereignty.* He was a member of [the Continental] Congress at the time the federal articles were formed. The injustice of allowing each State an equal vote was long insisted on. He voted for it, but it was ag[ain]st his Judgment, and under the pressure of public danger, and the obstinacy of the lesser States. The present confederation he considered as dissolving. The fate of the Union will be decided by the Convention. If they do not agree on something, few delegates will probably be appointed to [the Confederation] Cong[res]s. If they do Cong[res]s

will probably be kept up till the new System should be adopted—He lamented that instead of coming here like a band of brothers, belonging to the same family, we seemed to have brought with us the spirit of political nego[t]iators.[13]

On Tuesday, July 17, the Convention gave Congress broad discretionary legislative powers, but Madison's proposal that it have the power to review and veto state laws went down again in crashing defeat, with only three states (MA, VA, and NC) voting for it.[14] In its place, Luther Martin proposed what would eventually become the Constitution's supremacy clause.[15] Martin's resolution, taken from the New Jersey Plan, affirmed that all laws and treaties passed by Congress would be the "supreme law of the respective states" and that state courts were obliged to follow them in their rulings, regardless of state laws.[16] It passed without any dissent.[17] Meanwhile, on July 18, the delegates moved on to the issue of inferior national courts.[18] Although this issue had proved contentious earlier and divisions over it remained, the Convention quickly accepted the compromise fashioned by the Committee of the Whole to authorize (rather than mandate) the creation of such courts.[19]

12. Resol[ution]: "that Nat[iona]l <legislature> be empowered to appoint inferior tribunals[.]"

Mr. [Pierce] Butler could see no necessity for such tribunals. The State Tribunals might do the business.

Mr. [Luther] Martin concurred. They will create jealousies [and] oppositions in the State tribunals, with the jurisdiction of which they will interfere.

Mr. [Nathanial] Ghorum.... Inferior tribunals are essential to render the authority of the Nat[iona]l Legislature effectual[.]

Mr. Randolph observed that the Courts of the States can not be trusted with the administration of the National laws. The objects of jurisdiction are such as will often place the General [and] local policy at variance.

Mr. G[ouverneur] Morris urged also the necessity of such a provision.

Mr. Sherman was willing to give the power to the Legislature but wished them to make use of the State Tribunals whenever it could be done[] with safety to the general interest.

Col. Mason thought many circumstances might arise not now to be foreseen, which might render such a power absolutely necessary.

On question for agreeing to 12. Resol[ution]: <empowering> the National Legislature to appoint> "inferior tribunals[.]" Ag[ree]d to nem. con.[20]

After working through the Virginia Plan, the Convention sent the various resolutions as amended to a Committee of Detail, which fashioned those resolutions into twenty-three articles.[21] The Convention then worked through these articles. On August 23 it came to Article VIII: a supremacy clause based on the one approved by the Convention on July 17.[22] The Committee of Detail strengthened this clause slightly.[23] Where Martin's version followed the New Jersey Plan by instructing state judges that Congressional acts were "the supreme law of the several states" and preempted state laws, the new version stated that acts passed by Congress also preempted state constitutions.[24] John Rutledge proposed adding "This Constitution" to the beginning of the article, making it clear that the Constitution itself (as well as Congressional acts) preempted state laws and constitutions, and that state judges were bound to comply.[25] Rutledge's motion was approved.[26] When this clause reached the final draft of the Constitution as Article VI, Section 2, "supreme law of the several states"[27] became the "supreme [l]aw of the [l]and,"[28] to underscore that the United States was now a nation, not a confederacy.[29]

On their last working day (Saturday, September 15) the delegates made a variety of corrections and changes to the Constitution.[30] Incorporating provisions approved by the Convention, the Constitution gave Congress the power "to lay and collect taxes, duties, imposts and excises," and "to regulate commerce with foreign nations."[31] It specifically barred states from laying duties on imports or exports without Congressional consent.[32] A proposal to qualify this restriction led to a brief exchange between Gouverneur Morris and James Madison on the negative reach of Congressional power to regulate commerce.[33] The extent of that power would become a significant and much litigated issue in American constitutional law.[34]

Mr. [William] Mc.Henry [and] Mr. [John] Carroll moved that "no State shall be restrained from laying duties of tonnage for the purpose of clearing [harbors] and erecting light-houses[.]"

Col. Mason in support of this explained and urged the situation of the Chesapeak which peculiarly required [expenses] of this sort.

Mr. Govr. Morris. The States are not restrained from laying tonnage as the Constitution now [s]tands. The exception proposed will imply the [c]ontrary, and will put the States in a worse condition than the gentleman (Col[.] Mason) wishes.

Mr. Madison. Whether the States are now restrained from laying tonnage duties depends on the extent of the power "to regulate commerce[.]" These terms are vague but seem to exclude this power of the States—They may certainly be restrained by Treaty. He observed that there were other objects for tonnage Duties as the support of Seamen &c. He was more [and] more convinced that the regulation of Commerce was in its nature indivisible and ought to be wholly under one authority.

Mr. Sherman. The power of the U[nited] States to regulate trade being supreme can [control] interferences of the State regulations <when>such interferences happen; so that there is no danger to be apprehended from a concurrent jurisdiction.

Mr. [Stephen] Langdon insisted that the regulation of tonnage was an essential part of the regulation of trade, and that the States ought to have nothing to do with it. On motion "that no [']State shall lay any duty on tonnage without the Consent['] of Congress."[35]

NH, MA, NJ, DL, MD, SC, aye 6; PA, VA, NC, GA, no 4; CT divided.[36]

As the Convention moved toward adopting the Constitution, several delegates led by Governor Edmund Randolph, who had originally offered the Virginia Plan, rose to state their objections to the document. Several of those objections speak to the broad powers envisioned for the new national government over the states.

Mr. Randolph animadverting on the indefinite and dangerous power given by the Constitution to Congress, expressing the pain he felt at differing from the body of the Convention, on the close of the great [and] awful subject of their [labors], and anxiously wishing for some accommodating expedient which would relieve him from his embarrassments, made a motion importing "that amendments to the plan might be offered by the State Conventions, which should be submitted to and finally decided on by another general Convention." Should this proposition be disregarded, it would he said be impossible for him to put his name to the instrument. Whether he should oppose it afterwards he would not then decide but he would not deprive himself of the freedom to do so in his own State, if that course should be prescribed by his final judgment—

Col: Mason [second]ded [and] followed Mr. Randolph in animadversions on the dangerous power and structure of the Government, concluding that it would end either in monarchy, or a tyrannical aristocracy; which, he was in doubt[,] but one or other, he was sure. This Constitution had been formed without the knowledge or idea of the people. A second Convention will know more of the sense of the people, and be able to provide a system more consonant to it. It was improper to say to the people, take this or nothing. As the Constitution now stands, he could neither give it his support or vote in Virginia; and he could not sign here what he could not support there. With the expedient of another Convention as proposed, he could sign.

Mr. [Charles] Pinkney. These declarations from members so respectable at the close of this important scene, give a peculiar solemnity to the present moment. He descanted on the consequences of calling forth the deliberations [and] amendments of the different States on the subject of Government at large. Nothing but confusion [and] contrariety could spring from the experiment. The States will never agree in their plans—And the Deputies to a second Convention coming together under the discordant impressions of their Constituents, will never agree. Conventions are serious things, and ought not to be repeated—He was not without objections as well as others to the plan. He objected to the contemptible weakness [and] dependence of the Executive. He objected to the power of a majority only of Cong[res]s over Commerce. But apprehending the danger of a general confusion, and an ultimate decision by the Sword, he should give the plan his support.

Mr. Gerry, stated the objections which determined him to withhold his name from the Constitution. 1. the duration and re-eligibility of the Senate. 2. the power of the House of Representatives to conceal their journals. 3[.]—the power of Congress over the places of election. 4[.] the unlimited power of Congress over their own compensations. 5[.] Massachusetts has not a due share of Representatives allotted to her. 6. 3/5 of the Blacks are to be represented as if they were freemen[.] 7. *Under* the power over commerce, monopolies may be established. 8. The vice president being made head of the Senate. He could however he said get over all these, if the rights of the Citizens were not rendered insecure[.] 1. by the general power of the Legislature to make what laws they may please to call necessary and proper. 2. raise armies and money without limit. 3. to establish a tribunal without juries, which will be a Star-chamber as to Civil cases. Under such a view of the Constitution, the best that could be done he conceived was to provide for a second general Convention.

On the question on the proposition of Mr. Randolph. All the States answered—no.

On the question to agree to the Constitution[] as amended. All the States aye.

Notes

1. James Madison, Convention Notes (June 7), *in* 1 The Records of Convention of 1787, *supra* note 10, at 152–53 (footnote omitted).

2. *Id.* at 155–56.

3. *Id.* at 156.

4. *Id.*

5. Larson & Winship, *supra* note 1 (manuscript at 31).

6. *Id.*

7. *Id.* (manuscript at 36).

8. *Id.*

9. James Madison, Convention Notes (June 16), *in* 1 The Records of the Federal Convention of 1787, *supra* note 10, at 249.

10. James Madison, Convention Notes (June 29), *in* 1 The Records of the Federal Convention of 1787, *supra* note 10, at 465–66.

11. *Id.* at 466–67.

12. Robert Yates, Convention Notes (June 29), *in* 1 The Records of the Federal Convention of 1787, *supra* note 10, at 474.

13. James Madison, Convention Notes (June 29), *in* 1 The Records of the Federal Convention of 1787, *supra* note 10, at 467.

14. Larson & Winship, *supra* note 1 (manuscript at 70).

15. *Id.*

16. *Id.;* James Madison, Convention Notes (July 17), *in* 2 The Records of the Federal Convention of 1787, at 28–29 (Max Farrand ed., rev. ed. 1937).

17. Larson & Winship, *supra* note 1 (manuscript at 70); James Madison, Convention Notes (July 17), *in* 2 The Records of the Federal Convention of 1787, *supra* note 34, at 29.

18. Larson & Winship, *supra* note 1 (manuscript at 73).

19. *Id.*

20. James Madison, Convention Notes (July 18), *in* 2 The Records of The Federal Convention of 1787, *supra* note 34, at 45–46 (footnotes omitted).

21. Larson & Winship, *supra* note 1 (manuscript at 81).

22. *Id.* (manuscript at 101).

23. *Id.*

24. *Id.*

25. *Id.;* James Madison, Convention Notes (Aug. 23), *in* 2 The Records of the Federal Convention of 1787, *supra* note 34, at 389.

26. James Madison, Convention Notes (Aug. 23), *in* 2 The Records of the Federal Convention of 1787, *supra* note 34, at 389.

27. *Id.*

28. U.S. Const. art. VI, § 2.

29. Larson & Winship, *supra* note 1 (manuscript at 101).

30. *Id.* (manuscript at 113).

31. *Id.;* U.S. Const. art. 1, § 8, cl. 1.

32. Larson & Winship, *supra* note 1 (manuscript at 113).

33. *Id.*

34. *Id.*

35. James Madison, Convention Notes (Sept. 15), *in* 2 The Records of the Federal Convention of 1787, *supra* note 34, at 625 (footnote omitted).

36. *Id.* at 625–26.

Critical Thinking

1. Where do states rights end and federal government rights begin?

2. Why did the federal government not usurp more state power until the second industrial revolution?

3. Why were the framers so passionate about limiting the power of the federal government?

Create Central

www.mhhe.com/createcentral

Internet References

State versus Federal Power
http://law2.umkc.edu/faculty/projects/ftrials/conlaw/StatevFederalPower2.html

Exploring Constitutional Conflicts
http://law2.umkc.edu/faculty/projects/ftrials/conlaw/statesrights.html

AntiFederalists versus Federalists
http://staff.gps.edu/mines/APUSH%20-antifederalists_vs_federalists.htm

The Court and Constitutional Intepretation
www.supremecourt.gov/about/constitutional.aspx

Article   Prepared by: Wendy A. Maier-Sarti, *Oakton Community College*

America's Worst Winter Ever
And Why Mythmakers Chose to Forget It

RAY RAPHAEL

Learning Outcomes

After reading this article, you will be able to:

- Explain the reason this winter encampment is rarely discussed.

- Recount the trials and tribulations endured by Patriot soldiers during the winter of 1780.

- Analyze why the near mutiny was seldom discussed as the story of the encampment was passed on generationally.

In January 1780, fighting in the Revolutionary War came to a standstill as Mother Nature transformed America into a frigid hell. For the only time in recorded history, all of the saltwater inlets, harbors and sounds of the Atlantic coastal plain, from North Carolina northeastward, froze over and remained closed to navigation for a period of a month or more. Sleighs, not boats, carried cords of firewood across New York Harbor from New Jersey to Manhattan. The upper Chesapeake Bay in Maryland and the York and James rivers in Virginia turned to ice. In Philadelphia, the daily *high* temperature topped the freezing mark only once during the month of January, prompting Timothy Matlack, the patriot who had inscribed the official copy of the Declaration of Independence, to complain that "the ink now freezes in my pen within five feet of the fire in my parlour, at 4 o'clock in the afternoon."

The weather took an especially harsh toll on the 7,460 patriot troops holed up with General George Washington in Morristown, N.J., a strategic site 30 miles west of the British command in New York City. On January 3, the encampment was engulfed by "one of the most tremendous snowstorms ever remembered," army surgeon James Thacher wrote in his journal. "No man could endure its violence many minutes without danger of his life." When tents blew off, soldiers were "buried like sheep under the snow . . . almost smothered in the storm." The weather made it impossible to get supplies to the men, many of whom had no coats, shirts or shoes and were on the verge of starvation. "For a Fortnight past the Troops both Officers and Men, have been almost perishing for want," George Washington wrote in a letter to civilian officials dated January 8.

The winter at Valley Forge two years earlier is a celebrated part of America's Revolutionary mythology, while its sequel at Morristown is now largely forgotten. And therein lies a paradoxical tale. The climatic conditions the Continental Army faced at Valley Forge and a year later at Middlebrook, N.J., were mild compared to those they endured at Morristown during the harshest winter in American history. "Those who have only been in Valley Forge and Middlebrook during the last two winters, but have not tasted the cruelties of this one, know not what it is to suffer," wrote Baron Johann de Kalb, a German soldier who served as a major general in the Continental Army.

So why do we remember Valley Forge and not Morristown? The answer, in a nutshell, is that Valley Forge better fits the triumphal story of the Revolution passed down from generation to generation, while Morristown is viewed as an embarrassment. At Valley Forge, the story goes, soldiers suffered quietly and patiently. They remained true to their leader. At Morristown, on the other hand, they threatened to mutiny.

Nobody celebrated either Valley Forge or Morristown during the Revolution itself. The sorry plight of the poor men and teenage boys who comprised the Continental Army was a guarded secret, kept from the British, who must not know their vulnerability, and from the French, who might deny aid to a weak ally. Further, the failure of civilian governments to supply troops was just that—a failure, not to be publicized.

By the early 19th century, however, writers who looked to the Revolutionary War to inspire a new wave of patriotism developed a storyline that transformed the troubled winter at Valley Forge into a source of pride. Soldiers had endured their sufferings without complaint, drilled obediently under the instructions of Baron Von Steuben, and emerged strong and ready to fight. "How strong must have been their love of liberty?" Salma Hale asked rhetorically in a romanticized history written in 1822 for schoolchildren as well as adults. If Valley Forge was the low point of the war, the story went, it was also the turning point. After that, things got better.

For the Valley Forge story to work, a climatically normal winter was transformed into one of the most severe—something akin to the one soldiers experienced at Morristown two years later. Historical memory of Morristown was conveniently suppressed, in part because it revealed that the soldiers' hardships continued throughout the war, virtually unabated. Even worse, Morristown afforded clear proof that the soldiers' suffering was not always so silent.

At Morristown "we were absolutely, literally starved," Private Joseph Plumb Martin recalled after the war. "I do solemnly declare that I did not put a single morsel of victuals into my mouth for four days and as many nights, except a little black birch bark which I gnawed off a stick of wood, if that can be called victuals. I saw several of the men roast their old shoes and eat them, and I was afterwards informed by one of the officers' waiters, that some of the officers killed and ate a favorite little dog that belonged to one of them."

The prospect of mass desertions worried General Nathanael Greene. "Here we are surrounded with Snow banks, and it is well we are, for if it was good for traveling, I believe the Soldiers would take up their pack and march," he reported on January 5. The following day, Greene's fears were almost realized. "The Army is upon the eve of disbanding for want of Provisions," he wrote. Although the army did not break up as Greene feared, men deserted almost daily, about at the same rate as they had been leaving throughout the war, including the winter spent at Valley Forge. The rest toughed it out, and most of those survived.

Ironically, the largest threat to the continued existence of the Continental Army came in the spring, with the passing of harsh weather. Then, soldiers hoped for better fare at their mess, and they did get some food—but not with the regularity they would have preferred. The army's supply line continued to experience periodic lapses. When nature was to blame, soldiers found the inner strength to endure, but when human error was the cause of their discontent, they were less tolerant. So when little meat turned to no meat in the middle of May, many felt it was time to force the issue.

"The men were now exasperated beyond endurance; they could not stand it any longer," Private Martin recalled. "They saw no alternative but to starve to death, or break up the army, give all up and go home. This was a hard matter for the soldiers to think upon. They were truly patriotic, they loved their country, and they had already suffered everything short of death in its cause; and now, after such extreme hardships to give up all was too much, but to starve to death was too much also. What was to be done?"

Finally, on May 25, Martin and his fellow soldiers in the Connecticut line snapped. It was a "pleasant day," Martin recalled, but as the troops paraded, they started "growling like soreheaded dogs." That evening they disregarded their officers and acted "contrary to their orders." When an officer called one of the soldiers "a mutinous rascal," the rebel defiantly pounded the ground with his musket and called out, "Who will parade with me?" Martin reported the response: "The whole regiment immediately fell in and formed" with the dissenter. Then another regiment joined in, and they both started marching to the beat of the drums—without orders. Officers who stepped in to quell the incipient mutiny found bayonets pointed at their chests. Meanwhile, the defiant troops continued parading and "venting our spleen at our country and government, then at our officers, and then at ourselves for our imbecility in staying there and starving in detail for an ungrateful people who did not care what became of us."

Two days after the men had so dramatically registered their complaints, a shipment of pork and 30 head of cattle arrived in camp. The immediate crisis was over, but a series of escalating protests occurred in and around Morristown the following winter as well. Throughout the war, American soldiers did not suffer in silence, as the Valley Forge myth suggests. They kept themselves fed and alive however they could, even when that meant speaking out. By remembering Morristown, we acknowledge the can-do, rambunctious spirit that characterized Revolutionary soldiers and helped them carry on.

Critical Thinking

1. Why was the truth of what the soldiers faced covered up?

2. How would colonial opinion have changed toward the war if the truth of the near mutiny came out?

3. Why did patriotism trump the true events of this winter?

Create Central

www.mhhe.com/createcentral

Internet References

Why Is Valley Forge So Famous When the 1779–1780 Morristown Encampment Had the Worst Winter of the 18th Century?
www.nps.gov/morr/faqs.htm

Winter 1779–80 in New Jersey
www.revolutionarywararchives.org/coldwinter.html

RAY RAPHAEL is the author of *Founding Myths* and *Founders*.

Raphael, Ray. From *American History*, April 2010, pp. 52–55. Copyright © 2010 by Weider History Group. Reprinted by permission.

Article   Prepared by: Wendy A. Maier-Sarti, *Oakton Community College*

Franklin Saves the Peace

Shrewd negotiating by America's premier diplomat forced the British to sign an anything-but-inevitable peace treaty with the new republic.

Thomas Fleming

Learning Outcomes

After reading this article, you will be able to:

- Analyze Benjamin Franklin's role in resolving the Revolutionary War.
- Recount Franklin's skill as a statemen and negotiator.

Most people think that George Washington's 1781 triumph at York town ended the American Revolution. In fact the victory set in motion a peace process that imperiled America's independence as virulently as the invading armies George III had dispatched in 1776. No one understood this more clearly than 76-year-old Benjamin Franklin, the American ambassador to Paris.

Franklin had first rescued the infant nation in 1777, when he persuaded the wary French to sign a treaty of alliance, a coup that revived the Revolution's faltering hopes and transformed the contest into a global war from the West Indies to distant India. But as 1782 began, France was teetering on bankruptcy and ready to sign a face-saving peace that might not include American independence. As an ominous sign of their intentions, French diplomats had browbeaten the Continental Congress into ordering Franklin to keep them fully informed of any peace negotiations and to sign nothing without French approval.

The British were not merely indifferent to America's independence; they were still set on aborting it. When peace negotiations began in April 1782, Lord Shelburne, the double-talking secretary of state for home, Irish, and American affairs, simultaneously dispatched letters to his generals in America, directing them to send envoys to the leaders of the 13 rebel states, urging each to consider reconciliation with the mother country. The commission of the British envoy to the peace conference, Richard Oswald, omitted any mention of a United States of America. Instead Oswald was empowered to negotiate "with the said colonies or any of them or any parts thereof."

Redoubling Franklin's problems was the knowledge that his country was totally bankrupt and dependent on loans and gifts from France to keep even a semblance of a government and army operating. His desk was thick with frantic dispatches from Congress begging him to raise another multimillion-dollar loan. He also had to deal with his fellow negotiators, John Adams and John Jay, contentious lawyers determined to fake no advice or guidance, from France, no matter how instructed by Congress.

The ambassador decided to live dangerously. While maintaining a cordial face-to-face relationship with the French foreign secretary, the Comte de Vergennes, he told Adams and Jay: "I am of your opinion and will go on [with the negotiations] without consulting this court."

The Americans swiftly agreed on four goals: certifying their "full and complete" independence; designating the Mississippi River as the western border of the United States; determining the new nation's northern and southern borders; and obtaining the right to fish on the Grand Banks of Newfoundland, vital to New England's prosperity.

The British began the talks in an aggressive mood. In the West Indies, the Royal Navy had recently shattered the French fleet that had trapped Cornwallis at Yorktown. In India their army had routed the French and their allies. But the Americans blustered the British into conceding all four of their primary goals.

Finally, just one thorny issue divided the antagonists: compensation for the colonial loyalists who had lost millions of dollars' worth of property to confiscation by the rebel states, a concession the British were determined to exact. For a few days the conference teetered on the edge of dissolution. Franklin broke the impasse with a letter that he read aloud, which declared that the Americans would insist on a counterclaim for all the damages the British army and navy had inflicted since 1775. He listed burned towns such as Norfolk, Virginia, and Falmouth, Massachusetts, and reviewed the thousands of wrecked and looted houses in New Jersey, Pennsylvania, and the southern states. The British negotiators sat in stunned silence for a long time—and then agreed to sign.

Now came the great unanswered question: what would the French do when Franklin sent them the treaty? For several days nothing but frigid silence emanated from Versailles. Undeterred, Franklin visited Vergennes, who icily informed him there was "little in [the document] that could be agreeable to the king."

Franklin pointed out that, in the preface, the Americans said they would not sign a final treaty until France had negotiated a satisfactory separate peace. He then asked Vergennes for another loan of 6 million livres—a considerable sum considering the tiny American economy of 1782.

Franklin heard nothing for a week, whereupon he wrote a letter telling Vergennes that the appropriately named American vessel *Washington* was going home with a copy of the treaty. Could it possibly also carry the first installment of the 6-million-livre loan? "I fear Congress will be reduced to despair when they find that nothing is yet obtained."

Vergennes fired off a furious letter denouncing the Americans' conduct as a betrayal of France. Franklin pondered this missive for 36 hours and replied with his ultimate diplomatic master-piece. He admitted that, in failing to inform France about the treaty in advance, America had neglected a point of *bienséance* (propriety), but not out of any lack of respect for King Louis XVI, "whom we all love and honor." Should Vergennes refuse any further assistance, "the whole edifice sinks to the ground immediately."

Franklin would hold the *Washington* until the end of the week, awaiting the foreign minister's reply. Then came a threat, delivered in the same smooth style, and underlined: *the English, I just now learn, flatter themselves that they have already divided us*—all the more reason to hope that this "little misunderstanding" would be kept secret until George III and his followers found themselves "totally mistaken."

A few days later the *Washington* sailed for America with 600,000 gold livres in her hold. The ship's passport was made out to the United States of America and contained George III's signature—his first written acknowledgment of American independence.

That was when everyone realized the United States was going to happen.

Critical Thinking

1. What skills and/or qualities did Franklin possess that allowed him to work so well with the British?

2. How did Franklin negotiate for a treaty?

3. Did the French lend money to the United States only because of Franklin's negotiating skills?

Create Central

www.mhhe.com/createcentral

Internet References

The Definitive Treaty, Between Great Britain and the United States of America . . . [Passy] 1783
 www.indiana.edu/~liblilly/history/treaty.html

Treaty of Paris, 1783
 http://history.state.gov/milestones/1776-1783/Treaty

Benjamin Franklin in His Own Words
 www.loc.gov/exhibits/treasures/franklin-treaty.html

THOMAS FLEMING, author most recently of *The Intimate Lives of the Founding Fathers* (Harper 2009), has served as president of the Society of American Historians.

Unit 3

UNIT

Prepared by: Wendy A. Maier-Sarti, *Oakton Community College*

National Consolidation and Expansion

Officials during the first few years after 1789 were conscious that practically everything they did would be regarded as setting precedents for the future. Even such apparently trivial matters as the proper form of addressing the president caused debate. From hindsight of more than 200 years, it is difficult to appreciate how tentative they had to be in establishing this new government.

The most fundamental question about the Constitution arose over whether it should be interpreted strictly or loosely. That is, should governmental powers be limited to those expressly granted in the document, or were there "implied" powers that could be exercised as long as they were not expressly prohibited? Many of the disputes were argued on principles, but the truth is that most individuals were trying to promote programs that would benefit the interests they represented. The first financial crisis of the new government embodied the struggle between Thomas Jefferson and Alexander Hamilton over the future course of the United States.

George Washington, as first president, was a towering figure who provided a stabilizing presence during the seemingly endless squabbles. He believed that he served the entire nation, and that there was no need for political parties (he disdainfully referred to them as "factions"), which he regarded as divisive. Despite his disapproval, nascent political parties did begin to develop fairly early on in his first administration. By the time of John Adams' presidency the party system was almost fully established. Chief Justice John Marshall's brilliant performance in steering between the parties to establish the Supreme Court as a coequal arm of the federal government was unparalleled.

The United States already was a large country by 1803, stretching from the Atlantic Ocean to the Mississippi River. Some said it was too large. Propertied Easterners complained that the western migration lowered property values and raised wages, and they feared population shifts would weaken their section's influence in government. Others thought that the great distances involved might cause the system to fly apart, given the primitive means of communication and transportation at the time. When Thomas Jefferson had the unexpected opportunity to double the nation's size by purchasing the huge Louisiana Territory, he altered the course of American history.

The Second War for Independence, or the War of 1812, did not go well for the United States at first. It began the conflict with virtually no army and a tiny navy. Except for a few isolated naval victories, American forces suffered defeat after defeat. Indeed, by the summer of 1814, British forces invaded Washington, DC, and burned the White House. Through all of this, first lady Dolley

Madison's heroic performance in saving national treasures from British seizure made her a symbol of patriotism. Another patriot, Abigail Adams, during the American Revolution famously wrote to her husband John Adams to remember the ladies, an early call for rights for women. Years later, she showed her disdain for laws that privileged men by writing her own will in which she left most of her assets to other women. It had no legal standing but, to his credit, John carried it out to the letter.

The invention of the cotton gin in the 1790s had an enormous impact on the institution of slavery and resulted in the large-scale migration of slaves from the Upper South to states such as Mississippi and Alabama. Working conditions in the new areas were extremely harsh and many slave families were broken apart in the process. Few slave owners provided slaves with adequate food, shelter, or clothing, and human suffering knew no bounds. Much has been written about the Underground Railway and its part in spiriting runaway slaves to freedom. In 1833 there was a case in which a Detroit judge ruled that a young black couple who had escaped must be returned to their owners. His decision touched off a number of riots in Detroit. When both husband and wife escaped again, this time to Canada, demands were made that they be extradited back to the United States. These demands were refused, thereby serving notice that Canada would be a refuge for slaves seeking their freedom. Activism continued to grow. American women writers used literature, religious texts, and basic Christian constructs to challenge positions people held concerning race, slavery, segregation, and gender superiority. Women continued to fight for educational rights, and also for larger sections of society to be able to obtain an education. But often women themselves fought against educational equality, arguing that the advance of learning—especially for women—would lead to a destruction of the private, familial sphere.

Accounts of settling the west have changed over the years. Once presented in the relatively simplistic terms of "taming the wilderness," the westward movement was far more complicated than the story of hardy pioneers overcoming obstacles. Artifacts uncovered during the Lewis and Clark expedition revealed how generations of Native American history were captured in objects developed by native peoples as a way to preserve tradition and genealogy. These complex, advanced tribes were still seen as subversive, and their very existence in some areas proved challenging to westward expansion. One of the tragedies of this expansion was the forcible removal of the so-called Southern Tribes from their homes to west of the Mississippi. Two leaders of the Cherokee Nation tried to prevent the Cherokees from being displaced. The election of Andrew Jackson to the presidency dashed their hopes.

The Mexican War, dubbed "Polk's War," because President James K. Polk had precipitated it, was a divisive and costly conflict. When a treaty with Mexico was negotiated that was very favorable to the United States, Polk submitted it to the Senate for approval. The problem was that the President had earlier dismissed the man who negotiated the treaty. The treaty finally went through and thereby increased the size of the United States by nearly one-third.

Article   Prepared by: Wendy A. Maier-Sarti, *Oakton Community College*

Madison's Radical Agenda

A diminutive, persuasive Virginian hijacked the Constitutional Convention and forced the moderates to accept a national government with vastly expanded powers.

JOSEPH J. ELLIS

Learning Outcomes

After reading this article, you will be able to:

- Explain the elements of the Virginia Plan.

- Analyze the reasons Madison felt it was important to have a strong central government.

- Analyze the compromises made to create the Virginia Plan.

On May 5, 1787, James Madison arrived in Philadelphia. He was a diminutive young Virginian—about five feet three inches tall, 130 pounds, 36 years old—who, it so happened, had thought more deeply about the political problems posed by the current government under the Articles of Confederation than any other American.

Madison had concluded that the loose confederation of states was about to collapse, that the full promise of the American Revolution—liberty and order in an independent American nation—was about to be lost, and that only the wholesale replacement of the feeble authority of the Articles by a central government of vastly expanded, truly national powers could rescue the infant republic from anarchy, possible civil and petty interstate war, and the likely return of predatory European powers to American soil. He was poised to make that case to the other delegates gathering in Philadelphia for the Constitutional Convention, most of whom were moderates who presumed they were there to reform the Articles, whereas Madison was one of the radical minority that regarded the Articles as beyond repair and wished to replace them altogether.

He quickly discovered that he was the beneficiary of two pieces of good luck. The first was that the leading member of the Virginia delegation—none other than George Washington—agreed with his political diagnosis. "The situation of the General Government (if it can be called a government) is shaken to its foundations," Washington declared upon his arrival in Philadelphia. "In a word, it is at an end, and unless a remedy is soon applied, anarchy and confusion will inevitably ensue."

Madison's second stroke of good fortune was that the entire Virginia delegation had arrived on time, while the other state delegations took three weeks to gather and create a quorum. This meant that Madison enjoyed a providential interval during which he could lobby his fellow Virginians about the acute character of the political crisis and the radical reforms necessary to avert it.

There are no records of the many conversations that occurred in the boarding houses and taverns between May 5 and May 29, when the Constitutional Congress officially assembled. But going by the document that emerged from these deliberations—known as the Virginia Plan—Madison most probably conducted a nonstop seminar. He had all the information at his fingertips: the sorry history of all European confederacies; the abject failure of the state governments to maintain fiscal discipline; the inability of the Confederation Congress to raise revenue to pay off debts incurred during the war; the lack of any coherent foreign policy.

All of these concerns resulted in the fifteen-point plan, which recommended a fully empowered central government consisting of three branches—executive, legislative, and judicial. In effect it posited the wholesale replacement of a confederation where sovereignty resided in the states by a truly national government. Madison pushed hard for a provision that gave the new federal government a veto over state laws, but Edmund Randolph and George Mason insisted on softening this bold assertion of federal power with more ambiguous language. As a result, when the Constitutional Convention officially assembled on May 29, Madison's extraordinary diligence enabled the Virginia delegation to seize the initiative. No one on the moderate side of the argument had come to Philadelphia with equivalently clear proposals for a simple tinkering with the Articles, so the radical agenda embodied in the Virginia Plan commanded the field by default.

From the moderate point of view, and even more so from that of those delegates who opposed any reform of the Articles, Madison's maneuvers behind the scenes represented an orchestrated coup de main, a remarkably deft hijacking of the debate by a minority of radical nationalists. Over the next three months Madison was forced into repeated compromises. His proposal for a federal power to override state laws never gained any traction. And his insistence that both branches of the legislature be based on population was rejected in favor of a state-based

Senate and population-based House. Madison took both of these defeats hard, and when the convention adjourned, he departed Philadelphia fearful that the final document would prove inadequate to sustain the United States as a coherent union.

He was wrong about that, at least until 1861, when the core question of federal against state sovereignty became necessary to resolve on the battlefield. But by defining the terms of the debate with his Virginia colleagues in late May of 1787, Madison had established a framework that placed advocates of modest reform on the defensive throughout the convention, and thereby made some kind of consolidated American nation not only possible but likely.

In retrospect, the most important conversations that occurred during that sweltering summer took place before the delegates convened. This was "little Jemmy Madison's" most influential and consequential moment, because it defined the terms of the debate in collective terms that made the federal government a supportive embodiment of "us," or "We the People," rather than an alien embodiment of "them."

Madison had almost 50 years of public service before him, to include the secretaryship of state under Thomas Jefferson and the presidency in his own right. His constitutional posture shifted on several occasions over those years, and he had the misfortune to be the only sitting president to have the national capital laid waste by invaders' fire during his tenure. Life during the most formative phase of a nation's identity, especially political life at the highest level, is always hard. But looking back, with all the advantages of hindsight, we can say without much doubt that May 1787 was Madison's finest hour.

Critical Thinking

1. Why was it so important for Madison to create a new government that was much stronger than what was laid out by the Articles of Confederation?

2. Had George Washington not been an ally of Madison, would the newly forming government have accepted his policies?

3. What type of government did Madison envision?

Create Central

www.mhhe.com/createcentral

Internet References

The Virginia Plan
   www.ourdocuments.gov/doc.php?flash=true&doc=7

Variant Texts of the Virginia Plan, Presented by Edmund Randolph to the Federal Convention, May 29, 1787. Text A
   http://avalon.law.yale.edu/18th_century/vatexta.asp

Madison Debates May 29
   http://avalon.law.yale.edu/18th_century/debates_529.asp

Virginia Plan
   http://billofrightsinstitute.org/resources/educator-resources/americapedia/americapedia-constitution/virginia-plan/

JOSEPH J. ELLIS, winner of the 2001 Pulitzer Prize in History for *Founding Brothers: The Revolutionary Generation* (Knopf 2000), is the Ford Foundation Professor of History at Mount Holyoke College.

Ellis, Joseph J. From *American Heritage*, Winter 2010, pp. 39–40. Copyright © 2010 by American Heritage, Inc. Reprinted by permission of American Heritage Publishing and Joseph J. Ellis.

Article Prepared by: Wendy A. Maier-Sarti, *Oakton Community College*

Wall Street's First Collapse

Speculators caused a stock market crash in 1792, forcing the federal government to bail out New York bankers—and the nation.

THOMAS FLEMING

Learning Outcomes

After reading this article, you will be able to:

- Explain the reasons behind the panic of 1792.

- Analyze the impact of the panic of 1792 on the U.S. economy.

- Describe the precarious financial situation of the new United States of America.

Wall Street's first bubble swelled and burst in the spring of 1792, exerting a profound effect on American politics and society. Nine years after the Treaty of Paris and the acknowledgment of the former colonies' independence, both Europe and America lay in turmoil. The French Revolution was showing its first symptoms of radical violence. In March an assassin's bullet felled Sweden's King Gustav III, who had called for a crusade against France. In the United States, President Washington struggled to fight a war against British-backed Indians in the Midwest. Closer to home, a savage feud had exploded between his secretary of state, Thomas Jefferson, and his secretary of the treasury, Alexander Hamilton.

In spite of strenuous opposition by the supporters of Jefferson, Hamilton had persuaded Congress to set up a financial system designed to rescue the Republic from the humiliating bankruptcy that had almost destroyed the nation after the Revolution. In 1791 Congress chartered the Bank of the United States with the intention that it would buy up the millions of dollars in promissory notes issued by the Continental Congress when its paper money became worthless in the final years of the Revolution. "A public debt," Hamilton said, "was a public blessing." It could be used to pump new life into the all-but-dormant American economy. The Jeffersonians accused the secretary of trying to turn the new nation into a mirror image of Great Britain, which was not far from the truth.

Hamilton did not inspire confidence in average Americans. Born illegitimate in the West Indies, he had served as General Washington's chief aide-de-camp during the Revolution. The public neither saw nor appreciated his contributions. As the war ended, he married a daughter of Gen. Philip Schuyler, one of the nation's richest men. In the struggle to create a new constitution and federal government, he had displayed a no-holds-barred political style and a disdain, even contempt, for popular government. Hamilton regarded democracy as a "disease," dangerous to the nation's stability.

After winning the brawl over the bank, Hamilton and his followers clashed further with the Jeffersonians over how to deal with the debt. Haunted by the memory of the financial collapse of the 1780s, Hamilton decided to concentrate the wealth of the new republic in the hands of a relatively few men so that the nation would have capital when and if it was needed. He decided to buy at par value the millions of dollars in promissory notes that the bankrupt Continental Congress and state governments had issued to soldiers, farmers, and others who had supported the Revolution.

Hamilton knew that much of this federal debt was already in the hands of speculators. Most of the original holders of government paper had long since given up any hope of being paid its full value. They had either stuffed their certificates in drawers and forgotten them or sold them at heavy discounts. Hamilton permitted—and perhaps collaborated in—leaking his plan to numerous wealthy Americans. Chief among the leakers was almost certainly William Duer, the assistant secretary of the treasury, who combined government service with a passion for quick profits.

The son of a rich West Indies planter, Duer had come to New York on business in 1768 and stayed. He had joined the American side in the Revolution and served ably in the Continental Congress, where he had won Hamilton's friendship by defending General Washington against his critics. Later Duer became secretary of the Confederation government's Treasury Board. In 1779 he married Catherine Alexander, daughter of Maj. Gen. William Alexander of New Jersey, also known as Lord Stirling thanks to his somewhat dubious claim to a Scottish title. "Lady Kitty," as she was called, liked a splendid lifestyle as much as did Duer. They rode around New York in a coach and four with a coat of arms emblazoned on the doors, and they often served 15 different wines at their dinner parties.

leadership, the Court retreated from some of the advanced positions that the Federalists had tried to establish for the judiciary in the 1790s. He rejected the contentious idea that the common law of crimes ran in the federal courts, and repudiated the broad definition of treason that the Federalists had brought down upon the Whiskey and Fries rebels in the 1790s. Even Marshall's assertion of the Court's role in interpreting the Constitution in *Marbury v. Madison* was so subtle and indirect that it aroused little Republican hostility. It was the Federalists who were the angriest at the *Marbury* decision, having wanted to declare the Republicans' repeal of the Judiciary Act of 1801 unconstitutional. But Marshall knew better. That would have brought down the full fury of the Republican Congress.

In a variety of ways, therefore, Marshall sought to escape the partisan politics of the 1790s. All of his evasion and caution, he said, was based on a quite reasonable fear that otherwise he and his brethren would have been "condemned as a pack of consolidating aristocratic." He did much more than affirm the Court's authority to oversee the Constitution. He actually saved the Court's independence and thereby made possible its subsequent vast-ranging role in American history.

Critical Thinking

1. What was Jeffersonian opposition to Marshall based on?
2. How did Marshall elevate the status of the Supreme Court?

Create Central

www.mhhe.com/createcentral

Internet References

John Marshall, 1801–1835
www.pbs.org/wnet/supremecourt/democracy/robes_marshall.html
John Marshall Biography
www.biography.com/people/john-marshall-9400148
The Great Chief Justice: John Marshall and the Rule of Law
www.gvpt.umd.edu/lpbr/subpages/reviews/hobson.htm

GORDON S. WOOD, winner of the 1993 Pulitzer Prize for *The Radicalism of the American Revolution* (Knopf 1992), is the Alvo O. Way Professor of History emeritus at Brown University.

Wood, Gordon S. From *American Heritage*, Winter 2010, pp. 40–41. Copyright © 2010 by American Heritage, Inc. Reprinted by permission of American Heritage Publishing and Gordon S. Wood.

Article   Prepared by: Wendy A. Maier-Sarti, *Oakton Community College*

The Revolution of 1803

The Louisiana Purchase of 1803 was "the event which more than any other, after the foundation of the Government and always excepting its preservation, determined the character of our national life." So said President Theodore Roosevelt on the 100th anniversary of this momentous acquisition. As we celebrate the 200th anniversary, it's clear that the extraordinary real estate deal also shaped America's perception of its role in the world.

PETER S. ONUF

Learning Outcomes

After reading this article, you will be able to:

- Analyze the impetus behind the Louisiana Purchase.

- Describe the impact the purchase had on the United States.

- Discuss the factors that allowed the purchase to come together.

If there was one thing the United States did not seem to need in 1803, it was more land. The federal government had plenty to sell settlers in the new state of Ohio and throughout the Old Northwest (stretching from the Ohio and Mississippi rivers to the Great Lakes), as did New York, Pennsylvania, and other states. New Englanders were already complaining that the westward exodus was driving up wages and depressing real estate prices in the East.

The United States then consisted of 16 states: the original 13, strung along the Atlantic seaboard, and three recent additions on the frontier: Vermont, which had declared its independence from New York during the Revolution, was finally recognized and admitted in 1791, and Kentucky and Tennessee, carved out of the western reaches of Virginia and North Carolina in 1792 and 1796, respectively, extended the union of states as far as the Mississippi River. The entire area east of the Mississippi had been nominally secured to the United States by the Peace of Paris in 1783, though vast regions remained under the control of Indian nations and subject to the influence of various European imperial powers.

Many skeptical commentators believed that the United States was already too big and that the bonds of union would weaken and snap if new settlements spread too far and too fast. "No paper engagements" could secure the connection of East and West, Massachusetts congressman Rufus King wrote in 1786, and separatist movements and disunionist plots kept such concerns alive in subsequent years. Expansionists had a penchant for naturalistic language: At best, the "surge" or "tide" of white settlement might be channeled, but it was ultimately irresistible.

Though President Thomas Jefferson and the American negotiators who secured the Louisiana Purchase in 1803 had not even dreamed of acquiring such a vast territory, stretching from the Mississippi to the Rockies, the expansion of the United States has the retrospective feel of inevitability, however much some modern Americans may bemoan the patriotic passions and imperialistic excesses of "Manifest Destiny" and its "legacies of conquest." Indeed, it's almost impossible for us to imagine any other outcome now, or to recapture the decidedly mixed feelings of Americans about their country's expansion at the start of the 19th century.

Jefferson and his contemporaries understood that they were at a crossroads, and that the American experiment in republican self-government and the fragile federal union on which it depended could easily fail. They understood that the United States was a second-rate power, without the "energy" or military means to project—or possibly even to defend—its vital interests in a world almost constantly at war. And they understood all too well that the loyalties of their countrymen—and, if they were honest with themselves, their own loyalties—were volatile and unpredictable.

There were good reasons for such doubts about American allegiances. Facing an uncertain future, patriotic (and not so patriotic) Americans had only the dimmest sense of who or what should command their loyalty. The Union had nearly collapsed on more than one occasion, most recently during the presidential succession crisis of 1800–01, which saw a tie in the Electoral College and 36 contentious ballots in the House of Representatives before Jefferson was elevated to the presidency. During the tumultuous 1790s, rampant partisan political strife between Federalists and Jefferson's Republicans roiled the nation, and before that, under the Articles of Confederation (1781–89), the central government ground to a virtual halt and the Union almost withered away before the new constitution saved it. Of course, everyone professed to be a patriot, dedicated to preserving American independence. But what did that mean? Federalists such as Alexander Hamilton preached fealty to a powerful, consolidated central government capable of doing the people's will (as they loosely construed it); Republican oppositionists championed a strictly construed federal constitution that left power in the hands of the people's (or peoples') state governments. Each side accused the other of being subject to the corrupt influence of a foreign power: counterrevolutionary England in the case of Federalist "aristocrats" and "monocrats"; revolutionary France for Republican "Jacobins."

I n Jefferson's mind, and in the minds of his many followers, the new Republican dispensation initiated by his ascension to power in "the Revolution of 1800" provided a hopeful answer to all these doubts and anxieties. Jefferson's First Inaugural Address, which the soft-spoken, 57-year-old president delivered to Congress in a nearly inaudible whisper in March 1801, seemed to his followers to herald a new epoch in American affairs. "We are all republicans, we are all federalists," he insisted in the speech. "Let us, then, unite with one heart and one mind." The president's inspiring vision of the nation's future augured, as he told the English radical Joseph Priestley, then a refugee in republican Pennsylvania, something "new under the sun."

While Jefferson's conciliatory language in the inaugural address famously helped mend the partisan breach—and, not coincidentally, helped cast Hamilton and his High Federalist minions far beyond the republican pale—it also anticipated the issues that would come to the fore during the period leading up to the Louisiana Purchase.

First, the new president addressed the issue of the nation's size. Could an expanding union of free republican states survive without jeopardizing the liberties won at such great cost by the revolutionary generation? Jefferson reassured the rising, post-revolutionary generation that it too had sufficient virtue and patriotism to make the republican experiment work and to pass on its beneficent legacy. "Entertaining a due sense of our equal right to the use of our own faculties" and "enlightened by a benign religion, professed, indeed, and practiced in various forms, yet all of them inculcating honesty, truth, temperance, gratitude, and the love of man; acknowledging and adoring an over-ruling Providence, which by all its dispensations proves that it delights in the happiness of man here and his greater happiness hereafter," Americans were bound to be "a happy and a prosperous people."

Jefferson congratulated his fellow Americans on "possessing a chosen country, with room enough for our descendants to the thousandth and thousandth generation," a vast domain that was "separated by nature and a wide ocean from the exterminating havoc of one quarter of the globe." Jefferson's vision of nationhood was inscribed on the American landscape: "An overruling Providence, which by all its dispensations proves that it delights in the happiness of man here and his greater happiness hereafter" provided this fortunate people with land enough to survive and prosper forever. But Jefferson knew that he was not offering

an accurate description of the nation's current condition. Given the frenzied pace of westward settlement, it would take only a generation or two—not a thousand—to fill out the new nation's existing limits, which were still marked in the west by the Mississippi. Nor was the United States as happily insulated from Europe's "exterminating havoc" as the new president suggested. The Spanish remained in control of New Orleans, the key to the great river system that controlled the continent's heartland, and the British remained a powerful presence to the north.

J efferson's vision of the future was, in fact, the mirror opposite of America's present situation at the onset of the 19th century. The nation was encircled by enemies and deeply divided by partisan and sectional differences. The domain the president envisioned was boundless, continent-wide, a virgin land waiting to be taken up by virtuous, liberty-loving American farmers. In this providential perspective, Indian nations and European empires simply disappeared from view, and the acquisition of new territory and the expansion of the Union seemed preordained. It would take an unimaginable miracle, acquisition of the entire Louisiana territory, to begin to consummate Jefferson's inaugural promise.

Jefferson's expansionist vision also violated the accepted axioms of contemporary political science. In his *Spirit of the Laws* (1748), the great French philosopher Montesquieu taught that the republican form of government could survive only in small states, where a virtuous and vigilant citizenry could effectively monitor the exercise of power. A large state, by contrast, could be sustained only if power were concentrated in a more energetic central government; republicanism in an expanding state would give way to more "despotic," aristocratic, and monarchical regimes. This "law" of political science was commonly understood in mechanical terms: Centrifugal forces, pulling a state apart, gained momentum as territory expanded, and they could be checked only by the "energy" of strong government.

James Madison had grappled with the problem in his famous *Federalist* 10, in which he argued that an "extended republic" would "take in a greater variety of parties and interests," making it "less probable that a majority of the whole will have a common motive to invade the rights of other citizens." Modern pluralists have embraced this argument, but it was not particularly persuasive to Madison's generation—or even to Madison himself a decade later. During the struggle over ratification of the Constitution, Antifederalists effectively invoked Montesquieu's dictum against Federalist "consolidationism," and in the 1790s, Jeffersonian defenders of states' rights offered the same arguments against Hamiltonian High Federalism. And Jefferson's "Revolution of 1800," vindicating the claims of (relatively) small state-republics against an overly energetic central government, seemed to confirm Montesquieu's wisdom. Montesquieu's notion was also the basis for the popular interpretation of what had caused the rise of British tyranny in the colonies before the American Revolution.

At the same time, however, Montesquieu's logic posed a problem for Jefferson. How could he imagine a continental republic in 1801 and negotiate a land cession that doubled the country's size in 1803? To put the problem somewhat differently, how could Jefferson—who had, after all, drafted the controversial Kentucky Resolutions of 1798, which threatened state nullification of federal authority—overcome his own disunionist tendencies?

Jefferson's response in his inaugural was to call on his fellow Americans to "pursue our own federal and republican principles, our attachment to union and representative government," with "courage and confidence." In other words, a sacred regard for states' rights ("federal principles") was essential to the preservation and strength of a "union" that depended on the "attachment" of a people determined to secure its liberties ("republican principles"). This conception of states as republics would have been familiar and appealing to many Americans, but Jefferson's vision of the United States as a *powerful* nation, spreading across the continent, was breathtaking in its boldness. How could he promise Americans that they could have it both ways, that they could be secure in their liberties yet have a federal government with enough "energy" to preserve itself? How could he believe that the American government, which had only recently endured a near-fatal succession crisis and which had a pathetically small army and navy, was "the strongest Government on earth"?

Jefferson responded to these questions resoundingly by invoking—or perhaps more accurately, inventing—an American people or nation, united in devotion to common principles, and coming together over the course of succeeding generations to constitute one great family. Thus, the unity the president imagined was prospective. Divided as they might now be, Americans would soon come to realize that they were destined to be a great nation, freed from "the throes and convulsions of the ancient world" and willing to sacrifice everything in defense of their country. In Jefferson's vision of progressive continental development, the defensive vigilance of virtuous republicans, who were always ready to resist the encroachments of power from any and every source, would be transformed into a patriotic devotion to the transcendent community of an inclusive and expanding nation, "the world's best hope." "At the call of the law," Jefferson predicted, "every man . . . would fly to the standard of the law, and would meet invasions of the public order as his own personal concern."

Jefferson thus invoked an idealized vision of the American Revolution, in which patriotic citizen-soldiers rallied against British tyranny, as a model for future mobilizations against internal as well as external threats. (It was an extraordinary—and extraordinarily influential—exercise in revisionist history. More dispassionate observers, including those who, unlike Jefferson, actually had some military experience, were not inclined to give the militias much, if any, credit for winning the war.)

Jefferson's conception of the American nation imaginatively countered the centrifugal forces, the tendency toward anarchy and disunion, that republicanism authorized and unleashed. Devotion to the Union would reverse this tendency and draw Americans together, even as their private pursuits of happiness drew them to the far frontiers of their continental domain. It was a paradoxical, mystifying formulation. What seemed to be weakness—the absence of a strong central government—was,

in fact, strength. Expansion did not attenuate social and political ties; rather, it secured a powerful, effective, and affective union. The imagined obliteration of all possible obstacles to the enactment of this great national story—the removal of Indians and foreigners—was the greatest mystification of all, for it disguised how the power of the federal state was to be deployed to clear the way for "nature's nation."

In retrospect, the peaceful acquisition of the Louisiana Territory, at the bargain-basement price of $15 million, seemed to conform to the expansionist scenario in Jefferson's First Inaugural Address. The United States bought land from France, just as individuals bought land from federal and state land offices, demonstrating good intentions (to be fruitful and multiply, to cultivate the earth) and their respect for property rights and the rule of law. Yet the progress of settlement was inexorable, a "natural" force, as the French wisely recognized in ceding their claims.

The threat of armed conflict was, nonetheless, never far below the surface. When the chilling news reached America in 1802 that Spain had retroceded Louisiana to France, under pressure from Napoleon Bonaparte, some Federalists agitated for a preemptive strike against New Orleans before Napoleon could land troops there and begin to carry out his plan for a reinvigorated French empire in the Western Hemisphere. As if to provide a taste of the future, Spanish authorities in New Orleans revoked the right of American traders to store goods in the city for export, thereby sending ripples of alarm and economic distress through farms and plantations of the Mississippi valley. Americans might like to think, with Jefferson, that the West was a vast land reserve for their future generations, but nature would issue a different decree if the French gained control of the Mississippi River system.

As Senator William Wells of Delaware warned the Senate in February 1803, if Napoleon were ensconced in New Orleans, "the whole of your Southern States" would be at his mercy; the French ruler would not hesitate to foment rebellion among the slaves, that "inveterate enemy in the very bosom of those States." A North Carolina congressman expected the French emperor to do even worse: "The tomahawk of the savage and the knife of the negro would confederate in the league, and there would be no interval of peace." Such a confederation—a powerful, unholy alliance of Europeans, Indians, and slaves—was the nightmarish antithesis of the Americans' own weak union. The French might even use their influence in Congress to revive the vicious party struggles that had crippled the national government during the 1790s.

Jefferson had no idea how to respond to the looming threat, beyond sending his friend and protégé James Monroe to join U.S. Minister to France Robert R. Livingston in a desperate bid to negotiate a way out of the crisis. At most, they hoped that Napoleon would sell New Orleans and the Floridas to the United States, perhaps with a view to preempting an Anglo-American alliance. Jefferson dropped a broad hint to Livingston (undoubtedly for Napoleon's edification) that if France ever took "possession of N. Orleans . . . we must marry ourselves to the British fleet and nation." For the Anglophobe Jefferson this must have been a horrible thought, even if it was a bluff. But then, happily for Jefferson—and crucially for his historical reputation—fortune intervened.

Napoleon's intentions for the New World hinged on control of Saint-Domingue (now Haiti), but a slave revolt there, led by the brilliant Toussaint L'Ouverture, complicated the emperor's plans. With a strong assist from yellow fever and other devastating diseases, the rebels fought a French expeditionary force of more than 20,000 to a standstill. Thwarted in his western design and facing the imminent resumption of war in Europe, Napoleon decided to cut his losses. In April 1803, his representative offered the entire Louisiana Territory to a surprised Livingston. By the end of the month, the negotiators had arrived at a price. For $15 million, the United States would acquire 828,000 square miles of North America, stretching from the Mississippi River to the Rocky Mountains and from the Gulf of Mexico to the Canadian border. Over time 13 states would be carved from the new lands.

When the news reached America in July, it proved a great deal more than anyone had been contemplating but was met with general jubilation. There was widespread agreement that national security depended on gaining control of the region around New Orleans; and Spanish Florida, occupying the critical area south of Georgia and the territory that the state had finally ceded to Congress in 1802, was high on southern planters' wish list of territorial acquisitions. But it was hard to imagine any immediate use for the trans-Mississippi region, notwithstanding Jefferson's inspiring rhetoric, and there was some grumbling that the negotiators had spent more than Congress had authorized. A few public figures, mostly New England Federalists, even opposed the transaction on political and constitutional grounds.

The Lewis and Clark expedition, authorized before the Purchase was completed, testifies to Americans' utter ignorance of the West in 1803. The two explorers were sent, in effect, to feel around in the dark. Perhaps, Jefferson mused, the trans-Mississippi region could be used as a kind of toxic waste dump, a place to send emancipated slaves beyond harm's way. Or, a more portentous thought, Indian nations might be relocated west of the river—an idea President Andrew Jackson later put into effect with his infamous removal policy.

What gripped most commentators as they celebrated the news of the Purchase in 1803 was simply that the Union had survived another awful crisis. They tended to see the new lands as a buffer. "The wilderness itself," Representative Joseph Nicholson of Maryland exclaimed, "will now present an almost insurmountable barrier to any nation that inclined to disturb us in that quarter." And another congressman exulted that America was now "insulated from the rest of the world."

David Ramsay, the South Carolina historian and devout Republican, offered the most full-blown paean to the future of the "chosen country" as Jefferson had envisioned it. Echoing Jefferson's First Inaugural, he asked, "What is to hinder our extension on the same liberal principles of equal rights till we have increased to twenty-seven, thirty-seven, or any other number of states that will conveniently embrace, in one happy union, the whole country from the Atlantic to the Pacific ocean, and from the lakes of Canada to the Gulf of Mexico?" In his Second Inaugural, in 1805, Jefferson himself would ask, "Who can limit the extent to which the federative principle may operate effectively?" Gone were his doubts about the uses to which the new lands could be put. "Is it not better that the opposite bank of the Mississippi should be settled by our own brethren and children, than by strangers of another family?"

Jefferson's vision of the American future has ever since provided the mythic master narrative of American history. In the western domains that Jefferson imagined as a kind of blank slate on which succeeding generations would inscribe the image of American nationhood, it would be all too easy to overlook other peoples and other possibilities. It would be all too easy as well to overlook the critical role of the state in the progress of settlement and development. When Americans looked back on events, they would confuse effects with causes: War and diplomacy eliminated rival empires and dispossessed native peoples; an activist federal state played a critical role in pacifying a "lawless" frontier by privatizing public lands and promoting economic development. In the mythic history of Jefferson's West, an irresistible westward tide of settlement appears to be its own cause, the manifest destiny of nature's nation.

Yet if the reality of power remains submerged in Jefferson's thought, it's not at any great depth. The very idea of the nation implies enormous force, the power of a people enacting the will of "an overruling Providence." In Jefferson's Declaration of Independence, Americans claimed "the separate & equal station to which the laws of nature and of nature's God entitle them." The first law of nature, the great natural law proclaimed by writers of the day, was self-preservation, and the defining moment in American history was the great mobilization of American power to secure independence in the Revolution. President Jefferson's vision of westward expansion projected that glorious struggle into the future and across the continent. It was a kind of permanent revolution, reenacting the nation's beginnings in the multiplication of new, self-governing republican states.

Born in war, Jefferson's conception of an expanding union of free states constituted a peace plan for the New World. But until it was insulated from Europe's "exterminating havoc," the new nation would remain vulnerable, unable to realize its historic destiny. By eliminating the clear and present danger of a powerful French presence at the mouth of the Mississippi, the Louisiana Purchase guaranteed the survival of the Union—for the time being, at least. By opening the West to white American settlers, it all but guaranteed that subsequent generations would see their own history in Jefferson's vision of their future, a mythic, nation-making vision yoking individual liberty and national power and promising a future of peace and security in a dangerous world. Two hundred years later, that vision remains compelling to many Americans.

Critical Thinking

1. How did the Louisiana Purchase alter the course of American history?

2. How was the purchase negotiated and at what expense?

Create Central

www.mhhe.com/createcentral

Internet References

The Louisiana Purchase
www.loc.gov/rr/program/bib/ourdocs/Louisiana.html

The Louisiana Purchase
www.monticello.org/site/jefferson/louisiana-purchase

The Louisiana Purchase Treaty
www.archives.gov/historical-docs/document.html?doc=5&title.
raw=Louisiana%20Purchase%20Treaty

PETER S. ONUF is a professor of history at the University of Virginia. His most recent book is *Jefferson's Empire: The Language of American Nationhood* (2001). Copyright © 2003 by Peter Onuf.

Onuf, Peter S. From *Wilson Quarterly*, Winter 2003, pp. 22–29. Copyright © 2003 by Wilson Quarterly. Reprinted by permission of Peter S. Onuf and Woodrow Wilson International Center for Scholars.

torches. Dolley placed candles in every window of Octagon House. In the tumult, the Hartford Convention delegates stole out of town, never to be heard from again.

Ten days later, on February 14, came even more astonishing news: Henry Carroll, secretary to the American peace delegation, had returned from Ghent, Belgium. A buoyant Dolley urged her friends to attend a reception that evening. When they arrived, they were told that Carroll had brought a draft of a peace treaty; the president was upstairs in his study, discussing it with his cabinet.

The house was jammed with representatives and senators from both parties. A reporter from *The National Intelligencer* marveled at the way these political adversaries were congratulating each other, thanks to the warmth of Dolley's smile and rising hopes that the war was over. "No one . . . who beheld the radiance of joy which lighted up her countenance," the reporter wrote, could doubt "that all uncertainty was at an end." This was a good deal less than true. In fact, the president had been less than thrilled by Carroll's document, which offered little more than an end to the fighting and dying. But he decided that accepting it on the heels of the news from New Orleans would make Americans feel they had won a second war of independence.

Dolley had shrewdly stationed her cousin, Sally Coles, outside the room where the president was making up his mind. When the door opened and Sally saw smiles on every face, she rushed to the head of the stairs and cried: "Peace, Peace." Octagon House exploded with joy. People rushed to embrace and congratulate Dolley. The butler began filling every wineglass in sight. Even the servants were invited to drink, and according to one account, would take two days to recover from the celebration.

Overnight, James Madison had gone from being a potentially impeachable president to a national hero, thanks to Gen. Andrew Jackson's—and Dolley Madison's—resolve. Demobilized soldiers were soon marching past Octagon House. Dolley stood on the steps beside her husband, accepting their salutes.

Critical Thinking

1. Why was it important for Madison to act in the way that she did?

2. Were the British actions against Washington city considered an act of terrorism?

3. Why did the British invade the United States in 1812?

Create Central

www.mhhe.com/createcentral

Internet References

Dolley Madison
www.thejamesmadisonmuseum.org/biographies/dolley-madison
The Dolley Madison Project
www2.vcdh.virginia.edu/madison/
Dolley Madison
http://millercenter.org/president/madison/essays/firstlady
Dolley Madison
www.whitehouse.gov/about/first-ladies/dolleymadison

Fleming, Thomas. From *The Intimate Lives of Our Founding Fathers*, as seen in Smithsonian, April 2010, Pgs. 50–56. Copyright © 2009 by Thomas Fleming. Reprinted by permission of HarperCollins Publishers.

Article   Prepared by: Wendy A. Maier-Sarti, *Oakton Community College*

Abigail Adams' Last Act of Defiance

Our nation's most outspoken founding mother fired the final salvo of her revolutionary quest for women's rights when she scratched out her will.

WOODY HOLTON

Learning Outcomes

After reading this article, you will be able to:

- Describe Abigail Adams' fight for women's rights.
- Discuss how her relationship with her husband allowed for her to have unprecedented knowledge of the newly forming government of the United States.
- Describe how women were defined legally at this time.

Weeks before the Continental Congress issued the Declaration of Independence in 1776, Abigail Adams penned a now famous letter to her husband, John, admonishing him to "Remember the Ladies" when drawing up a new code of laws. "If particuliar care and attention is not paid to the Laidies," she wrote, "we are determined to foment a Rebelion, and will not hold ourselves bound by any Laws in which we have no voice, or Representation." Within a few years of writing these words, Adams did something that has never been revealed until now. She carried out a mini-revolution in the arena that mattered to her the most: her own household.

In the new Code of Laws which I suppose it will be necessary for you to make I desire you would Remember the Ladies, and be more generous and favourable to them than your ancestors.

Of all the means by which the Founding Fathers and other men lorded it over women, none annoyed Adams more than the legal degradation that women had to submit to the moment they got married. Single women, including widows, were allowed to own and control property. Yet as Adams complained to her husband in a June 1782 letter, wives' property was "subject to the controul and disposal of our partners, to whom the Laws have given a soverign Authority." Historians have studied Abigail Adams' denunciations of married

women's inability to control property for decades. But what they have overlooked is that she did not simply complain about the government's denial of married women's property rights. She defied it.

As the Revolutionary War drew to a close, Adams started setting aside a portion of her husband's property and declaring it her own. She added more and more to this stash over the ensuing decades, and she invested it wisely. By the end of 1815 her "pocket money," as she sometimes called it, had grown to more than $5,000—which would be about $100,000 today.

Finally in 1816, racked with pain and convinced she was dying, Adams delivered the parting shot in her household revolution. On January 18, she sat down to write a will. Since she had no legal right as a married woman to own property in her name and her husband was still very much alive, scratching out the four-page document was the ultimate act of rebellion. Moreover, a close look at the will reveals a curious fact that historians have mostly ignored. Apart from a couple of token gifts to her two sons, all the people Adams chose to bequeath money to were women. And many of those women were married.

You know my situation, and that a rigid economy is necessary for me to preserve that independancy which has always been my ambition.

Adams' personal property rights revolution had its roots in her struggle to shield her family from the financial destruction that accompanied the Revolutionary War. Of all the patriot soldiers and statesmen who were forced to abandon their families for long periods, few stayed away as long as John Adams, who saw very little of his Braintree, Mass., farm from 1774 to 1784. John put Abigail in charge of all of the Adams family finances, and she ended up handling her husband's money much better than he ever had, primarily because she was more open to risk. During the course of the war she became an import merchant and then a speculator

What Would Abigail Do?

Americans struggling to weather the economic recession could learn a few things from Abigail Adams, who made money during one of the rockiest periods of our nation's history. If you were to hire her as your financial adviser, here's some advice she might offer.

- **Invest with your head, not your heart.** John Adams wanted to invest all his savings in real estate. But his farmland returned as little as 1 percent annually, and Abigail proved she could earn as much as 25 percent each year speculating in depreciated government securities.
- **Wait for the motivated seller.** In 1785 the Adamses daughter, Abigail, jilted her fiancé, Royall Tyler, who then stopped making payments on the home they planned to move into after they wed. The frustrated seller agreed to sell the house at a bargain price to Abigail and John Adams.
- **Stay coy while bargaining.** When buying real estate, Abigail instructed her business agent not to reveal that he was representing her until a hard bargain was struck. She worried that a seller who knew he was dealing with the wealthy Adams would demand a higher price.
- **Negotiate with the taxman.** After John became president, a tax collector tried to pay him the compliment of giving the Adams mansion in Quincy, Mass., the highest valuation in town. When Abigail protested, the assessed value of the house was lowered and they paid less tax.
- **Be fearless.** When the Dow dipped below 7,000 a year ago, many Americans dumped their stocks, only to kick themselves when the market later rallied. Abigail would not have joined the panic. Shays' Rebellion, a farmers' revolt in Massachusetts, sent bond prices plummeting in late 1786, but she ignored advice from her uncle Cotton Tufts to sell her federal securities and instead instructed him to buy more. "Do not be affraid," she wrote.
- **Keep a close eye on your spouse.** While the Adamses were living in Europe, Abigail routinely read letters John sent from Europe to his business agent in America. As a result, she discovered that her husband planned to purchase a notoriously unproductive farm near their own. She talked him out of it.
- **Share the credit.** Abigail never objected when John took credit for investment decisions that she had actually made. And she tended to portray herself as just the passive consumer of the investment advice she received from her uncle—though she actually managed her portfolio quite aggressively.

—Woody Holton

---

in depreciated government securities and Vermont land titles. And as she repeatedly reinvested her profits, she increasingly thought of the money she earned as her own.

Abigail lived by the credo "nothing venture nothing have"—a notion that John found somewhat alarming. While he was an envoy in France, the couple confronted a seemingly mundane problem. How could he remit a portion of his salary home? Her solution was audacious. If he shipped her trunkloads of merchandise from Europe, she could extract the few items her family needed and arrange to sell the rest to New England shopkeepers whose shelves were nearly empty because of the war. She convinced John the scheme would allow her to avoid having to "pay extravagant prices" for basic necessities, downplaying that she could also turn a healthy profit by selling the imported goods at an enormous markup. When some of these shipments were captured by the British, John wanted to abandon the whole thing, but she wrote back, "If one in 3 arrives I should be a gainer."

In the fall of 1781, Abigail decided to turn some income from her import business into productive capital. As she later reported to John, she placed 100 pounds sterling "in the hands of a Friend"—her uncle, Cotton Tufts—to invest for her. John, who had seen wartime inflation devastate his, savings, reacted with the curt instruction: "Don't trust Money to any Body." But she chose not to call in the loan. She even speculated in depreciated government securities that had been inveigled from Continental Army soldiers at a fraction of their face value. John hated bond speculators, and used anti-Semitic language against them,

but Abigail turned him into one, and she got him an annual return of as much as 24 percent.

By the winter of 1782, Adams had her sights on a new commercial venture. She set about purchasing a 1,650-acre tract in the projected town of Salem, Vt., near the Canadian border. The purchase would be highly speculative, for the sellers had a less than perfect right to the land. Moreover, the town charter prohibited anyone from buying more than 330 acres, but Adams was able to obtain one grant for her husband and one each in the name of four straw men, who then deeded their tracts to the Adams children. The only member of the family who received no parcel was Abigail herself, since as a married woman she was not allowed to purchase real estate in her own name. John thought the venture was far too risky and told Abigail in no uncertain terms, "Don't meddle any more with Vermont." But after the war, she pressed him to expand the family holdings there.

There was scarce ever any such thing under the Sun as an inconsolable widow.

Out of all the money Abigail made for her husband, she set aside some of it and declared it "my own pocket money," "my pin money" and "this money which I call mine." She used it to help out her kids, her sisters, her father's former slave Phoebe Abdee, and other needy neighbors. Even though Abigail believed she had full authority over these funds, she often concealed her activities from her husband. For example, since John had an annoying habit of opening her mail, she once devised a way for her correspondent to enclose her message in a letter addressed to her daughter, Nabby. "It will then fall into no hands but my own," she explained.

But she didn't always conceal her savings from her husband. Once, in December 1783, she tried to use some of this money to bribe John, who had spent the previous five years in Europe as an American diplomat, into coming home to her.

There was a farm he wanted to buy, but he didn't have enough money on hand to complete the deal. So Abigail wrote him, "If my dear Friend you will promise to come home, take the Farm into your own hands and improve it, let me turn dairy woman, and assist you in getting our living this way; instead of running away to foreign courts and leaving me half my Life to mourn in widowhood, then I will run you in debt for this Farm." Most of Abigail's biographers quote this statement, since it went against Abigail and John's shared abhorrence for borrowing money. But they haven't noticed *who it was* that she was proposing John borrow money from. It was Abigail herself. Even though in the eyes of the law she owned *no* personal property, here she was offering to lend her husband a portion of what was technically his own money—but only if he would come home to her. John insisted on staying in Europe, and Abigail held on to the money.

Nearly all of Abigail Adams' biographers mention her will, but they usually move on, overlooking not only the remarkable fact of its existence but its contents. In it, she made token gifts to her two surviving sons, but she gave nothing to her grandsons, nephews or male servants. Everything went to her granddaughters, nieces, female servants and daughters-in-law. In addition to gowns and small sums of cash to pay for mourning rings, Abigail handed out more than $4,000 worth of bank stock, a $1,200 IOU and a total of seven shares of stock in the companies managing the Weymouth and Haverhill toll bridges.

Each granddaughter received clothing, jewelry and a cash payment of anywhere from $400 to $750, depending on how wealthy she was. Her granddaughters Caroline De Windt and Susanna Adams each received $750. Susanna also got a gold watch, several gowns, "the upper part of my pearl Earings" and a share in the Haverhill toll-bridge company. The smallest bequests, $400 each, went to her son Thomas' daughters, both of whom were still children. The cluster of granddaughters that headed up Abigail's roll call of heirs contained one anomaly: Adams included Louisa Smith in this list, even though she was actually a niece. Having never married, Smith had become her aunt's steadiest companion, her most faithful nurse—and her honorary granddaughter. Indeed, her inheritance was the largest of all. In addition to transferring the $1,200 promissory note to her, Abigail gave her a share in the company managing the Haverhill toll bridge. Additional bequests went to Adams' nieces, her sister-in-law Catherine Smith, a pair of distant cousins who were sisters, and two female servants.

There is no indication that Adams had any animus against her male relatives. So why did she exclude all but two of them from her will? Having spent three decades asserting control over land and ownership of personal property despite being married, Adams now bequeathed the bulk of her estate to her granddaughters, nieces, daughters-in-law and female servants in order to enable them, as far as lay in her power, to make the same claim.

To her own surprise, Abigail held on for another year and a half after writing her will. She died about 1 P.M. on October 28, 1818, a few weeks shy of her 74th birthday. Abigail's will was not a legal document that any court was bound to respect, and John would have been within his rights in throwing it in the fire. But he honored it to the letter.

Whilst you are proclaiming peace and good will to Men, Emancipating all Nations, you insist upon retaining an absolute power over Wives.

Abigail had assigned her son Thomas the responsibility of supervising the distribution of her property. Thomas' brother, John Quincy Adams, and their father assisted him in carrying out Abigail's wishes. On November 9, less than two weeks after her death, John transferred the $1,200 promissory note to Louisa Smith, just as Abigail had directed. The former president's compliance with the provisions of his wife's will transformed it into a legally valid document. In the eyes of the law, she had acted as his agent and distributed property that belonged to him. In 1819 John Quincy replaced the promissory note he had given his mother years earlier with a new one made out to Louisa herself. No one could ever challenge his cousin's legal right to recover these funds, for she had never married.

In January 1819, when Louisa Catherine Adams, John Quincy's wife, learned that Abigail had left her an inheritance of $150, she set aside half of the bequest to be divided equally among her three sons, who seemed "to have a better title to it than I could boast." By passing this money on to Abigail's grandsons, Louisa may have indicated disapproval of her mother-in-law's decision to exclude all male descendants other than her own sons from her will. Yet it seems unlikely that Abigail would have considered the younger woman's gift a defeat. After all, by deciding on her own authority to present the money to her children instead of her husband, Louisa acknowledged what the law of the land denied and Abigail had always affirmed: that the money was hers to give.

Critical Thinking

1. Did Adams expect full civil equality or simply just voting rights?

2. Why were married women legally not allowed to own property?

3. Did Adams' fight for acknowledgment of women's issues and rights happen? Why or why not?

Create Central

www.mhhe.com/createcentral

Internet References

Abigail Smith Adams
www.whitehouse.gov/about/first-ladies/abigailadams
Abigail Smith Adams
www.abigailadams.org

Correspondence Between John and Abigail Adams
www.masshist.org/digitaladams/aea/letter/index.html
First Lady Abigail Adams
www.firstladies.org/biographies/firstladies.aspx?biography=2

WOODY HOLTON, an associate professor of history at the University of Richmond, is the author of *Abigail Adams* and *Unruly Americans*. For a glimpse of a woman's life at the other end of the economic spectrum in early America, see the online extra "Abigail Adams and Phoebe Abdee" at www.historynet.com.

Article   Prepared by: Wendy A. Maier-Sarti, *Oakton Community College*

Fashioning Slavery: Slaves and Clothing in the United States South, 1830–1865

KATIE KNOWLES

Learning Outcomes

After reading this article, you will be able to:

- Explain the impact clothing had on slaves.
- Evaluate clothing in the overall sphere of slave life.

By 1830, the slave economy was firmly entrenched in the United States South. The cotton revolution and the spread of white settlement into the Southwest furthered the system of slave labor. From growing urban centers such as Savannah and Charleston to the backcountry yeoman farms of Tennessee to the massive cotton plantations of Mississippi, enslaved people of African heritage worked as the backbone of the southern labor force.[1] Planters who owned larger numbers of slaves usually distributed clothing all at the same time. Sometimes this happened twice a year around December and in late spring. Other large plantation owners only distributed cloth or clothing in December. While the December date often corresponded with Christmas, both of these times were slower work periods within yearly crop cycles. Slaveholders who owned ten or fewer slaves tended to give clothing out as it was needed.

Slaves in the antebellum South wore a variety of clothing styles made out of several different materials. Most summer clothing was made from cheap cotton, while winter clothing was usually made from wool. Other materials included linen, hemp, and various mixtures of fibers.[2] A woman's sleeveless white cotton apron provides an example of everyday work clothing worn by many slaves in the antebellum South. The apron is open at the back but closes at the neck with a drawstring, and the hem is trimmed with five tucks ending with a picot edge. An old card that likely came with the apron when it found its home in the Charleston Museum says: 'Slave apron, worn when serving.[3] This brief card provides a hint as to why this apron has a fancy edging. The person who wore it likely did so while serving the white owners and their guests either in a city house or in the plantation's Big House.

A second apron, also made of cotton, is another example of typical work clothing worn by slaves. This fabric is of a rougher, cheaper quality than the first apron. This piece also has sleeves, which probably served the important purpose of protecting the wearer's arms. Like the first apron, this piece came with a small card when it entered the collection of the Charleston Museum. The plain-weave cotton fabric is referred to as "osnaberg" and the note says this apron was "worn when working."[4] The placement of the sleeves in relation to the neckline and the lack of any shaping at the shoulders are intriguing, as are the reddish stains that appear all over the garment. The stains, which might be anything from remnants of foodstuffs to some sort of cleaning agent, may provide a clue as to how this apron was used. Chemical analysis could provide more conclusive answers, but like so many details of history, the specific work the apron's wearer performed will likely remain a mystery.

These two aprons look similar in appearance at first glance, but they served two very different purposes. The first higher-quality apron was worn by a woman who worked around white owners and their guests. Enslaved people who worked in the homes of slaveholders often had better-quality clothing than their field-working counterparts. In part, this was due to the use of slave bodies as a locale for displaying wealth. A healthy, clean, and well-dressed house slave was a sign to white visitors that the master had the income to not only own slaves, but to provide amply for their care. The second apron was probably used by an enslaved woman who worked out in the fields or in the kitchen of the house, away from the prying eyes of fellow slaveholders come to call. This slave's physical appearance was not as valuable to the plantation owner as her physical labor.

The plantation books of James Heyward of South Carolina provide a good example of how slave clothing appears in the historical record. The surviving plantation books cover the years 1852–1858 and contain cloth and blanket distribution lists for three different plantations he owned. Heyward gave clothing out to his slaves once a year in late November or early December.[5] Many slaveholders gave clothing in the late spring as well as in winter, while others distributed clothing throughout the year as it was needed. Others such as Heyward only handed out clothing in the winter, reasoning that by summer the cloth would be worn enough to be thinner, but substantial enough to last until the next winter. Although the rhythm of plantation life differed slightly by the crops grown, most of the heavy work would be completed in the late spring and by mid-winter. Clothing goods would be given out at these times for a variety of reasons such as a reward for the work done during the year or as a Christmas or New Year present.

Often, as is the case with Heyward's plantations, slaves were not given completely finished clothing. Having time to sew the yards of cloth that were doled out presented another reason for giving it at a relatively idle time in the crop cycle, since slaves would have more of their own time to devote to making finished clothing. Heyward's lists are organized with the first column listing male and female slaves by name followed by several columns with different types of apparel. These columns are named "white cloth," "blue cloth," "shoes," "blankets," "caps," "handkerchiefs," "great coats," and "homespun." Different yardage amounts of cloth are given under the appropriate columns, with the majority of people listed receiving five and a half yards of white cloth and six yards of homespun. Only the first four people listed received blue cloth, each receiving six yards. The first person listed has the word "driver" after his name, indicating that this slave had a certain amount of authority over the others.[6] By giving slaves with higher authority or special skills different clothing goods, which were often of better quality than what the majority received, slaveholders were able to establish a visual hierarchy among the enslaved population.

Toward the end of Heyward's list the yardage amounts become progressively smaller, indicating that children appear at the bottom. Being smaller, children's bodies would not require the same amount of yardage as an adult body. Slaveholders also reasoned that, since children did not work as full hands, they did not need all of the clothing items given to adults. In Heyward's case, none of the children received shoes and some did not receive blankets.[7]

Although children did not get shoes, almost all of the adults on the list received a pair. It appears that Heyward ordered ready-made shoes in various sizes for his plantation. In the shoe column of the list the numbers four through eleven are listed by each person's name, indicating what size of shoe each needed. Heyward could have gotten these shoes from a number of sources. In many areas of the South, itinerant craftsmen traveled among the plantations making shoes and other specialty goods. Or Heyward may have ordered them from a local merchant who bought goods from the northern states.

The burgeoning ready-made apparel industry in New England and the Mid-Atlantic found one of its best markets in Southern slaveholders.[8] In an 1848 account with a Philadelphia merchant, planter John Devereux purchased "66 large size negro Blankets" for one dollar apiece.[9] Another planter from South Carolina listed coats ordered by size, including two frock coats, in his plantation journal.[10] The higher cost of finished goods may have been worth the extra labor saved for the slaves who would have otherwise made them.

An Alabama planter noted at the end of his clothing distribution list for 1854, "Clothing this year has been entirely of woolen goods. The men and women of the Pine [K]not plains [fabric] manufactured at the Eagle Factory in Columbus, Ga. That for the men cost 30 cents. Women 28 cents. The children

are of northern satinets, cost 25 cents."[11] Rather than produce finished cloth from raw goods raised on his plantation, this man purchased finished cloth from both northern and southern manufacturers.[12] Other planters purchased tools for carding, spinning, and weaving cloth and some plantations even included loom houses.[13]

Some plantation managers considered clothing to be a privilege earned by obedient workers. Davison McDowell, who kept a journal for his plantation in South Carolina, often noted times when he withheld clothing as punishment for various infractions. After returning from a trip in the fall of 1827 he noted in his journal, "Jerry and Jackson has killed a beef. The runaway Marlbro was concerned in it also…Give them no Christmas nor Summer cloths."[14] Enslaved people used stealing and truancy as forms of resistance against their oppressors. In this case, two men fed themselves and another likely hiding nearby by killing one of the plantation's cows and eating the meat. As punishment, McDowell withheld their clothing allowance for the entire year. Four years later, McDowell recounted the return of two truant male slaves: "This day makes 4 weeks since they went away. As they have come home themselves (agreeable to a Rule of the Plantation) they are not to be whipped! [B]ut they are to be deprived of all the comforts of the Plantation: they are to get no Summer cloth's, Christmas; and as the offence appears to [be] one of great enormity (my Crop being very grassy when they went away) I think I will give them no Winter cloth's."[15] These men likely relied on other slaves in the community to help them find enough clothing to keep sufficiently warm and suitably covered.[16]

Besides fieldwork, nursing, cooking, cleaning, and waiting, enslaved women were often employed in making their own clothing. In some cases this involved constructing apparel from cloth purchased by the owner. On other plantations, women made finished garments from the cotton and wool raised right on the land. In the Southern Historical Collection at the University of North Carolina, a plantation book provides a glimpse into this work.[17] An overseer employed on a plantation owned by Rice Ballard took notes of the work slaves performed each day. Several entries include information about cloth production. On November 23, 1848, the overseer wrote, "Wet day, nothing at all done of any importance the women engaged at the House Spinning, Sewing Thread, Karding Bats, & making Comforts."[18] That the overseer considered all of this labor of no importance to the overall productivity of the plantation is a common perception of women's work. In many other sources studied for this project, spinning, weaving, sewing, and laundering are not considered to be work by plantation owners or overseers. Slave women and single men often spent their so-called Saturday "free time" in laundering their clothing and taking care of their living quarters.

Slaves were closely involved with the production of their apparel. Knowing the amount of work hours that went into making a simple shirt or chemise made the clothing that slaves received all the more valuable. On some plantations, this meant helping to grow the cotton and linen and raising sheep for wool. Included in many plantation accounts are purchases of cards, spinning wheels, needles, pins, and shears. These implements were either distributed to the slaves with their cloth allotments, or used by a small group of slaves to produce finished goods for all. In her plantation records, Mistress Mary Pringle lists "work cut out and put under Celia's care" that includes fourteen servants' shirts along with eight shirts apiece for the master and his three sons and ten chemises for Mary Pringle.[19] In this case, the plantation mistress likely did the cutting, and then gave the cut garments to the enslaved woman Celia for finishing. White women were often involved in the distribution and making of plantation clothing, but the extent differed from plantation to plantation.[20]

Because of their higher cost relative to other garments, shoes were a commodity to many enslaved people. [A] shoe dating to about 1860 came to the South Carolina State History Museum from Darlington County, South Carolina. The heeled wooden sole is very typical of other surviving examples and written descriptions of shoes worn by slaves. The upper part of the shoe is made of cotton and ticking, with a leather strap to hold it on; this type is less common in written descriptions of slave shoes. Most shoes used by slaves were of a type referred to as brogans. They usually had wooden soles with leather uppers. These were of the roughest hide, ill-fitting, and of poor quality. In written accounts slaves often describe their shoes as so uncomfortable they preferred to go barefoot.[21] By the time the leather was softened enough to bear, the cheap brogans were worn through or broken.

Shoes were one of the first types of wearing apparel to be produced in mass quantity to a standard size. These ready-made shoes often cost between two and three dollars throughout the antebellum period, depending on the size of the shoe.[22] Some planters, particularly those with larger plantations, had shoes made for their slaves. Itinerant shoemakers, enslaved and free, traveled from plantation to plantation making up shoes for the slave population and then moved on to the next job.[23] A few plantations had a designated shoemaker who spent all of his work time in making shoes for his fellow slaves. The process began when an animal was slaughtered. The hides had to go through a long, arduous processing before the shoemaker could work with them. The period from slaughter to prepared hide took several weeks. While sewing was left to the women, cobbling was an exclusively male job. Conventional male tasks such as carving, blacksmithing, and tanning were all components of shoe making.

In the records of James Heyward, as in those of many planters, children did not receive footwear.[24] In his list of rules for the plantations, Edward Spann Hammond lists detailed instructions for overseers regarding when and how much cloth should be given to men, women, and children. For children he writes:

> Each child gets 2 shirts of cotton drilling every fall, & 2 of shirting in the spring made very long. The girls get a frock, & the boys a pr. of pants reaching the neck & with sleeves, every fall & spring—of lighter woolens in the fall than that given to the work hands. . . . Mothers are required to put entirely clean clothes on their children twice a week, & it is the duty of the nurse to report any omission to do so.[25]

Notes

1. John B. Boles, *The South Through Time: A History of an American Region,* vol. I, 3rd ed. (Upper Saddle River, NJ: Pearson Education, Inc., 2004). This first volume in a two-volume set provides an excellent overall introduction to the history of the southern United States. Chapters eleven through fourteen are particularly relevant to the antebellum years discussed in this study, as is the accompanying "Guide to Further Reading."

2. Many different terms are used in sources referring to the fabrics used for making slave clothing, including osnaburg, linsey-woolsey, plains, negro cloth, woolen plains, and kersey. Sometimes different terms were used colloquially to refer to the same type of fabric. Meanings also changed over time, as in the word linsey-woolsey, which usually referred to a cotton and wool blend in the nineteenth century period studied here, but meant a linen and wool blend in the eighteenth century. For a good resource on textile definitions, see Phyllis G. Tortora and Robert S. Merkel, eds. *Fairchild's Dictionary of Textiles,* 7th ed. (New York: Fairchild Publications, 2007). For an example of cost comparison, in 1833 a planter purchased 294 yards of osnaburg at a total of $32.34, or roughly nine cents per yard. In the same transaction he also bought 6½ yards of Paris muslin for a total of $6.50, or one dollar per yard. Bill for A. North Jr. from David Hopkins, May 2, 1833, Hopkins Family Papers, South Carolina Historical Society (SCHS), Charleston, SC.

3. Note in Object File, HT2902, Charleston Museum (CM), Charleston, SC.

4. Note in Object File, HT2903, CM.

5. James Heyward Plantation Book, 1852–1858, James Barnwell Heyward Papers, SCHS.

6. Heyward Plantation Book. All of the numbers given here are taken from the entry for Rotterdam plantation on November 16, 1852. The number of total slaves and the yardage received by the people varies little over the six-year span of the plantation book. This is one of the most complete lists throughout the record. Not all of them include columns for entering caps, handkerchiefs, and great-coats. This may be because Heyward did not give out these items every year, or it may be that he simply varied in how he kept his records. These record books were often filled out by plantation overseers rather than the owner. The changing of overseers happened more frequently than the changing of owners and may account for the discrepancy in record keeping as well.

7. Heyward Plantation Book.

8. For work on the ready-made industry, see Michael Zakim, *Ready-Made Democracy: A History of Men's Dress in the American Republic, 1760–1860* (Chicago: University of Chicago Press, 2003); Tom Downey, *Planting a Capitalist South: Masters, Merchants, and Manufacturers in the Southern Interior, 1760–1860* (Baton Rouge: Louisiana State University Press, 2009); Michele Gillespie, "Building Networks of Knowledge: Henry Merrell and Textile Manufacturing in the Antebellum South," in *Technology, Innovation, and Southern Industrialization: From the Antebellum Era to the Computer Age,* ed. Susanna Delfino and Michelle Gillespie (Columbia: University of Missouri Press, 2008), 97–124. Dr. Seth Rockman at Brown University is currently conducting research on the industry of goods

made in the North specifically for sale and use to southern plantations, including shoes made in Massachusetts and negro cloth manufactured in Rhode Island.

9. John Devereux in account with M. Furrall, September 4, 1848, Devereux Family Papers, Duke University Special Collections (Duke), Durham, NC.

10. Blanket List for 1853, Slave Blanket Book 1853–1860, SCHS.

11. Clothing List Fall of 1854, John Horry Dent Farm Journals and Account Books, South Caroliniana Library (SCL), Columbia, SC.

12. For work on the burgeoning southern textile industry see: Tom Downey; Gillespie, 97–124.

13. List of Tools, Edward Dromgoole Plantation Book 1853–1865, Duke.

14. Asylum Plantation Journal, August 7, 1827, Davison McDowell Plantation Journal, SCL.

15. Asylum Plantation Journal, August 24, 1831.

16. For further studies regarding everyday resistance tactics of enslaved African Americans, see John Blassingame, *The Slave Community: Plantation Life in the Antebellum South* (New York: Oxford University Press, 1972); Stephanie Camp, *Closer to Freedom: Enslaved Women and Everyday Resistance in the Plantation South* (Chapel Hill: The University of North Carolina Press, 2004); Sharon Ann Holt, "Symbol, Memory, and Service: Resistance and Family in Nineteenth-Century African America," in *Working Toward Freedom: Slave Society and Domestic Economy in the American South,* ed. Larry E. Hudson Jr. (Rochester, NY: University of Rochester Press, 1994), 192–210; Charles Joyner, *Down by the Riverside: A South Carolina Slave Community* (Urbana: University of Illinois Press, 1984).

17. Patricia K. Hunt, "Fabric Production in the 19th-Century African American Slave Community," *Ars Textrina* 15 (July 1991): 83–92.

18. Plantation Book for Magnolia Plantation, November 23, 1848, Rice C. Ballard Papers, Southern Historical Collection at the University of North Carolina, Chapel Hill, NC. There are several other similar entries in this plantation journal by the same overseer.

19. Mary Pringle, Record of Servants, June 7, 1852, Alston-Pringle Papers, SCHS.

20. Scholars have long debated how much actual physical labor was done by the plantation mistress. See Fox-Genovese, *Within the Plantation Household;* Deborah Gray White, *Ar'n't I a Woman?: Female Slaves in the Plantation South,* rev. ed. (New York: W.W. Norton and Company, 1999) for examples of differing views on this issue.

21. Rawick, *American Slave.*

22. List of Expenses, 1850–1858, Morris Conley Account Book, Duke.

23. Rawick, *American Slave.*

24. James Heyward Plantation Books, SCHS.

25. Undated Plantation Journal, Edward Spann Hammond Plantation Books, SCL.

Critical Thinking

1. Why did clothing have such a dramatic impact on slaves?

2. Why did slave owners not provide adequate clothing for their slaves?

Create Central

www.mhhe.com/createcentral

Internet Reference

The Role of Women in Slave Communities
www3.gettysburg.edu/~tshannon/hist106web/Slave%20Communities/atlantic_world/gender.htm

Slavery Mississippi
www.sc.edu/uscpress/books/2013/7332.html

Sports in Shackles: The Athletic and Recreational Habits of Slaves on Southern Plantations
http://journals.chapman.edu/ojs/index.php/VocesNovae/article/view/55/229

KATIE KNOWLES is a PhD student in history at Rice University in Houston, Texas. This article encompasses portions of her dissertation, also entitled "Fashioning Slavery: Slaves and Clothing in the United States South, 1830–1865." Her research interests include nineteenth-century American history, the US South, and gender studies.

Article

Prepared by: Wendy A. Maier-Sarti, *Oakton Community College*

Circumcision of the Female Intellect

19th Century Women Who Opposed Scholarly Education

MARBETH HOLMES

Learning Outcomes

After reading this article, you will be able to:

- Explain what influences led to some women opposing scholarly education for females.
- Explain the concept of Republican Motherhood and the impact of that concept.

In 19th century America, some women decried the opportunity for scholarly education as rebellion against religion and predicted a grim decline in the quality of life, home, and hearth for American families and for American culture and politics. In particular, women who opposed scholarly education argued that God had not created men and women equally; therefore, women should not desire nor be granted equality in social expectations or roles but remain in the sphere of gender difference. These women preferred the Biblical submission to male-dominant authority, the domestic tranquility of doilies and embroidery, the notion of the morality of motherhood, and the absence of intellectual stimulation and development—objecting to academic education and its consequential outgrowths of political participation, gainful employment, matrimonial choice, and independent living. It is here among these women we find the desire for womanly piety, purity, social graces, and the necessity of the development of Christian character. The intellectual circumcision was deeply rooted in the Protestant faith and was fostered through all branches of religious service. The idea that harmonious development of Christian character was more rewarding and stimulating than scholarly education pulverized the intellectual growth of women. The examination of the pursuit of perfected womanhood and the damning predictions regarding the quality of life for those women who stray from their true purpose is a fascinating reflection of a truly circumcised female intellect and a thoroughly mutilated spirit. Or is it?

Pomp and Piety: Marriage to God and Man

As immigrants flocked to the newly Revolutionized America, Land of the Free, they brought with them in full force:

Religion. Though there were many denominations and various forms, in them all was a common theme: the God-given Divinity of gender inequity and difference. From the very Creation of the first social community, the Garden of Eden, the purpose of woman has been clear. She is to be the helpmate and companion of man and submissive to his authority. She also is the instigator of temptation and sin. Ironically, in the biting of the forbidden fruit, it was Eve who first sought knowledge, and Adam who was weak and succumbed to her feminine prowess. However, that was not the message that came to the shores of America. Woman was weak. When left to her own devices, woman was disobedient and sinful, the downfall of man. This was the religious message that resounded from pulpits across the land.

This sentiment is echoed in the writings of M. Carey Thomas—even after she became president of Bryn Mawr, one of the most prestigious women's colleges in the country at this time. In her essay, "Present Tendencies in Women's Education," she recalls the horror she experienced as a child reading the Bible, most particularly the letters of Paul that define clearly the pious role of women as subservient to men. She says she even prayed that God would kill her if that was all she had to aspire to—a life inferior to men.[1] Although she rose above the examples she detested in Milton, Shakespeare, and the Bible of the non-intellectual woman, even in her own success, she limits the benefits of education for women to making them better wives and "vastly better mothers."[2] Although she became quite a trailblazer, in her essay, we see the lessons taught at home and in the pulpit that women's "brains were too light, their foreheads too small, their reasoning powers too defective, their emotions too easily worked upon" to be anything other than domestic beings.[3] This is the identity that prevailed in American thought.

Women are the vessels of God, the nurturers of moral growth and the very givers of life. Biblical teaching instructs women to be submissive to their husbands as they are the Lord, going so far as to specifically state that a husband is the head of his wife. Women are taught to be silent in church, not even daring to question except in the privacy of the home. Older women are to teach what is good and religious and to train the younger generation to love their husbands, to live pure lives above reproach, to take care of the home and the sexual needs of their husbands so as not to bring shame on the Lord God. In the pursuit of Piety, wives even sacrifice their bodies to the sensual whims of husbands. The desire to be a wife of noble character that well pleases both God and Man is the central and initial education for women. Although by law his legal property, a good Christian wife is trustworthy and greatly enhances the life of her husband. She makes clothing and provides food, getting up before dawn to prepare the meal for the household and to plan the work for the day. Her frugality and energy are deeply admired and bring pride to her family.

Caroline Gillman epitomizes these pious beliefs in her book, *Recollections of a Southern Matron,* written in 1838. Her observations of the male-dominant South are especially noteworthy. She professes that in order to form a harmonious marriage, women must "sacrifice thought and action."[4] Here, we find the Godly wife denies herself and submits to her first priority: the pleasing of her husband, and she did so out of love for both God and duty. She notes that when she became bored, she turned her attentions to the beautification of the home, "careful to consult my husband in those points which interested him, without annoying him with mere trifles." She admits that she "sacrificed" her own desires and preferences to a feeling of domestic contentment that she calls, "a more sacred feeling." While noting the absence of much intellectual stimulation of her own, she found delight in being a good wife to her beloved husband. A good wife, she asserts, "must smile amid a thousand perplexities, and clear her voice to tones of cheerfulness when her frame is drooping with disease."[5] Wifely duty preceded the caretaking of one's self even in sickness. And in the interest of submissive harmony, there must be "no scenes of tears and apologies be acted to agitate" the husband. Instead, a Christian wife must be "the star of domestic peace" that "arises in fixedness and beauty . . . and shines down in gentle light" on the life of the family unit.[6] Though she clearly has an inquiring mind that desires stimulation, she passively submits to the circumcision that the role of submissive wife fosters.

In addition to being a good wife, the woman is Biblically charged to help the poor and the needy. Motivated out of pious fear of the Lord and damnation, many women embraced these Biblical instructions and began seminaries and academies solely for the purpose of educating women to be worthy Christian wives. Although the antebellum period saw rise to activism and feminism in its early forms, the majority of women were not yet ready to embrace such immoral and irreligious notions as independence and scholarly education. They were, however, forming social organizations to fulfill their inherent benevolent natures and administer the Graces of God. One such organization was the Ladies Society of New York formed under its Constitution in 1800 and in direct cooperation with Protestant clergymen. Another was Colored Female Religious and Moral Society of Salem, Massachusetts, founded in 1818. These benevolent groups enabled women to assist widows, the poor and needy, and the sick. Interestingly, the women who applied for assistance from these organizations were required to be women who had fallen on hard times due to widowhood or poverty[7] and were of strict moral rectitude and demonstrative of excellent moral behavior. Through these social outreach ministries, women of both races networked and offered emotional support and conversation for one another to nourish the piety of their souls. They used this forum to instruct and be instructed more deeply in the ways of Godly service.

Purity of body and mind is also an essential element of the Godly wife. In her essay analyzing the peculiar nature of woman as it was viewed in the 19th century, "The Cult of True Womanhood," Barbara Welter asserts by Divine right, "religion or piety was the core of woman's virtue, the source of her strength."[8] In fact, religion was so very valuable because it did confine woman to her domestic sphere and served as a "kind of tranquilizer" for those young females who may feel restless in youth and experience what she calls "undefined longings . . . about which it is better to pray than to think."[9] In her discussion of the rigors of pious domesticity, she declares it is woman's "solemn responsibility . . . to uphold the pillars of the temple with her frail white hand."[10] The purity of woman's physical body was also a condition of the Divine expectation for the Christian woman. She must at all cost "preserve her virtue until marriage and marriage was necessary for her happiness."[11] And even the wardrobe of the 19th century American woman with all its corsets, sheaths, and bustles did just that—protected her chastity. Yet, ironically, marriage for her was an end to her innocence and a Divine charge to accept the husbandly attentions even in the absence of affection or desire.

Gender Spheres and Family Valued

It was also in the 19th century that we saw the emergence of the middle-class and the "doctrine of separate spheres became an important ideology" as noted in *Women and the Making of America.*[12] Since the family was the first social organization, the woman's role in the creation of family was paramount. Suddenly a man's worth was in part estimated by the social graces and domestic talents of his wife and the production of a well-run household and a religious family unit. Mary Virginia Hawes Terhune, a writer and opponent of women's rights, asserted that developing a quality family and home was the best profession a woman could have. She "justified female education and training only in relation to domesticity, as preparation for homemaking or in family need."[13] In her estimation, marriage was the only profession of women. In the separate sphere of public (male) and private (female) identities, women were cautioned to maintain virtue and propriety.

While white middle-class men worked for material gain and professional advancement, "women accepted as their female duty the obligation of providing husbands with a much needed refuge from the wider world."[14] In general, women kept to themselves and had little contact with men, and therefore little opportunity to defile their reputations or stimulate their curiosity beyond domesticity. The correlation between a happy family and a successful man became quite apparent during this time. Yet, the wife at home remained the "keeper of the spiritual values of the family" and her competence in house-keeping and entertaining and the development of a good family was her measure of success.[15] However, compliance to the idea of separate spheres earned women a measure of respect even in the pulpit as long as women maintained their subservient obedience to male authority and adherence to their Divine purpose.

Another woman writer and teacher, Mary Lyon suggests that once married the wife's domestic duties must be done with "courage, patience, and submission. Men are to earn support, and the women are to save."[16] Zilpah Grant phrased it slightly differently in her teachings to promote submission claiming that in marriage "where there are only two there can be no majority, and the supremacy must rest on one."[17] Both of these women were teachers who forged the instruction of the religious necessity for maintaining separate spheres in order to fulfill the woman's destiny as wife. Mary Beth Norton writes that the education of women, especially among the emerging middle class, was "limited to the bare essentials of basic literacy, domestic skills, and perhaps the female 'accomplishments' of music and painting. She asserts that too much education—of the scholarly nature—"rendered a woman decidedly unfeminine."[18] Margaret Nash, author of *Women's Education in the United States,* attributes the content of the female education as mostly "ornamental" as she says, "confined to music, needlework, or the fine arts."[19]

Even when educated by intellectual women at formal academies, the curriculum circumcised the female possibilities to the limits and the confines of the home. Interestingly, the educators who were teaching at these female academies and seminaries believed strongly that women should have "proper diction, tone, and pronunciation," not to become orators but to "please listeners." In the instruction of these young intellectual American women, reading aloud "'with propriety and grace,'" as one academy trustee called it, was deemed a "'charming accomplishment.'"[20] Ah, the necessity to provide delightful and soothing entertainment at one's dinner party.

Perhaps no other writer sounded the trumpet of family and the differing roles therein more than Lyman Abbot in his article, "Why Women Do Not Wish the Suffrage." He speaks well for the many women who truly did not desire to separate themselves from domesticity. Here, we are reminded of the predisposed separateness of gender in the public and private sectors of life and the religious implications for all of womanhood—even after nearly a century of feminism and activism. His call to home and hearth is a reflection of the conflict of the women who were at war with the culture of independence, and with it a reaffirmation of the value of family and the Divinity of femininity. In keeping with the Biblical identity of the first family as Adam and Eve, he asserts also that the "family was the first church," citing Abraham's alter and Sarah and the servants gathering to worship. The family is the first labor union, the first army, and even the first government.[21] In the evolution of that initial society, it is the act of marriage that unites them—and us today—one to another. The family is "historically," "organically," and "biologically" the component of all social organization.[22] Then, quite revealing is the assertion that the "most patent fact in the family is the differences in the sexes" and it is here in these separate spheres that the family finds its "sweet and sacred bond."[23] Abbott did, however, assert that different did not necessitate any one being more essential or superior to the other, which aids in his review as a proponent of feminism of sorts. The claim that women are "different in nature, in temperament, in function…[and] in preserving it lies the joy of the family; the peace, prosperity, and well-being of society"[24] is a common theme among women teachers at seminary as well. Catharine Beecher taught that if women ventured beyond the realm of domesticity, they would meet with failure and then become inferior. Understanding and submitting to the "law of Nature, that is the law of God," as Mr. Abbott describes it is essential not only to the success of the family unit, but also to the success of society and ultimately humanity,[25] which is the very lesson of Biblical and academic instruction.

Notes

1. Ellen Skinner. *Women and the National Experience—Primary Sources in American History,* (United States: Addison-Wesley Educational Publishers, 2003), 133.

2. Skinner, 113.

3. Skinner, 114.

4. Skinner, 76.

5. Skinner, 78.

6. Skinner, 78.

7. Skinner, 28.

8. Barbara Welter. *The Cult of True Womanhood: 1820–1860,* Summer 1966, http://www.pinzler.com/ushistory/cultwo.html (8 May 2009), 1.

9. Welter, 1.

10. Welter, 1.

11. Welter, 2.

12. Mari Jo Buhle, Teresa Murphy, and Jane Garland, *Women and the Making of America,* (New Jersey, US: Pearson Education, 2009), 145.

13. Barbara Miller Solomon. *In the Company of Educated Women,* (New Haven: Yale University Press, 1985),

14. Solomon, 37.

15. Solomon, 37.

16. Solomon, 26.

17. Solomon, 26.

18. Margaret A. Nash. *Women's Education in the United States,* (New York: Palgrave MacMillan, 2005), 26.

19. Nash, 36.

20. Nash, 44.

21. Lyman Abbott. *Why Women Do Not Wish the Suffrage,*

22. Abbott, 2.

23. Abbott, 2.

24. Abott 3.

25. Abbott, 4.

Critical Thinking

1. What made Republican Motherhood so important and impactful?

2. Why did some women oppose the concept of scholarly education?

Create Central

www.mhhe.com/createcentral

Internet References

The Cult of Domesticity and Womanhood
www.library.csi.cuny.edu/dept/history/lavender/386/truewoman.html

Challenging Gender Stereotypes during the Depression: Female Students at the University of Washington
http://depts.washington.edu/depress/women_uw_changing_roles.shtml

National Organization of Women Statement of Purpose
http://history.hanover.edu/courses/excerpts/111now.html

Article

Prepared by: Wendy A. Maier-Sarti, *Oakton Community College*

Education and Access to Christian Thought in the Writing of Harriet Beecher Stowe and Anna Julia Cooper

JOJO MAGNO

> *Let them give to the slave . . . the right to read the word of God, and to have such education as will fully develop his intellectual and moral nature; the right of free religious opinion and worship.*
>
> —Harriet Beecher Stowe, *The Key to Uncle Tom's Cabin*

> *A boy . . . had only to declare a floating intention to study theology and he could get all the support . . . he needed . . . [w]hile a self-supporting girl had to struggle on by teaching . . . and actually to fight her way against positive discouragements to the higher education.*
>
> —Anna Julia Cooper, "The Higher Education of Women"

Learning Outcomes

After reading this article, you will be able to:

• Explain Stowe and Cooper's position on slavery.

• Define why some women opposed slavery and became abolitionists.

In attempting to climb past the racist and sexist barriers which existed in nineteenth-century America, women could look to writers such as Harriet Beecher Stowe and Anna Julia Cooper. Their works not only reflect the conditions of women and African-American women in particular, but also call for access to educational opportunities for these women to provide a gateway to Christian thought. Bible study and theological education extended the idea of women and blacks as God's creatures, possessed of a soul, and rebutted the use of Scripture by Southern white males to promote slavery and segregation.

Reviled as sentimental and considered little more than armchair sociology from a woman whose experience in the South consisted of "a visit of a few days' duration to friends in Kentucky,"[1] Harriet Beecher Stowe's *Uncle Tom's Cabin* (1852) is in fact full of challenges that go beyond emotion and abolitionist arguments. When read in connection with Stowe's other works, and in contrast to the writings of contemporary preachers, *Uncle Tom's Cabin* presents a clear call for increased

understanding of Christian theology in general and Scripture particularly, for the good of blacks and women in the South. This call was picked up by Anna Julia Cooper, whose *A Voice From the South* (1892) lauds *Uncle Tom's Cabin* and Stowe and frequently associates ideas of education with the social and moral benefits of intelligent Christian understanding.

Why was it necessary for Stowe and later Cooper to call for learned approaches to Christian ideals? Both before *Uncle Tom's Cabin*'s publication and in response to its message, some Southern Christian thinkers used a certain interpretation of Old (and sometimes New) Testament teachings to defend slavery (and later, segregation and disenfranchisement). If Stowe was no expert in Southern life or the true lot of the slave, she was undoubtedly an expert in Christian thought. Her detractors picked, in this area at least, a very poor platform on which to stand against her. It would take all of her considerable knowledge of Christian ideals to rebut the strident moralizing of the pro-slavery preachers, and she therefore concluded that it was in the best interests of all who shared her desire for abolition to also educate themselves in this area. Since women play the most significant role in the education of children, Stowe's female characters demonstrate how a command of Scripture is essential in opposing the white males who make the pro-slavery or Jim Crow laws; their education must not be neglected. But above all, Stowe tells us, blacks should learn to read and have access to their Bibles. Like Martin Luther, who objected to the Word of God transmitted to laypeople via a priestly scholar of Latin, Stowe recognized that secondhand knowledge of the

Bible was acceptable when nothing else was available, but inferior to direct apprehension of Scripture. She places this sentiment into the mouth of her "little evangelist," Evangeline "Eva" St. Clare:

> "But they ought to read the Bible, mamma, to learn God's will."
>
> "O! They can get that read to them all they need."
>
> "It seems to me, mamma, the Bible is for every one to read themselves."[2]

And Uncle Tom himself does the best he can despite his limited literacy:

> As for Tom's Bible, though it had no annotations and helps in margin from learned commentators, still it had been embellished with certain way-marks and guideboards of Tom's own invention, and which helped him more than the most learned expositions could have.[3]

Education is not a certain line of defense against misapprehension of God's word on slavery and the state of the Southern black. Stowe creates a hierarchy of Biblical education and enlightenment among her white characters. At the lowest order is Eva's cousin Henrique, who replies to Eva's question, "Doesn't the Bible say we must love everybody?" with "O, the Bible! To be sure, it says a great many such things; but then, nobody ever thinks of doing them,—you know, Eva, nobody does."[4] Eva's mother, Marie St. Clare, moves past Henrique's ignorance into a dangerous bit of learning as she parrots her preacher's assertion that the text "He hath made everything beautiful in its season" (a conflation of Ecclesiastes 3:1 and 3:11) shows how "all the orders and distinctions in society came from God . . . and he applied [the text] so well to all this ridiculous fuss that is made about slavery, and he proved distinctly that the Bible was on our side."[5]

But these half-literate interpretations are easily dismissed by Eva's intense faith. Much harder to challenge, and requiring more sophisticated Biblical understanding than that of Tom or Eva, are the messages by the Southern preachers who use Scripture to defend, and even sanctify, slavery. When these are invoked by Stowe's more learned white characters, she counters them with intelligent educated women like Miss Ophelia, the New England cousin of St. Clare; Mrs. Bird, the Senator's wife in the free state of Ohio; Rachel Halliday, the Quaker woman who runs the Underground Railroad sanctuary; and most notably Mrs. Shelby, the wife of Tom's first, humane, owner. Upon her husband's reminder of such a preacher's sermon, Mrs. Shelby heatedly replies: "I don't want to hear such sermons; I never wish to hear Mr. B. in our church again. Ministers can't help the evil, perhaps . . . any more than we can,—but defend it!—it always went against my common sense."[6]

Close reading reveals Stowe's unequivocal rejection of Southern male preachers' use of Biblical admonition. Largely demonstrated by her female, black, and child characters, but also by her own didactic voice, the message of *Uncle Tom's Cabin* is one of internalization of New Testament ideology. Eva preaches love to Topsy, and succeeds where Ophelia's moralizing has failed; Tom preaches patience and empathy to the Shelby slaves who wish that the slave trader Haley would burn in hell forever: "I'm afeared you don't know what ye're sayin'. Forever is a *dre'ful* word . . . you oughtenter wish that ar to any human crittur."[7] Mrs. Shelby believes that the best Christian lesson she can give her maid Eliza regards how she should love and care for her husband and son: "I have talked with Eliza about her boy—her duty to him as a Christian mother, to watch over him, pray for him, and bring him up in a Christian way . . . I have told her that one soul is worth more than all the money in the world."[8]

At times the instruction of the pro-slavery ministers is deemed so pernicious that Stowe must insert her authorial voice and didactic tone in response, for not Eva's sincerity, Tom's simple piety nor Mrs. Shelby's impassioned humanity will suffice. Such a challenge comes when Tom contemplates the suicide of a young slave whose infant has been sold while she is distractedly looking over the railing of the *La Belle Rivière* to try to catch sight of her husband. Stowe explains Tom's thoughts as they might be viewed by the Southern preachers:

> To him, it looked like something unutterably horrible and cruel, because, poor, ignorant black soul! he had not learned to generalize, and to take enlarged views. If he had only been instructed by certain ministers of Christianity, he might have thought better of it . . . but Tom, as we see, being a poor ignorant fellow, whose reading had been confined entirely to the New Testament, could not comfort and solace himself with views like these.[9]

In Chapter 12, a conversation in the passengers' quarters aboard the *La Belle Rivière* ensues when one of the children reports that there are slaves in the hold. After a light and sentimental regret is expressed by one of the women and contradicted by another, who claims that "they are better off than they would be to be free," a preacher begins careful instruction in Scripture:

> "It's undoubtedly the intention of Providence that the African race should be servants,—kept in a low condition," said a grave-looking . . . clergyman . . . "'Cursed be Canaan; a servant of servants shall he be,' the scripture says."
>
> "I say, stranger, is that ar what that text means?" said a tall man, standing by.
>
> "Undoubtedly. It pleased Providence, for some inscrutable reason, to doom the race to bondage, ages ago; and we must not set up our opinion against that."[10]

This preacher of Stowe's will not question with his intellect the "inscrutable" wisdom of Providence, and so she can only challenge him though the words of "an honest drover" who slyly remarks, "See what 'tis, now, to know scripture. If ye'd only studied yer Bible, like this yer good man, ye . . . could jist have said, 'Cussed be'—what's his name?—'and 'twould all have come right.'"[11]

The citation "Cursed be Canaan" (Gen. 9:25–27) is an encapsulation of the major Southern Christian justification of slavery, segregation, and disenfranchisement which was elucidated in lengthy "scholarly" publications. In 1843, Josiah Priest published the 570-page *Bible Defence of Slavery, or, The Negro Race as Deduced from History, Both Sacred and Profane, Their Natural Relations—Moral, Mental, and Physical—to the Other Races of Mankind, Compared and Illustrated—Their Future Destiny Predicted, Etc.* which asserts explicit Old Testament authority: ". . . the institution of slavery received 'the sanction of the Almighty in the Patriarchal age."[12] Jesus, Priest claimed, intimated approval of slavery ("its legality was recognised, and its relative duties regulated by our Saviour, when upon earth;"[13]) by pointed silence on the issue: "the practice passed by without reproof in the New Testament."[14] Priest stipulates that the numerous Old Testament comments concerning "bondsmen" or "bought servants" are in fact references to "the Negro or Canaanite slave."[15] Without further explanation, throughout he equates the Negro race with those descendants of Noah's grandson Canaan, son of Ham, whom Noah declares were to be "cursed" servants to the descendants of Noah's other sons, Shem and Japheth. Although the text is indistinct—Noah's wrath is incurred by Ham's witnessing him drunk and "uncovered" and may refer to the vintner Noah's shame as the descendant of Cain the husbandman[16]—eighteenth and nineteenth-century commentary clearly asserts that

> This [Gen. 9] certainly points at the victories in aftertimes obtained by Israel over the Canaanites . . . The whole continent of Africa was peopled mostly by the descendants of Ham; and for how many ages have the better parts of that country lain under the dominion of the Romans, then of the Saracens, and now of the Turks! In what wickedness, ignorance, barbarity, slavery, and misery most of the inhabitants live![17]

Therefore, "Canaanites" equals "Negroes," and any scriptural admonition regarding the slavery of Canaanites is plainly applicable to the American South. The connection is so commonplace that this commentator, Matthew Henry, feels compelled to add:

> But this in no way excuses the covetousness and barbarity of those who enrich themselves with the product of their sweat and blood. God has not commanded us to enslave negroes; and, without doubt, he will severely punish all such cruel wrongs.[18]

In 1856 *Scriptural and Statistical Views in Favor of Slavery*, by Thornton Stringfellow, D.D. was presented to the public. In addition to the same claims rooted in Mosaic law as those of Priest, Stringfellow develops the "Cursed be Canaan" motif at length:

> Here, language is used, showing the favor which God would exercise to the posterity of Shem and Japheth, while they were holding the posterity of Ham in a state of abject bondage. May it not be said in truth, that God decreed this institution before it existed; and has he not connected its existence with prophetic tokens of special favor, to those who should be slave owners or masters? He is the same God now, that he was when he gave these views of his moral character to the world; and unless the posterity of Shem and Japheth, from whom have sprung the Jews, and all the nations of Europe and America,

and a great part of Asia, (the African race that is in them excepted,)—I say, unless they are all dead, as well as the Canaanites or Africans who descended from Ham, then it is quite possible that his favor may now be found with one class of men who are holding another class in bondage. Be this as it may, God decreed slavery—and shows in that decree, tokens of good-will to the master.[19]

It is noteworthy, though understandable, that more attention should be paid to these scholarly discourses on a vague text than to Stowe's own indirect jab at that same text. Written in 1956, J. C. Furnas's *Goodbye to Uncle Tom* devotes five full pages to atrocities perpetuated on blacks in the name of the curse of Canaan: ". . . [C]hurchgoers were not inclined to question the parson's authority for identifying the seed of Canaan with the field hands of Georgia. . .[n]either was Mrs. Stowe so inclined . . . she did not touch on 'Cursed be Canaan . . .'"[20] Furnas may be referring to Stowe's omission in her *Key to Uncle Tom's Cabin* (1854) but he significantly fails to mention the reference in the novel itself. Clearly, education in Bible interpretation and textual exegesis remains sorely lacking among Stowe's detractors even into the twentieth century. Furnas's criticisms ring especially hollow when we read Chapter 14 of *The Key to Uncle Tom's Cabin*, entitled "The Hebrew Slave-Law Compared with the American Slave-Law." This chapter does little *but* question the authority of parsons who would use the former to justify the latter. The principle of her argument[21] is threefold: first, that many things justified in Mosaic law are no longer deemed acceptable, such as polygamy (Ex. 21:9–11), genocide (Deut. 9:12; 20:16–18) and murderous retribution (Num. 35:9–39); second, that even these activities are given strict parameters in Mosaic law because, she contends, each was "an ameliorating law", designed to take the place of some barbarous abuse . . . because the attempt to enforce a more stringent system . . . would have only produced greater abuses"[22]; and finally, that St. Paul had declared the Hebrew system "imperfect" and "superseded by the Christian dispensation.—Heb. viii. 13."[23] Beyond these interpretations is a mitigating factor, applicable even if Stowe had found no other weaknesses in the comparison between Hebrew and American slave-law. The goal of Hebrew slave-law was to assure the education and elevation of the "debased, half-civilised race, which had been degraded by slavery in its worst form among the Egyptians, was gradually elevated to refinement and humanity." The American slaveholder has no such obligation even with the advantages offered by "printing and books."[24]

Note Stowe's use of the word "degraded."[25] Used frequently by Priest and Stringfellow, this term became popular even among African-Americans to explain their own condition. As early as 1768, Phillis Wheatley referred to hers as a "benighted" race, "black as Cain"[26] still in the thrall of African paganism. Degradation was as often a self-inflicted condition as one imposed upon the race. In 1831, Maria Stewart expressed concern for her race's "wretched and degraded situation" and declared herself "sensible of the gross ignorance that prevails among us."[27] For Wheatley, improvement lay in Christian education from her master and mistress; for Stewart, only with knowledge of the principles of religion and morality could the "the chains of slavery and ignorance burst."[28] Priest is confident

U.S. citizens, the court was forced to act. On March 3, 1832, the justices declared the arrests unconstitutional and said Georgia could not extend its laws to Cherokee land. They also ruled that the federal government, by treaty, had the authority to protect Indian tribes from state intrusions. Taking aim at removal, Marshall wrote, "Protection does not imply the destruction of the protected."

Ross wrote to some Cherokee delegates in Washington, "[T]here are great rejoicings throughout the [Cherokee] nation."

But Jackson declared the ruling "stillborn."

A month later, Major Ridge's son John and two other Cherokees were in Washington, trying to determine whether the federal government would enforce the court's decision. Jackson met with them only to send them home to tell their people "that their only hope of relief was in abandoning their country and removing to the West."

The Cherokees' "only hope of relief," Jackson said, "was in abandoning their country and removing to the West."

Jackson's resolve unnerved the younger Ridge. Gradually, he realized that court victory or not, his people were losing ground. But he could not relay that message to the tribe for fear of being branded a traitor, or killed. He was even hesitant to confide in his father, believing Major Ridge would be ashamed of him.

But the son underestimated his father. Major Ridge judged his people's prospects by their suffering, and he knew the situation was far worse than anyone had dared to admit. Forbidden to meet by Georgia law, the Cherokees had abandoned New Echota in 1831. Settlers were confiscating their homesteads and livestock. By sharing his thoughts on Jackson, John Ridge helped his father come to the conclusion that the tribe had to at least consider going west.

But Major Ridge kept his feelings private, believing he needed to buy time to persuade his people to think about uprooting. At the same time, he began to wonder how Ross could remain so strident in his resistance. Couldn't he see that his strategy was bearing no fruit?

Ross met twice with Jackson at the White House, to no avail. When Jackson offered $3 million to move the Cherokees west, arguing that Georgia would not give up its claims to Cherokee land, Ross suggested he use the money to buy off the Georgia settlers.

By spring 1833, the Cherokees were split between a National Party, opposed to removal, and a Treaty Party, in favor of it. As factional violence flared, some of the most influential Cherokees signed a letter to Ross saying their ongoing "course of policy" would "not result in the restoration of those rights" that had been taken from them. In signing the letter, Ridge acknowledged that he had softened on removal. In a closed meeting, the chiefs gave Ross until fall to resolve the impasse with the government before they made the letter public.

Under so much pressure—from the state of Georgia, the federal government and a stream of settlers—the tribe began to disintegrate. Some Cherokees—including Ross' brother Andrew—set out for Washington to broker their own deals. John Ridge quietly continued to recruit members to the Treaty Party and make overtures to Jackson. When Ross learned of these efforts, he tried to pre-empt them, proposing to cede Cherokee land in Georgia and to have Cherokees in other states become U.S. citizens.

By then, the rift between Ross and Major Ridge was widening: when Ridge heard of the chief's offer, he saw it not just as a bargaining ploy but as an abuse of power. Without the blessing of the other chiefs, Ridge said, Ross had no more power to make a treaty than his traitorous brother.

The majority of the tribe members remained opposed to removal, but the Ridges began advocating the idea more openly—and when they broached it at a council meeting in Red Clay, Tennessee, in August 1834, one Cherokee spoke of shooting them. Father and son slipped away unharmed, but by the end of the summer the Cherokees were trading rumors—false—that Ross and Major Ridge had each hired someone to kill the other.

In September 1834, Ridge visited Ross at his home to put the rumors to rest. They tried to talk as they once had, but the only thing they could agree on was that all talk of murder had to stop. Ridge believed Ross' intransigence was leading the Cherokees to destruction. Ross thought his oldest friend had become soft, unduly influenced by his son.

By January 1835, the council had sent Ross back to Washington with instructions to again seek federal protection, and the Treaty Party had sent John Ridge to broker a deal. Afraid of being outflanked by the Treaty Party, Ross told Jackson the Cherokees would leave their land for $20 million. He was stalling; he knew the federal government would never pay that much. When Jackson rejected him, Ross proposed that the Senate come up with an offer. When the Senate named its price as $5 million, Ross said he would take the offer to the council but wouldn't be bound by that figure. By then Jackson had lost his patience. In late 1835, he dispatched a commissioner to Georgia to seal an agreement with the Treaty Party leaders.

They met in New Echota, the deserted Cherokee capital. The terms were simple: the Cherokees would receive $5 million for all their land east of the Mississippi. The government would help them move and promise never to take their new land or incorporate it into the United States. The Cherokees would have two years to leave.

It was Major Ridge who outlined the final argument to those present. "They are strong and we are weak," he said. "We are few, they are many. . . . We can never forget these homes, I know, but an unbending, iron necessity tells us we must leave them. I would willingly die to preserve them, but any forcible effort to keep them will cost us our lands, our lives and the lives of our children. There is but one path to safety, one road to future existence as a Nation."

On December 29, a small group of Cherokees gathered at the home of Ridge's nephew Elias Boudinot to sign the Treaty of New Echota. After Ridge made his mark, he paused and said, "I have signed my death warrant."

John Ross tried to overturn the treaty for two years but failed. In May 1838, U.S. troops herded more than 16,000 Cherokees into holding camps to await removal to present-day Oklahoma. Indians who tried to flee were shot, while those who waited in the camps suffered from malnutrition, dysentery and even sexual assault by the troops guarding them. Within a month, the first Cherokees were moved out in detachments of around a thousand, with the first groups leaving in the summer heat and a severe drought. So many died that the Army delayed further removal until the fall, which meant the Cherokees would be on the trail in winter. At least a quarter of them—4,000—would perish during the relocation.

Ridge headed west ahead of his tribesmen and survived the journey, but on the morning of June 22, 1839, separate groups of vengeful Cherokees murdered him, John Ridge and Boudinot. Ross, appalled, publicly mourned the deaths. "Once I saved Major Ridge at Red Clay, and would have done so again had I known of the plot," he told friends.

John Ross served as principal chief for 27 more years. He oversaw the construction of schools and a courthouse for the new capital, and spent years petitioning the federal government to pay the $5 million it owed his people. (It wasn't fully paid until 1852.) Even as his health failed, Ross would not quit. In 1866, he was in Washington to sign yet another treaty—one that would extend Cherokee citizenship to freed Cherokee slaves—when he died on August 1, two months shy of his 76th birthday More than three decades later, the federal government appropriated Indian property in the West and forced the tribes to accept land reservations. Today, many of the country's 300,000 Cherokees still live in Oklahoma.

Critical Thinking

1. What led to the removal of the five Civilized Tribes?

2. Why has the Trail of Tears not been classified as a genocidal act? Should it be? Consider this article: http://hnn.us/article/7302 and then decide whether or not actions such as the Trail of Tears should be defined as genocidal.

3. Why did the Native Americans who were relocated have a hard time assimilating into the areas where they were forcibly relocated?

Create Central

www.mhhe.com/createcentral

Internet References

The Trail of Tears, The Indian Removals
www.ushistory.org/us/24f.asp

Trail of Tears
www.nps.gov/trte/index.htm

Trail of Tears
www.cherokee.org/AboutTheNation/History/TrailofTears.aspx

John Ridge
http://digital.library.okstate.edu/encyclopedia/entries/R/RI003.html

The Life of Major Ridge
http://chieftainsmuseum.org/2011/05/history-of-chieftains/

Hicks, Brian. From *Smithsonian*, March 2011, pp. 51–60. Copyright © 2011 by Brian Hicks. Reprinted by permission of the author.

Article   Prepared by: Wendy A. Maier-Sarti, *Oakton Community College*

A Unique Northern Plains Ceramic Vessel in the Museum's Lewis and Clark Collection

Mark D. Mitchell

Learning Outcomes

After reading this article, you will be able to:

- Describe the culture of the Mandan and the Hidatsa tribes.

- Explain the significance of the ceramic discovery.

- Understand how primary sources have taken on many forms.

Even well-known artifacts can yield surprising new discoveries. Scholars have long believed that fragments of pottery in the Penn Museum's collection represented the remains of two nearly identical vessels collected during the winter of 1804–1805 by Meriwether Lewis and William Clark. However, a recent attempt to reassemble the remaining pieces, undertaken in conjunction with research on 19th century northern Plains pottery production, has instead demonstrated that they belong to a single oblong pot with two necks. No vessel of this type has ever been observed in archaeological collections from the upper Missouri River region.

Lewis and Clark and the men of the Corps of Discovery reached the Mandan and Hidatsa villages near the confluence of the Knife and Missouri rivers in late October 1804. They spent most of the next month building a V-shaped log structure, dubbed Fort Mandan, in which they would pass the winter.

In his instructions to Lewis, President Jefferson had asked the captains to learn as much as they could about the native inhabitants of Louisiana and the Northwest. Throughout the long northern winter they visited the Mandan and Hidatsa villages, interviewing political and military leaders, making observations, and participating in community activities. They also collected ethnographic objects, animal skins and skeletons, minerals, and dried plants and seeds.

In early April 1805, with the spring thaw on the Missouri just underway, the Corps began making preparations for their journey to the Pacific. Six men were delegated to return to the United States with Clark's journals and maps and the objects

that had been collected during the winter. Among the items listed on the accompanying inventory was "1 earthen pot, such as the Mandans manufacture and use for culinary purposes."

The shipment from Fort Mandan reached President Jefferson in August. Zoological specimens were sent to Charles Willson Peale's museum in Philadelphia. Mineral samples went to the American Philosophical Society. The pot, along with other ethnographic objects, may have been displayed for a time in Jefferson's "Indian Hall" at Monticello or it may have gone directly to the Philosophical Society. In either case, by the time it was finally transferred to the University Museum in 1937, by way of the Academy of Natural Sciences, it had been broken and some of the pieces had been lost.

The Lewis and Clark pot is classified by archaeologists as Knife River ware. The defining characteristic of this type of pottery is a vertical or out-flaring rim, reinforced at the lip by a narrow coil or strap of clay known as a "brace." In this case, a second strap, called a "fillet," has been added to each rim, a few centimeters below the lip. The potter decorated the vessel by pressing twine made from plant fibers into the wet clay. The downward-projecting tabs and strap handles attached to the fillet may have held a rope used to carry or suspend the vessel. The parallel grooves visible on the body of the pot were made by a carved wooden paddle, which was used to thin and shape the vessel's walls.

Knife River ware was first produced by Mandan and Hidatsa potters sometime before AD 1600, perhaps as early as AD 1500. Over time it slowly replaced other ceramic forms, becoming the dominant style produced in the upper Missouri by the middle of the 18th century.

The vessel's form sheds light on an enigmatic stereograph taken in 1879 by Orlando S. Goff. The image, which shows a set of six earthenware pots, was taken at Like-A-Fishhook Village, the last earthlodge settlement on the upper Missouri. Among them are two double-mouthed vessels remarkably similar to the Lewis and Clark pot. Until now scholars have not known whether the pots in the photo, especially the two double-mouthed vessels, represented indigenous ceramic forms. The Lewis and Clark pot demonstrates that upper Missouri potters already were producing a variety of decorative vessels by the time European explorers and traders first entered the region. It now seems likely that such imaginative shapes had been a part of the upper Missouri ceramic repertoire at least since AD 1600. Recent excavations at several Mandan villages near the confluence of the Heart and Missouri rivers, some 100 km below the Knife, have revealed a broad range of ceramic forms, including broad, flat-bottomed platters, boat-shaped bowls, and jars with hexagonal and octagonal mouths. No doubt many more shapes will be identified as research continues.

This newly documented ceramic diversity helps explain an observation made in 1832 by George Catlin. A self-taught artist who traveled extensively throughout the Plains from 1830 to 1836, Catlin observed that pottery was "a familiar part of the culinary furniture of every Mandan lodge, and [is] manufactured by the women of this tribe in great quantities, and modeled into a thousand forms and tastes." The Lewis and Clark pot shows that Catlin's statement is more than simply a case of dramatic embellishment, a trait for which he otherwise was justly famous.

Together, the Lewis and Clark pot and Goff's stereograph help tell a remarkable tale of cultural survival. Thirty years after the Corps of Discovery's transcontinental journey, smallpox struck the native villages of the upper Missouri. Thousands died. The Mandans were hit especially hard, losing as much as 90 percent of their population. Eventually, the survivors worked together with the Hidatsas to establish Like-A-Fishhook Village. In 1862 they were joined there by the Arikaras or Sahnish.

Many scholars have believed that the epidemic of 1837 was responsible for a tremendous loss of cultural knowledge. Among the Mandans and Hidatsas, specialists produced many crafts, including ceramic vessels, arrows, and bison-hide boats. Ritual and sacred knowledge also was restricted to people who had purchased the right to perform a particular ceremony. Pottery production, in particular, involves many steps and stages, each of which must be completed successfully to produce a serviceable vessel. Raw clay needs to be gathered from a suitable source and mixed with other minerals to create a workable clay body. Special skills, learned only through lengthy practice, are required to shape a pot, particularly one as complex as the Lewis and Clark pot. Firing requires expert knowledge about how to build a kiln and how much fuel to use. The deaths of craft specialists could have meant the loss of their proprietary skills. However, the Lewis and Clark pot and Goff's photo together demonstrate that the complex technical knowledge at the heart of the upper Missouri ceramic tradition survived the epidemic. As tragic as it was, the epidemic did not lead to the wholesale loss of critical cultural knowledge. People died, but the village cultures of the upper Missouri went on.

Critical Thinking

1. What makes discoveries on the Lewis and Clark expedition so important?
2. Why were Lewis and Clark so qualified to perform the exploration?
3. What would have happened if Lewis and Clark were sent 10 years later rather than when they were sent?

Create Central

www.mhhe.com/createcentral

Internet References

The Journey
    www.nps.gov/nr/travel/lewisandclark/journey.htm
Clark Journal
    http://lewisandclarkjournals.unl.edu/read/?_xmlsrc=1805-11-03
    .xml&_xslsrc=LCstyles,xsl

MARK D. MITCHELL is a Ph.D. candidate in the Department of Anthropology at the University of Colorado at Boulder.

Mitchell, Mark D. From *Expedition*, vol. 50, no. 3, 2012, pp. 45–47. Copyright © 2012 by University of Pennsylvania Museum of Archaeology and Anthropology. Reprinted by permission.

Unit 4

UNIT

Prepared by: Wendy A. Maier-Sarti, *Oakton Community College*

The Civil War and Reconstruction

Sectionalism plagued the United States from its inception. The Constitutional proviso that slaves would count as three-fifths of a person for representational purposes, for instance, or that treaties had to be passed by two-thirds majorities grew out of sectional compromises. Manufacturing and commercial interests were strong in the North. Such interests generally supported high tariffs to protect industries, and the construction of turnpikes, canals, and railroads to expand domestic markets. The South, largely rural and agricultural, strongly opposed such measures. Southerners believed that tariffs cost them money to line the pockets of Northern manufacturers, and had little interest in what were known as "internal improvements." Such differences were relatively easy to resolve because there were no moral issues involved, and matters such as tariffs aroused few emotions in the public.

The question of slavery added a different dimension. Part of the quarrel involved economic considerations. However, without multilevel institutional support from government, could slavery as an institution have survived as long as it did? Northerners feared that the spread of slavery would discriminate against "free" farming in the west. Southerners just as adamantly believed that the institution should be allowed to exist wherever it proved feasible. Disputes in 1820 and again in 1850 resulted in compromises that papered over these differences, but they satisfied no one. As time wore on, more and more Northerners came to regard slavery as sinful, an abomination that must be stamped out. Southerners, on the other hand, grew more receptive to the idea that slavery actually was beneficial to both blacks and whites and was condoned by the Bible. Now cast in moral terms, the issue could not be resolved in the fashion of tariff disputes by splitting differences.

In the years before the Civil War began, influential magazines and newspapers in the North already were advocating emancipation. The Underground Railroad functioned as an escape route for runaway slaves, and white Southerners detested and feared its existence for two reasons beyond the sheer number of escapees, which some scholars estimate to be around 150,000. First, it revealed the fallacy of Southern arguments that slavery was a benevolent institution and that slaves were a happy, contented lot. Second, it seemed clear that, whatever politicians might say, large numbers of Northerners were willing to break the law in order to undermine the "peculiar institution." Abolitionist John Brown led a raid on Harpers Ferry, demonstrating his willingness to defy the law. Brown's raid in particular touched off an explosion of feverish charges and countercharges by both sides. The tendency in the North to treat Brown as a martyr confirmed Southern suspicions that abolitionists meant to destroy slavery by violence if necessary. African Americans also played an important role in ending slavery, a fact that is often overlooked in a study of abolition.

Moderates in the two national parties, the Whigs and Democrats, tried to keep the slavery question from tearing the country in two. Though suffering some defections, the Democrats managed to stay together until the elections of 1860. The Whigs, however, fell apart during the 1850s. The emergence of the Republican Party, with its strength almost exclusively based in the North, signaled the beginning of the end. Southerners came to regard the Republicans as the party of abolitionism. Abraham Lincoln, Republican presidential candidate in 1860, tried to assure Southerners that, although he opposed the spread of slavery, he had no intentions of seeking to abolish the institution where it already existed. He was not widely believed in the South. Republican victory in 1860 seemed to them, or at least to the hotheads among them, to threaten not just slavery but the entire Southern way of life. One by one, Southern states began seceding, and Lincoln's unwillingness to let them destroy the union led to the Civil War.

In his inaugural address, Lincoln had promised to "hold, occupy, and possess" all government property, even if located within the Confederacy (which he never recognized as legitimate). Fort Sumter, in Charleston Harbor, presented a hard choice. To evacuate the post would appear to constitute a retreat before Confederate belligerency, to reinforce it not only would be difficult but would appear as an aggressive act. Lincoln cleverly escaped this dilemma by announcing that he would send only provisions, not troops, to Sumter. If the Southerners bombarded the fort, they would bear the onus of firing the first shots. They did.

The Civil War began as a struggle over national union, but ultimately became a conflict over the continued existence of slavery. Lincoln faced many obstacles that prevented him from issuing the preliminary Emancipation Proclamation before he actually did. Among the most important factors in Lincoln's mind was the Constitution's protection of property rights. Although he knew he would be criticized by some for not going far enough, he also knew he would be condemned for having exceeded his executive powers.

By April 1865, Southern forces were depleted and exhausted after four years of costly fighting. General Robert E. Lee realized that the Confederacy no longer could continue to sustain a conventional war. Some of his subordinates urged that he disband the army and have his troops regroup as guerilla bands. Such a course would have prolonged the fighting for the near future and would have fanned the flames of hatred on both sides.

Therefore, based on these conclusions, some believe that the Confederacy lost, rather than that the Union achieved victory.

A struggle took place, after the war ended, over how the South would be reintegrated into the Union. The most important issue was what status Blacks would have in the postwar society. Moderates, such as Lincoln, wished to make Reconstruction as painless as possible even though this meant continued white domination of Southern states. Radical Republicans sought to grant freed people the full rights of citizenship, and were willing to use force to attain this goal. Southern whites resisted "Radical Reconstruction" any way they could, and ultimately prevailed when Northern will eroded. With northern victory after the Civil War came the ascendancy of northern economic superiority over the southern agrarian based system. With the federal government willing to promote business, and with little initial regulation, industrialization swept many northern cities and outlying areas as the United States experienced a second industrial revolution. For women, with the passage of the third of the Reconstruction amendments, it appeared that suffrage was at last achieved; however, it was anything but. Women like Susan B. Anthony believed that the 15th amendment granted all citizens the right to vote, but an 1875 Supreme Court decision decided otherwise.

White encroachment on Indian lands continued up to and after the Civil War. Railroads constructed after the conflict ended speeded this process. One of the worst catastrophes for the Plains Indians was the destruction of the once huge buffalo herds that provided them with everything from food and clothing to weapons. The Indians fought back from time to time but confronted overwhelming odds. In the end most tribes were forced onto reservations where they became little more than wards of the state. To its great discredit, the United States made and broke countless treaties with the Indians over the years.

America's favorite pastime, baseball, grew rapidly in the post-Civil War years. Minority involvement in the sport allowed for expression of identity and solidification of community sport, but also saw racial struggles that would come to define professional sports for decades to come.

Article

Prepared by: Wendy A. Maier-Sarti, *Oakton Community College*

Deadweight Loss and the American Civil War: The Political Economy of Slavery, Secession, and Emancipation

JEFFREY ROGERS HUMMEL

Learning Outcomes

After reading this article, you will be able to:

- Define the term "Deadweight Loss."
- Provide two examples of how the federal government supported slavery.

No one attacked the black slavery prevailing throughout the southern states with greater vehemence than a group of young, radical abolitionists who burst upon the American landscape in the early 1830s. Exasperated at the betrayal of the Revolutionary promise that all forms of human bondage would disappear in this new land of liberty, and marshaling all the evangelical fervor of the religious revivals then sweeping the country, they demanded no less than the immediate emancipation of all slaves. They not only opposed any compensation to slaveholders and any colonization outside the country of freed slaves, but they also demanded full political rights for all blacks, North and South.

The most prominent of these abolitionists was William Lloyd Garrison. Son of a drunken sailor who had abandoned his family, Garrison grew up in a poor but piously Baptist household in Newburyport, Massachusetts. He served as a printer's apprentice and then made his first notable mark on antislavery activism when he went to jail rather than pay a fine for libeling as a "highway robber and murderer" a New England merchant who shipped slaves between Baltimore and New Orleans. From Boston on January 1, 1831, the near-sighted, prematurely balding, twenty-five-year-old editor brought out the first issue of a new weekly paper, *The Liberator*. Garrison left no doubt about his refusal to compromise with the sin of slavery:

> I will be as harsh as truth, and as uncompromising as justice. On this subject, I do not wish to think, or speak, or write with moderation. No! No! Tell a man whose house is on fire, to give a moderate alarm: tell him to moderately rescue his wife from the hands of the ravisher; tell the mother to gradually extricate her babe from the fire into which it has fallen;—but urge me not to use moderation in a cause like the present. I am in earnest—I will not equivocate—I will not excuse—I will not retreat a single inch—AND I WILL BE HEARD.

Garrison conceded that the elimination of slavery would take time in practice. But that should not inhibit forthright condemnation of moral evil. "Urge immediate abolition as earnestly as we may, it will alas! be gradual abolition in the end. We have never said that slavery would be overthrown by a single blow; that it ought to be we shall always contend."

The crusading editor, however, did not look to direct political action to eradicate slavery. Moral suasion and non-violent resistance were his strategies. With agitation, he hoped at first to shame slaveholders into repentance. By early 1842 Garrison had gone so far as to denounce the U.S. Constitution for its proslavery clauses as "a covenant with death and an agreement with hell." He publicly burned a copy during one 4th of July celebration, proclaiming: "So perish all compromises with tyranny!" He now believed that if anything the North should secede from central government. The slogan "No Union with Slave-Holders" appeared on the masthead of Garrison's *Liberator* for years.

Needless to say this disrespect for the Union did not go over well in the North. Throughout the 1830s, even before Garrison made his call for secession explicit, abolitionist lecturers, presses, and property were frequent targets of hostile violence, often instigated and directed by gentlemen of prominence and high rank. A Boston mob, enraged at reports that the editor of *The Liberator* had dared, while touring abroad in England, to condemn the United States for countenancing slavery, almost lynched him after he returned. Nor did every abolitionist embrace disunion. Many would turn away from Garrison's pacifism and anarchism to take up political activity in a quest for respectability and success. As the antislavery crusade split into doctrinal factions, the resort to the ballot box would bring both a broadened appeal and a dilution of purity.

Nonetheless, Garrison's strategic vision was hardly unique to him. Nearly all of slavery's most radical opponents at one time shared it, including, among others, Frederick Douglass, the free black leader who had escaped in 1838 from slavery in Maryland, and Wendell Phillips, a wealthy lawyer and Boston Brahmin converted to the cause by anti-abolitionist violence. When the American Anti-Slavery Society endorsed disunion in May of 1844, this radical tactic had already found expression in anti-slavery politics. Twelve northern Congressmen, led by the venerable former president, John Quincy Adams, had one year earlier issued an address to the people boldly asserting that the annexation of Texas as a slave state would "not only inevitably result in a dissolution of the Union, but fully justify it," and eight more Congressmen added their support to the statement in the newspapers. The legislatures of Massachusetts and Ohio passed similar resolutions in 1845, while the year after that, Congressman Joshua Giddings, influenced by his Garrisonian daughter, ran for reelection declaring that the unlawful annexation of Texas followed by the unconstitutional war with Mexico had annulled the Union's authority. Such sentiments, however, ultimately subsided, particularly after the Compromise of 1850 appeared to have settled the divisive issue of slavery at the national level. Subsequent efforts by Garrison and his associates in 1857 to get Republican Party politicians to attend disunionist conventions held in Worcester, Massachusetts, and Cleveland, Ohio, brought meager results.

The radical abolitionists, consequently, have too often been dismissed as hopelessly naive. Garrison's opposition to government was so intense that he and his followers refused even to vote. But this appearance of strategic naiveté is misleading. Once it became clear, for instance, that Southerners were not inclined to repent and free their chattels voluntarily, the Garrisonians fully understood that abolition would require some political act. They further realized, however, that the politics would take care of itself—indeed only could take care of itself—after moral suasion had first created a powerful anti-slavery constituency.

Critical Thinking

1. Was slavery actually the economic boom that supporters touted?

2. Why was it necessary for abolitionists to become politically active?

Create Central

www.mhhe.com/createcentral

Internet References

An Introduction to Slave Narratives
  http://docsouth.unc.edu/neh/intro.html
Deadweight Loss
  www.princeton.edu/~achaney/tmve/wiki100k/docs/Deadweight_loss.html
The New Man
  http://docsouth.unc.edu/fpn/bruce/bruce.html
Of Our Spiritual Strivings
  http://xroads.virginia.edu/~hyper/dubois/ch01.html

Hummel, Jeffrey Rogers. From *Deadweight Loss and the American Civil War: The Political Economy of Slavery, Secession, and Emancipation*, October 1, 2012, pp. Copyright © 2012 by Jeffrey Rogers Hummel. Reprinted by permission of the author.

Article   Prepared by: Wendy A. Maier-Sarti, *Oakton Community College*

What the Founders *Really* Thought About Race

JARED TAYLOR

Learning Outcomes

After reading this article, you will be able to:

- Explain the viewpoints held by founding fathers who were slave owners and who were not slave owners.

- Explain how some slave owners could still believe that "all men are created equal."

- Articulate how not solving the question of slavery was one of the causal factors that led to the Civil War.

The Abolition Movement

Today, it is common to think of the antebellum North as united in the desire to free the slaves and to establish them as the social and political equals of Whites. This is a distorted view. First of all, slavery persisted in the North well into the post-Revolutionary period. It was not abolished in New York State until 1827, and it continued in Connecticut until 1848.[1]

Nor was abolitionist sentiment anything close to universal. Many Northerners opposed abolition because they feared it would lead to race mixing. The easiest way to stir up opposition to Northern abolitionists was to claim that what they were really promoting was intermarriage. Many abolitionists expressed strong disapproval of miscegenation, but the fact that speakers at abolitionist meetings addressed racially mixed audiences was sufficiently shocking to make any charge believable. There were no fewer than 165 anti-abolition riots in the North during the 1820s alone, almost all of them prompted by the fear that abolition would lead to intermarriage.[2]

The 1830s saw further violence. On July 4, 1834, the American Anti-Slavery Society read its Declaration of Sentiments to a mixed-race audience in New York City. Rioters then broke up the meeting and went on a rampage that lasted 11 days. The National Guard managed to bring peace only after the society issued a "Disclaimer," the first point of which was: "We entirely disclaim any desire to promote or encourage intermarriages between white and colored persons."[3]

Philadelphia suffered a serious riot in 1838 after abolitionists, who had had trouble renting space to hold their meetings, built their own building. On May 17, the last day of a three-day dedication ceremony, several thousand people—many of high social standing—gathered at the hall and burned it down while the fire department stood by and did nothing.[4]

Sentiment against Blacks was so strong that many Northern Whites supported abolition only if it was linked, as Jefferson and Madison had proposed, to plans to deport or "colonize" Blacks. Most abolitionist activism therefore reflected a deep conviction that slavery was wrong, but not a desire to establish Blacks as social and political equals. William Lloyd Garrison and Angelina and Sarah Grimké favored equal treatment for Blacks in all respects, but theirs was very much a minority view. Henry Ward Beecher, brother of Harriet Beecher Stowe who wrote *Uncle Tom's Cabin,* expressed the majority view: "Do your duty first to the colored people here; educate them, Christianize them, and *then* colonize them."[5]

The American Colonization Society was only the best known of many organizations founded for the purpose of removing Blacks from North America. At its inaugural meeting in 1816, Henry Clay described its purpose: to "rid our country of a useless and pernicious, if not dangerous portion of the population."[6] The following prominent Americans were not just members but served as *officers* of the society: James Madison, Andrew Jackson, Daniel Webster, Stephen Douglas, William Seward, Francis Scott Key, Winfield Scott, John Marshall, and Roger Taney.[7] James Monroe, another President who owned slaves, worked so tirelessly in the cause of "colonization" that the capital of Liberia is named Monrovia in recognition of his efforts.

Early Americans wrote their opposition to miscegenation into law. Between 1661 and 1725, Massachusetts, Pennsylvania, and all the southern colonies passed laws prohibiting inter-racial marriage and, in some cases, fornication.[8] Of the 50 states, no fewer than 44 had laws prohibiting inter-racial marriage at some point in their past.[9] Many Northern Whites were horrified to discover that some Southern slave owners had Black concubines. When Bostonian Josiah Quincy wrote an account of his 1773 tour of South Carolina, he professed himself shocked to learn that a "gentleman" could have relations with a "negro or mulatto woman."[10]

Massachusetts prohibited miscegenation from 1705 to 1843, but repealed the ban only because most people thought it was unnecessary.[11] The new law noted that inter-racial relations were "evidence of vicious feeling, bad taste, and personal degradation," so were unlikely to be so common as to become a problem.[12]

The northern "free-soil" movement of the 1840s is often described as friendly to Blacks because it opposed the expansion of slavery into newly acquired territories. This is yet another misunderstanding. Pennsylvania Democrat David Wilmot started the movement when he introduced an amendment banning slavery from any territories acquired after the Mexican-American War. The "Wilmot Proviso" was certainly anti-slavery, but Wilmot was not an abolitionist. He did not object to slavery in the South; only to its spread into the Western territories. During the congressional debate, Wilmot asked:

> whether that vast country, between the Rio Grande and the Pacific, shall be given up to the servile labor of the black, or be preserved for the free labor of the white man? . . . The negro race already occupy enough of this fair continent; let us keep what remains for ourselves, and for our children.

Wilmot called his amendment the "white man's proviso."[13]

The history of the franchise reflects a clear conception of the United States as a nation ruled by and for Whites. Every state that entered the Union between 1819 and the Civil War denied Blacks the vote. In 1855, Blacks could vote only in Massachusetts, Vermont, New Hampshire, Maine, and Rhode Island, which together accounted for only four percent of the nation's Black population. The federal government prohibited free Blacks from voting in the territories it controlled.[14]

Several states that were established before the Civil War hoped to avoid race problems by remaining all White. The people of the Oregon Territory, for example, voted not to permit slavery, but voted in even greater numbers not to permit Blacks in the state at all. In language that survived until 2002, Oregon's 1857 constitution provided that "[n]o free negro, or mulatto, not residing in this state at the time of the adoption of this constitution, shall come, reside, or be within this State, or hold any real estate."[15]

Despite Charles Pinckney's confirmation in 1821 that no Black could be an American citizen, the question was taken up in the famous *Dred Scott* decision of 1857. The seven-to-two decision held that although they could be citizens of states, Blacks were not citizens of the United States and therefore had no standing to sue in federal court. Roger Taney, the chief justice who wrote the majority decision, noted that slavery arose out of an ancient American conviction about Negroes:

> They had for more than a century before been regarded as beings of an inferior order, and altogether unfit to associate with the white race, either in social or political relations; and so far inferior, that they had no rights which the

white man was bound to respect; and that the negro might justly and lawfully be reduced to slavery for his benefit.[16]

Abraham Lincoln's time was well beyond the era of the Founders, but many Americans believe it was "the Great Emancipator" who finally brought the egalitarian vision of Jefferson's generation to fruition.

Again, they are mistaken.

Lincoln considered Blacks to be—in his words—"a troublesome presence"[17] in the United States. During the Lincoln-Douglas debates he stated:

> I am not nor ever have been in favor of making voters or jurors of negroes, nor of qualifying them to hold office, nor to intermarry with white people; and I will say in addition to this that there is a physical difference between the white and black races which I believe will for ever forbid the two races living together on terms of social and political equality.[18]

His opponent Stephen Douglas was even more outspoken (in what follows, audience responses are recorded by the *Chicago Daily Times,* a Democratic paper):

> For one, I am opposed to negro citizenship in any form. [Cheers—*Times*] I believe that this government was made on the white basis. ['Good,'—*Times*] I believe it was made by white men for the benefit of white men and their posterity forever, and I am in favor of confining the citizenship to white men—men of European birth and European descent, instead of conferring it upon negroes and Indians, and other inferior races. ['Good for you. Douglas forever,'—*Times*][19]

Douglas, who was the more firmly anti-Black of the two candidates, won the election.

Lincoln opposed the expansion of slavery outside the South, but was not an abolitionist. He made war on the Confederacy only to preserve the Union, and would have accepted Southern slavery in perpetuity if that would have kept the South from seceding, as he stated explicitly.[20]

Indeed, Lincoln supported what is known as the Corwin Amendment to the Constitution, passed by Congress shortly before he took office, which forbade any attempt by Congress to amend the Constitution to give itself the power to "abolish or interfere" with slavery. The amendment therefore recognized that the federal government had no power over slavery where it already existed, and the amendment would have barred any future amendment to give the government that power. Outgoing President James Buchanan took the unusual step of signing the amendment, even though the President's signature is not necessary under the Constitution.

Lincoln referred to the Corwin Amendment in his first inaugural address[21], adding that he had "no objection" to its ratification, and he sent copies of the text to all state governors.[22] Ohio, Maryland, and Illinois eventually ratified the amendment. If the country had not been distracted by war, it could well have become law, making it more difficult or even impossible to pass the 13th Amendment.

Notes

1. Davis, *Inhuman Bondage,* p. 128.

2. Lemire, "*Miscegenation,*" p. 90. This count was reported by the three leading anti-slavery newspapers of the period.

3. Ibid., pp. 59, 83.

4. Ibid., pp. 87–91.

5. Quoted in Fredrickson, *The Black Image in the White Mind,* p. 115.

6. Weyl and Marina, *American Statesmen on Slavery and the Negro,* p. 133.

7. Ibid., p. 132.

8. Elise Lemire, "*Miscegenation,*" p. 57.

9. Ibid., p. 2.

10. Ibid., p. 11.

11. Legal opposition to miscegenation lasted many years. In 1967, when the Supreme Court finally ruled anti-miscegenation laws unconstitutional in *Loving v. Virginia,* 16 states still had them on the books. The laws were only sporadically enforced, but state legislatures were unwilling to rescind them.

12. Ibid., p. 139.

13. Earle, *Jacksonian Antislavery & the Politics of Free Soil, 1824–1854,* pp. 138–39.

14. Keyssar, *The Right to Vote,* p. 55.

15. Peter Prengaman, "Oregon's Racist Language Faces Vote," Associated Press, Sept. 27, 2002.

16. Full text of the decision is available here: http://caselaw .lp.findlaw.com/scripts/getcase.pl?navby=case&court=us&vol= 60&invol=393

17. Ginsberg and Eichner, *Troublesome Presence,* p. ix.

18. See Basler, *The Collected Works of Abraham Lincoln,* Vol. II, pp. 235–236.

19. Holzer, *The Lincoln-Douglas Debates,* pp. 54f.

20. See, for instance, Lincoln's 1862 letter to Horace Greeley, editor of the *New York Tribune:* "[M]y paramount object in this struggle is to save the Union, and it is not either to save or destroy slavery, If I could save the Union without freeing any slave, I would do it, and if I could save it by freeing all the slaves, I would do it; and if I could save it by freeing some and leaving others alone I would also do that." Available online: http://www.learner.org/workshops/primarysources/ emancipation/docs/lin_greeley.html

21. For the full text of the address, see http://www.bartleby .com/124/pres31.html.

22. Holzer, *Lincoln President-Elect,* p. 429.

Critical Thinking

1. Why do the different sources portray Thomas Jefferson in such a different light?

2. How did the founding fathers who owned slaves justify that practice in light of the phrase "All men are created equal"?

3. Why did the slave owning founding fathers not grant their slaves freedom?

Create Central

www.mhhe.com/createcentral

Internet References

Founding Fathers and Slave Holders
www.smithsonianmag.com/history-archaeology/Flawed_Founders.html

Thomas Jefferson
www.whitehouse.gov/about/presidents/thomasjefferson/

The Founding Father and His Slaves
http://gwpapers.virginia.edu/articles/conroy_2.html

Slavery and the American Founding: The "Inconsistency Not To Be Excused"
http://edsitement.neh.gov/lesson-plan/slavery-and-american-founding -inconsistency-not-be-excused

Taylor, Jared. From *The National Policy Institute,* February 17, 2012, pp. 7–13. Copyright © 2012 by National Policy Institute. Reprinted by permission.

Article   Prepared by: Wendy A. Maier-Sarti, *Oakton Community College*

John Brown's Raid on Harpers Ferry

RICHARD CAVENDISH

Learning Outcomes

After reading this article, you will be able to:

- Describe who John Brown was and why he was important to American history.
- Explain the basic foundation of the abolitionist movement.
- Analyze the significance of Harpers Ferry.

A virtual civil war over slavery in Kansas in the 1850s attracted the attention of John Brown, a devout Calvinist in his mid-fifties, who regarded slavery as an abominable sin against God and a breach of the principles of the Declaration of Independence. Five of his sons had moved to Kansas and in 1855 he joined them with a supply of rifles and swords. For several years after that he led a band of anti-slavery fighters in guerrilla warfare against pro-slavery activists.

Brown's plans changed over time. At one stage he hoped to create a new state for blacks, safe from attack in the Appalachian Mountains, to which all the slaves in the South would flock. Later he decided on an armed insurrection, which masses of blacks in both the South and the North would eagerly join. He would lead them to the mountains from which they would make raids into Virginia, Tennessee and Alabama. Black uprisings would then spread spontaneously throughout the South until slavery was no more. To get the weapons he needed, he decided to seize the United States armoury at Harpers Ferry in Virginia (now in West Virginia), on the Potomac and Shenandoah rivers within 60 miles of Washington DC, where there were thousands of rifles and muskets in store.

Brown assembled a small force of 16 whites and five blacks at a farmhouse outside Harpers Ferry. Leaving three of them behind as a temporary rearguard, he and his men cut the telegraph wires east and west of the town and stormed the armoury. It was a rainy Sunday night, there were few people about and only a single watchman in the armoury, who was easily overcome. Brown and his men took some townspeople prisoners as hostages and also some local slave-owners, forcibly liberating their slaves and arming them with pikes; to the dismay of many of the slaves, who feared the consequences. The raiders also stopped a Baltimore and Ohio Railroad train passing through, but then allowed it to go on its way, carrying word of what was happening. The news spread round the countryside

at lightning speed and the reaction was swift and ferocious. By Monday morning armed militiamen, townspeople and local farmers were keeping up a hail of fire on Brown and his men, who holed up with some of their prisoners in a fire-engine house. The militia seized the bridges over the two rivers, cutting off any retreat, and the hoped-for influx of blacks eager to join Brown and his men completely failed to materialize.

Hoping to negotiate, Brown sent his son Watson and another man out under a white flag, but they were both promptly shot, Watson being mortally wounded. One of the prisoners in the engine house said afterwards that 'Brown commanded his men with the utmost composure, encouraging them to sell their lives as dearly as they could.' The mayor of Harpers Ferry, Fontaine Beckham, was killed by a bullet from the engine house, which only increased the vengeful fury of the crowd, a good few of whom were by now drunk. Another of Brown's sons, Oliver, was mortally wounded by a bullet from outside. In agony, he begged his father to finish him off, but Brown said, 'If you must die, die like a man.'

During Monday night a company of United States Marines arrived at Harpers Ferry, under the command of a certain Colonel Robert E. Lee, the future Confederate general. His aide-de-camp was another celebrated Confederate figure of the future, Lieutenant J.E.B. Stuart. On Tuesday morning Lee sent Stuart to the engine house under a flag of truce to offer to spare the lives of Brown and his men if they surrendered. Brown refused and the Marines immediately attacked the door of the engine house with sledgehammers and an improvised battering ram and burst in, firing as they entered. Brown was wounded and knocked unconscious, others of the defenders were shot or bayoneted and it was all over in a matter of minutes. To protect him from lynching, Brown was hurried to Charlestown, where at the end of the month he was tried for treason against the state of Virginia, conspiracy with slaves, and murder. His defenders stressed the history of mental instability on his mother's side of his family, hoping to get his sentence commuted for insanity, but Brown himself spurned any such talk. Lying on a cot in the courtroom, 'composed and heroic' as his biographer Stephen B. Oates described him, he was duly sentenced to death. He was hanged on December 2nd, behaving calmly and bravely throughout.

One of the witnesses to the execution, oddly enough, was John Wilkes Booth, the future assassin of Abraham Lincoln. Lincoln himself thought Brown 'a misguided fanatic,' but his death gave him immortality as an abolitionist martyr, whose 'soul is marching on.'

Critical Thinking

1. Why did John Brown take so many risks to free slaves?
2. Was this one of the largest resistance movements against the instiution of slavey?

Create Central

www.mhhe.com/createcentral

Internet References

John Brown Harpers Ferry Historical Park
www.nps.gov/hafe/historyculture/john-brown.htm

The Battle of Harpers Ferry
www.civilwar.org/battlefields/harpers-ferry.html

John Brown's Raid 1859
www.eyewitnesstohistory.com/johnbrown.htm

The Raid on Harpers Ferry
www.smithsonianmag.com/multimedia/videos/The-Raid-on-Harpers
-Ferry.html

Cavendish, Richard. From *History Today*, October 2009. Copyright © 2009 by History Today, Ltd. Reprinted by permission.

Article   Prepared by: Wendy A. Maier-Sarti, *Oakton Community College*

Free at Last

A new museum celebrates the Underground Railroad. The secret network of people who bravely led slaves to liberty before the Civil War.

FERGUS M. BORDEWICH

Learning Outcomes

After reading this article, you will be able to:

- Explain the purpose of the underground railroad.
- Analyze the implications of the underground railroad.
- Assess the success of the underground railroad.

The phone rang one drizzly morning in Carl Westmoreland's office overlooking the gray ribbon of the Ohio River and downtown Cincinnati. It was February 1998. Westmoreland, a descendant of slaves, scholar of African-American history and former community organizer, had recently joined the staff of the National Underground Railroad Freedom Center. Then still in the planning stages, the center, which opened this past August in Cincinnati, is the nation's first institution dedicated to the clandestine pre-Civil War network that helped tens of thousands of fugitive slaves gain their freedom.

The caller, who identified himself as Raymond Evers, claimed that a 19th-century "slave jail" was located on his property in northern Kentucky; he wanted someone to come out to look at it. As word of the center had gotten around, Westmoreland had begun to receive a lot of calls like this one, from individuals who said their house contained secret hiding places or who reported mysterious tunnels on their property. He had investigated many of these sites. Virtually none turned out to have any connection with the Underground Railroad.

"I'll call you back tomorrow," Westmoreland said.

The next day, his phone rang again. It was Evers. "So when are you coming out?" he asked. Westmoreland sighed. "I'm on my way," he said.

An hour later, Westmoreland, a wiry man then in his early 60s, was slogging across a sodden alfalfa pasture in Mason County, Kentucky, eight miles south of the Ohio River, accompanied by Evers, 67, a retired businessman. The two made their way to a dilapidated tobacco barn at the top of a low hill.

"Where is it?" Westmoreland asked.

"Just open the door!" Evers replied.

In the darkened interior, Westmoreland made out a smaller structure built of rough-hewn logs and fitted with barred windows. Fastened to a joist inside the log hut were iron rings: fetters to which manacled slaves had once been chained. "I felt the way I did when I went to Auschwitz," Westmoreland later recalled. "I felt the power of the place—it was dark, ominous. When I saw the rings, I thought, it's like a slave-ship hold."

At first, Westmoreland had difficulty tracking down the history of the structure, where tobacco, corn and farm machinery had been stored for decades. But eventually Westmoreland located a Mason County resident who had heard from his father, who had heard from his grandfather, what had gone on in the little enclosure. "They chained 'em up over there, and sold 'em off like cattle," the Mason County man told Westmoreland.

At Westmoreland's urging, the Freedom Center accepted Evers' offer to donate the 32- by 27-foot structure. It was dismantled and transported to Cincinnati; the total cost for archaeological excavation and preservation was $2 million. When the Freedom Center opened its doors on August 23, the stark symbol of brutality was the first thing that visitors encountered in the lofty atrium facing the Ohio River. Says Westmoreland: "This institution represents the first time that there has been an honest effort to honor and preserve our collective memory, not in a basement or a slum somewhere, but at the front door of a major metropolitan community."

By its own definition a "museum of conscience," the 158,000-square-foot copper-roofed structure hopes to engage visitors in a visceral way. "This is not a slavery museum," says executive director Spencer Crew, who moved to Cincinnati from Washington, D.C., where he was director of the Smithsonian Institution's National Museum of American History. "Rather, it is a place to engage people on the subject of slavery and race without finger-pointing. Yes, the center shows that slavery was terrible. But it also shows that there were people who stood up against it."

Visitors will find, in addition to the slave jail, artifacts including abolitionists' diaries, wanted posters, ads for runaways, documents granting individual slaves their freedom and newspapers such as William Lloyd Garrison's militant *Liberator,* the first in the United States to call for immediate abolition. And they will encounter one of the most powerful symbols of slavery: shackles. "Shackles exert an almost mystical fascination," says Rita C. Organ, the center's director of exhibits and collections. "There were even small-sized shackles for children. By looking at them, you get a feeling of what our ancestors must have felt—suddenly you begin to imagine what it was like being huddled in a coffle of chained slaves on the march."

Additional galleries relate stories of the central figures in the Underground Railroad. Some, like Frederick Douglass and Harriet Tubman, are renowned. Many others, such as John P. Parker, a former slave who became a key activist in the Ohio underground, and his collaborator, abolitionist John Rankin, are little known.

Other galleries document the experiences of present-day Americans, people like Laquetta Shepard, a 24-year-old black West Virginia woman who in 2002 walked into the middle of a Ku Klux Klan rally and shamed the crowd into dispersing, and Syed Ali, a Middle Eastern gas station owner in New York City who prevented members of a radical Islamic group from setting fire to a neighborhood synagogue in 2003. Says Crew, "Ideally, we would like to create modern-day equivalents of the Underground Railroad conductors, who have the internal fortitude to buck society's norms and to stand up for the things they really believe in."

The center's concept grew out of a tumultuous period in the mid-1990s when Cincinnati was reeling from confrontations between the police and the African-American community and when Marge Schott, then the owner of the Cincinnati Reds, made comments widely regarded as racist. At a 1994 meeting of the Cincinnati chapter of the National Conference of Christians and Jews, its then-director, Robert "Chip" Harrod, proposed the idea of a museum devoted to the Underground Railroad. Since then, the center has raised some $60 million from private donations and another $50 million from public sources, including the Department of Education.

The term underground railroad is said to derive from the story of a frustrated slave hunter who, having failed to apprehend a runaway, exclaimed, "He must have gone off on an underground road!" In an age when smoke-belching locomotives and shining steel rails were novelties, activists from New York to Illinois, many of whom had never seen an actual railroad, readily adopted its terminology, describing guides as "conductors," safe houses as "stations," horse-drawn wagons as "cars," and fugitives as "passengers."

Says Ira Berlin, author of *Many Thousands Gone: The First Two Centuries of Slavery in North America:* "The Underground Railroad played a critical role, by making the nature of slavery clear to Northerners who had been indifferent to it, by showing that slaves who were running away were neither happy nor well-treated, as apologists for slavery claimed. And morally, it demonstrated the enormous resiliency of the human spirit in the collaboration of blacks and whites to help people gain their freedom."

Thanks to the clandestine network, as many as 150,000 slaves may have found their way to safe havens in the North and Canada. "We don't know the total number and we will probably never know," says James O. Horton, a professor of American studies and history at George Washington University in Washington, D.C. "Part of the reason is that the underground was so successful: it kept its secrets well."

By the 1850s, activists from Delaware to Kansas had joined the underground to help fugitives elude capture. Wrote abolitionist Gerrit Smith in 1836: "If there be human enactments against our opening our door to our colored brother. . . . We must obey God."

As the nation's second great civil disobedience movement— the first being the actions, including the Boston Tea Party, leading to the American Revolution—the Underground Railroad engaged thousands of citizens in the subversion of federal law. The movement provoked fear and anger in the South and prompted the enactment of draconian legislation, including the 1850 Fugitive Slave Law, which required Northerners to cooperate in the capture of escaped slaves. And at a time when proslavery advocates insisted that blacks were better off in bondage because they lacked the intelligence or ability to take care of themselves, it also gave many African-Americans experience in political organizing and resistance.

"The Underground Railroad symbolized the intensifying struggle over slavery," says Berlin. "It was the result of the ratcheting up of the earlier antislavery movement, which in the years after the American Revolution, had begun to call for compensated emancipation and gradualist solutions to slavery." In the North, it brought African-Americans, often for the first time, into white communities where they could be seen as real people, with real families and real feelings. Ultimately, Berlin says, "the Underground Railroad forced whites to confront the reality of race in American society and to begin to wrestle with the reality in which black people lived all the time. It was a transforming experience."

For blacks and whites alike the stakes were high. Underground agents faced a constant threat of punitive litigation, violent reprisal and possible death. "White participants in the underground found in themselves a depth of humanity that they hadn't realized they had," says Horton. "And for many of them, humanity won out over legality." As New York philanthropist Gerrit Smith, one of the most important financiers of the Underground Railroad, put it in 1836, "If there be human enactments against our entertaining the stricken stranger—against our opening our door to our poor, guiltless, and unaccused colored brother pursued by bloodthirsty kidnappers—we must, nevertheless, say with the apostle: 'We must obey God rather than man.'"

From the earliest years of American bondage—the Spanish held slaves in Florida in the late 1500s; Africans were sold to colonists at Jamestown in 1619—slaves had fled their masters. But until British Canada and some Northern states—including

Pennsylvania and Massachusetts—began abolishing slavery at the end of the 18th century, there were no permanent havens for fugitives. A handful of slaves found sanctuary among several Native American tribes deep in the swamps and forests of Florida. The first coordinated Underground Railroad activity can be traced to the early 19th century, perhaps when free blacks and white Quakers began to provide refuge for runaways in and around Philadelphia, or perhaps when activists organized in Ohio.

The process accelerated throughout the 1830s. "The whole country was like a huge pot in a furious state of boiling over," recalled Addison Coffin in 1897. Coffin served as an underground conductor in North Carolina and Indiana. "It was almost universal for ministers of the gospel to run into the subject in all their sermons; neighbors would stop and argue pro and con across the fence; people traveling along the road would stop and argue the point." Although abolitionists initially faced the contempt of a society that largely took the existence of slavery for granted, the underground would eventually count among its members Rutherford B. Hayes, the future president, who as a young lawyer in the 1850s defended fugitive slaves; William Seward, the future governor of New York and secretary of state, who provided financial support to Harriet Tubman and other underground activists; and Allan Pinkerton, founder of the Pinkerton Detective Agency, who in 1859 helped John Brown lead a band of fugitive slaves out of Chicago and on to Detroit, bound for Canada. By the 1850s, the underground ranged from the northern borders of states including Maryland, Virginia and Kentucky to Canada and numbered thousands among its ranks from Delaware to Kansas.

But its center was the Ohio River Valley, where scores of river crossings served as gateways from slave states to free and where, once across the Ohio, fugitives could hope to be passed from farm to farm all the way to the Great Lakes in a matter of days.

In practice, the underground functioned with a minimum of central direction and a maximum of grass-roots involvement, particularly among family members and church congregations. "The method of operating was not uniform but adapted to the requirements of each case," Isaac Beck, a veteran of Underground Railroad activity in southern Ohio, would recall in 1892. "There was no regular organization, no constitution, no officers, no laws or agreement or rule except the 'Golden Rule,' and every man did what seemed right in his own eyes." Travel was by foot, horseback or wagon. One stationmaster, Levi Coffin, an Indiana Quaker and Addison's uncle, kept a team of horses harnessed and a wagon ready to go at his farm in Newport (now Fountain City), Indiana. When additional teams were needed, Coffin wrote in his memoir, posthumously published in 1877, "the people at the livery stable seemed to understand what the teams were wanted for, and they asked no questions."

On occasion, fugitives might be transported in hearses or false-bottomed wagons, men might be disguised as women, women as men, blacks powdered white with talc. The volume of underground traffic varied widely. Levi Coffin estimated that during his lifetime he assisted 3,300 fugitives—some 100 or so annually—while others, who lived along more lightly traveled routes, took in perhaps two or three a month, or only a handful over several years.

The underground clarified the nature of slavery (fugitives brought ashore in Philadelphia in 1856) to Northerners. As the railroad accelerated, "the whole country," wrote conductor Addison Coffin in 1897, "was like a huge pot in a state of boiling over."

One of the most active underground centers—and the subject of a 15-minute docudrama, *Brothers of the Borderland,* produced for the Freedom Center and introduced by Oprah Winfrey—was Ripley, Ohio, about 50 miles east of Cincinnati. Today, Ripley is a sleepy village of two- and three-story 19th-century houses nestled at the foot of low bluffs, facing south toward the Ohio River and the cornfields of Kentucky beyond. But in the decades preceding the Civil War, it was one of the busiest ports between Pittsburgh and Cincinnati, its economy fueled by river traffic, shipbuilding and pork butchering. To slave owners, it was known as "a black, dirty Abolition hole"— and with good reason. Since the 1820s, a network of radical white Presbyterians, led by the Rev. John Rankin, a flinty Tennessean who had moved north to escape the atmosphere of slavery, collaborated with local blacks on both sides of the river in one of the most successful underground operations.

The Rankins' simple brick farmhouse still stands on a hilltop. It was visible for miles along the river and well into Kentucky. Arnold Gragston, who as a slave in Kentucky ferried scores of fugitives across the then 500- to 1,500-foot-wide Ohio River, later recalled that Rankin had a "lighthouse in his yard, about thirty feet high."

Recently, local preservationist Betty Campbell led the way into the austere parlor of the Rankin house, now a museum open to the public. She pointed out the fireplace where hundreds of runaways warmed themselves on winter nights, as well as the upstairs crawl space where, on occasion, they hid. Because the Rankins lived so close to the river and within easy reach of slave hunters, they generally sheltered fugitives only briefly before leading them on horseback along an overgrown streambed through a forest to a neighboring farmhouse a few miles north.

"The river divided the two worlds by law, the North and the South, but the cultures were porous," Campbell said, gazing across the river's gray trough toward the bluffs of Kentucky, a landscape not much altered since the mid-19th century. "There were antislavery men in Kentucky, and also proslavery men here in Ohio, where a lot of people had Southern origins and took slavery for granted. Frequently, trusted slaves were sent from Kentucky to the market at Ripley."

For families like the Rankins, the clandestine work became a full-time vocation. Jean Rankin, John's wife, was responsible for seeing that a fire was burning in the hearth and food kept on the table. At least one of the couple's nine sons remained on call, prepared to saddle up and hasten his charges to the next way station. "It was the custom with us not to talk among ourselves about the fugitives lest inadvertently a clue should be obtained of our modus operandi," the Rankins' eldest son, Adam, wrote years later in an unpublished memoir. " 'Another runaway went through at night' was all that would be said."

One Rankin collaborator, Methodist minister John B. Mahan, was arrested at his home and taken back to Kentucky, where after 16 months in jail he was made to pay a ruinous fine that impoverished his family and likely contributed to his early death. In the summer of 1841, Kentucky slaveholders assaulted the Rankins' hilltop stronghold. They were repulsed only after a gun battle that left one of the attackers dead. Not even the Rankins would cross the river into Kentucky, where the penalty for "slave stealing" was up to 21 years' imprisonment. One Ripley man who did so repeatedly was John P. Parker, a former slave who had bought his freedom in Mobile, Alabama; by day, he operated an iron foundry. By night, he ferried slaves from Kentucky plantations across the river to Ohio. Although no photograph of Parker has survived, his saga has been preserved in a series of interviews recorded in the 1880s and published in 1996 as *His Promised Land: The Autobiography of John P. Parker.*

On one occasion, Parker learned that a party of fugitives, stranded after the capture of their leader, was hiding about 20 miles south of the river. "Being new and zealous in this work, I volunteered to go to the rescue," Parker recalled. Armed with a pair of pistols and a knife, and guided by another slave, Parker reached the runaways at about dawn. He found them hidden in deep woods, paralyzed with fear and "so badly demoralized that some of them wanted to give themselves up rather than face the unknown." Parker led the ten men and women for miles through dense thickets.

As many as 150,000 slaves may have gained freedom. "We will probably never know [the total]," says historian James O. Horton. "Part of the reason is that the underground was so successful: it kept its secrets well."

With slave hunters closing in, one of the fugitives insisted on setting off in search of water. He had gone only a short way before he came hurtling through the brush, pursued by two white men. Parker turned to the slaves still in hiding. "Drawing my pistol," he recalled, "I quietly told them that I would shoot the first one that dared make a noise, which had a quieting effect." Through thickets, Parker saw the captured slave being led away, his arms tied behind his back. The group proceeded to the river, where a patroller spotted them.

Though the lights of Ripley were visible across the water, "they might as well have been [on] the moon so far as being a relief to me," Parker recalled. Bloodhounds baying in their ears, the runaways located a rowboat quickly enough, but it had room for only eight people. Two would have to be left behind. When the wife of one of the men picked to stay behind began to wail,

Parker would recall, "I witnessed an example of heroism that made me proud of my race." One of the men in the boat gave up his seat to the woman's husband. As Parker rowed toward Ohio and freedom, he saw slave hunters converge on the spot where the two men had been left behind. "I knew," he wrote later, "the poor fellow had been captured in sight of the promised land."

Parker carried a $2,500 price on his head. More than once, his house was searched and he was assaulted in the streets of Ripley. Yet he estimated that he managed to help some 440 fugitives to freedom. In 2002, Parker's house on the Ripley waterfront—restored by a local citizens' group headed by Campbell—opened to the public.

On a clear day last spring, Carl Westmoreland returned to the Evers farm. Since his first visit, he had learned that the slave jail had been built in the 1830s by a prosperous slave trader, John Anderson, who used it to hold slaves en route by flatboat to the huge slave market at Natchez, Mississippi, where auctions were held several times a year. Anderson's manor house is gone now, as are the cabins of the slaves who served in his household, tended his land and probably even operated the jail itself.

"The jail is a perfect symbol of forgetting," Westmoreland said at the time, not far from the slave trader's overgrown grave. "For their own reasons, whites and blacks both tried to forget about that jail, just as the rest of America tried to forget about slavery. But that building has already begun to teach, by causing people to go back and look at the local historical record. It's doing its job." Anderson died in 1834 at the age of 42. Westmoreland continued: "They say that he tripped over a grapevine and fell onto the sharp stump of a cornstalk, which penetrated his eye and entered his brain. He was chasing a runaway slave."

Critical Thinking

1. Why was the underground railroad so important?
2. How did its existence convince the slaveholding south that white northerners would end slavery?

Create Central

www.mhhe.com/createcentral

Internet References

Aboard the Underground Railroad
www.nps.gov/nr/travel/underground/
The Underground Railroad
www.math.buffalo.edu/~sww/0history/UndergroundRailRoad.html
Map of the Underground Railroad
www.nps.gov/nr/travel/underground/routes.htm
Harriet Tubman
www.americaslibrary.gov/aa/tubman/aa_tubman_subj.html

FERGUS M. BORDEWICH is the author of *Bound for Canaan: The Underground Railroad and the War for the Soul of America,* published by Amistad/HarperCollins.

Bordewich, Fergus M. From *Smithsonian*, December 2004. Copyright © 2004 by Fergus M. Bordewich. Reprinted by permission of the author.

Article   Prepared by: Wendy A. Maier-Sarti, *Oakton Community College*

There Goes the South

President-elect Abraham Lincoln remained strangely silent as threats of secession became a reality during the long winter before his inauguration.

H. W. BRANDS

Learning Outcomes

After reading this article, you will be able to:

- Explain the motivations behind secession.

- Analyze the alternatives to secession.

- Describe Lincoln's motives behind waiting until after his inauguration to denounce secession.

On the eve of his victory in the 1860 presidential election, Abraham Lincoln surprised a well-wisher by declaring, "For personal considerations, I would rather have a full term in the Senate—a place in which I would feel more consciously able to discharge the duties required and where there was more chance to make a reputation and less danger of losing it—than four years of the presidency."

Lincoln's expression of 11th-hour doubt was not merely the disclaimer of a self-deprecating politician. The nearer he got to fulfilling his ambition of becoming president, the more he realized how daunting the job would be. He did his best to maintain a cheerful front as he monitored the final election returns at the Springfield, Ill., telegraph office on November 6. But his private secretary John Nicolay watched "the appalling shadow of his mighty task and responsibility" pass over him as he donned his overcoat around 1:30 A.M. and headed home in a melancholy mood. "It seemed as if he suddenly bore the whole world upon his shoulders, and could not shake it off."

Lincoln faced the unnerving prospect that by the time he took his oath of office on March 4—four months after the election—the Union would be in ruins. Southern radicals were already clamoring for secession. Meanwhile, even though Lincoln lacked the constitutional authority to act as president, people in both the North and the South looked to him for leadership as the nation plunged into a period of dangerous uncertainty.

Years later, Lincoln's first vice president, Hannibal Hamlin, chided eulogists for "constructing a Lincoln who was as great the day he left Springfield as when he made his earthly exit four years later." As president-elect, Lincoln was uncertain about whether the secession movement represented the bluster of a minority or a groundswell of popular Southern sentiment. Nor could he confidently predict whether Northerners would insist on holding the Union together or bid good riddance to the slave states. Moreover, he struggled at first with his own natural tendency to let pressing questions simmer until solutions bubbled to the surface. Should he try to reach some accommodation with Southern moderates in hopes of averting war? Or would that merely encourage the radical secessionists, who would interpret any accommodation as weakness and grow more convinced the North would never fight?

Only at his inauguration did he muster the will to attack the secessionists head on. By then it was too late to save the Union peacefully.

During the long winter interlude before he took office, Lincoln initially did nothing, hoping the crisis would pass. But when his inaction proved counterproductive and the secessionist momentum intensified, he felt obliged to alter course. Still, he moved quietly and indirectly, fearing that his words and deeds might provoke Southern moderates into joining the secessionists. Only at his inauguration did he muster the will to speak boldly and attack the secessionists head on.

By then it was too late to save the Union peacefully.

Lincoln had sought the presidency by means that invited confusion. He won the Republican nomination largely on the strength of his House Divided speech of 1858, in which he declared that America could not continue half slave and half free. But in the general election the Republicans promised to leave slavery alone in the states where it existed, and Lincoln embraced that promise without ever overtly disavowing the uncompromising message of the House Divided address.

In the mid-19th century presidential candidates didn't campaign for themselves, nor was it thought seemly for

Rebel Administration. Jefferson Davis (left) and Alexander Stephens were sworn in as president and vice president of the new Confederacy a month before Lincoln's inauguration. Stephens was on friendly terms with Lincoln and initially argued against secession.

presidents-elect to speak on the record. But given the turmoil surrounding his election, many people thought Lincoln must explain his position on the unfolding crisis. A pointed appeal came from George Prentice, the editor of the *Louisville Journal.* Prentice was a discouraged Southern Unionist who urged Lincoln to make a public statement that would "take from the disunionists every excuse or pretext for treason."

"If what I have already said has failed to convince you, no repetition of it would convince you," Lincoln replied. His answer was a dodge; he wouldn't speak because he didn't want to commit himself before he had to.

The rumblings of secession increased, however, and Lincoln realized he had to give some sign of his thinking. Lyman Trumbull was a senator from Illinois who had been elected as a Democrat but subsequently converted to Republicanism. He and Lincoln were known to be close, and his words were often taken as coming from Lincoln. Two weeks after the election Lincoln wrote a brief passage for Trumbull to insert in a speech at Chicago. "I have labored in and for the Republican organization," Trumbull said, for himself and Lincoln, "with entire confidence that whenever it shall be in power, each and all of the states will be left in complete control of their own affairs respectively, and at as perfect liberty to choose, and employ,

their own means of protecting property, and preserving peace and order within their respective limits, as they have ever been under any administration."

Lincoln's proxy statement failed dismally. It lacked the authority that words spoken by Lincoln himself would have carried, and its second-hand character suggested a timidity that augured ill for Lincoln's administration or his cause. Southern secessionists concluded that a man without the courage to speak in his own voice would be a president without the nerve to challenge their separatist designs. Northern radicals complained that the Trumbull statement was a retreat from the moral clarity of the House Divided speech.

The criticism reinforced Lincoln's caution. "This is just what I expected, and just what would happen with any declaration I could make," he told a friend. "These political fiends are not half sick enough yet. 'Party malice' and not 'public good' possesses them entirely. 'They seek a sign, and no sign shall be given them.'"

Lincoln's diffidence encouraged others to take the stage. The secessionists called conventions and drafted resolutions to implement their separatist aims. Northern

Unionists and Southern moderates weighed a constitutional amendment guaranteeing the future of slavery in the states where it already existed. Lame duck president James Buchanan sent an envoy, Duff Green, to test Lincoln's thinking on such an amendment.

"I do not desire any amendment," Lincoln told Green. An amendment, he reasoned, would be difficult to pass and nearly impossible to repeal. He blanched at the idea of grafting slavery so egregiously onto America's fundamental law. But he wouldn't rule it out entirely, if only because amending the Constitution was the prerogative of Congress and the states, not the president.

More promising, to Lincoln's view, was the approach of Alexander Stephens, a Georgia moderate Lincoln had known since the 1840s, when they served in the House of Representatives together. As Georgians debated their response to Lincoln's election, Stephens gave a widely noted speech opposing rash action. "I do not anticipate that Mr. Lincoln will do anything to jeopardize our safety or security," he said. "He can do nothing unless he is backed by power in Congress. The House of Representatives is largely in the majority against him. In the Senate he will also be powerless."

Lincoln read newspaper summaries of Stephens' remarks, and he wrote Stephens asking if he had prepared them for publication. Stephens replied that he had not, but that the news reports fairly characterized what he had said. He went on to offer Lincoln encouragement in his efforts to hold the nation together. "The Country is certainly in great peril and no man ever had heavier or greater responsibilities resting upon him than you have in this present momentous crisis," he said.

Lincoln appreciated the gesture, and he tried, through Stephens, to allay the concerns of Southern moderates. "Do the people in the South really entertain fears that a Republican administration would, directly or indirectly, interfere with their slaves?" he asked Stephens. "If they do, I wish to assure you, as once a friend and still, I hope, not an enemy, that there is no cause for such fears. The South would be in no more danger in this respect than it was in the days of Washington."

You think slavery is right and ought to be extended, while we think it is wrong and ought to be restricted. That I suppose is the rub.

Yet Lincoln conceded to Stephens that the issue ran deeper than political assurances. Southerners and Northerners had irreconcilable views on the morality of slavery. "You think slavery is right and ought to be extended, while we think it is wrong and ought to be restricted. That I suppose is the rub."

That was the rub, and it chafed the more as Lincoln's inauguration neared. A desperate Congress convened committees to find an arrangement to hold the Union together. Proposals included one to resurrect a popular sovereignty scheme advanced by Lincoln's old nemesis Stephen Douglas, by which residents of frontier territories would vote to permit or ban slavery. Lincoln still declined to issue a public statement, but he wrote Republican members of Congress to stiffen their resolve against any retreat on slavery in the territories. "Entertain no proposition for a compromise in regard to extension of slavery," he urged William Kellogg, a Republican representative from Illinois. "The instant you do, they have us under again; all our labor is lost. . . . The tug has to come and better now than later." Lincoln told Elihu Washburne, another Illinois Republican: "Hold firm, as with a chain of steel."

Lincoln perceived Southerners' aggressiveness on the slave issue as inevitable. Their current demands were but the start. "If we surrender, it is the end of us, and of the government," he asserted privately. "They will repeat the experiment upon us ad libitum." The sole way out of the present impasse, Lincoln said, was by a route neither Northerners nor Southerners would accept: "a prohibition against acquiring any more territory." It was a great irony of American history that this very solution—which Lincoln and nearly every contemporary rejected as unworkable—had already been effected, in political practice if not in political theory. The continental expansion that was causing all the trouble had ended in 1848. The only substantial piece of North America to be added to the United States after 1860 was Alaska, which was unsuited to a large population of any sort, slave or otherwise.

As the winter dragged on, Lincoln realized he had underestimated the South. Those who spoke of secession were not bluffing. He decided he must state his position—albeit still not quite for public consumption. Thurlow Weed, the New York Republican boss whose support had been central to Lincoln's election, had convened Northern governors to prepare a riposte to the South. "I am unwilling to see a united South and a divided North," Weed wrote Lincoln. "Thus united, your administration will have its foundation upon a rock." What could Lincoln tell the governors, even in private, about his intentions?

Lincoln's response echoed what he had told other Republicans: He was "inflexible on the territorial question"—no slavery outside the Southern states. He added: "My opinion is that no state can, in any way lawfully, get out of the Union, without the consent of the others; and that it is the duty of the President, and other government functionaries, to run the machine as it is."

But the machine was already breaking up. South Carolina, amid great fanfare, had passed an ordinance of secession on December 20, and in the succeeding weeks several other states prepared to follow suit and leave the Union.

On February 11, Lincoln left Springfield for Washington. The psychological strain of the long, hard winter showed in his face and bearing; an acquaintance remarked that his body "heaved with emotion and he could scarcely command his feelings." Lincoln's voice broke as he told his Springfield neighbors, "I now leave, not knowing when, or whether ever, I may return."

The strain intensified as he headed east. The newspapers en route reported on the provisional Congress of the Confederate States of America, meeting in Montgomery, Ala. Seven states—South Carolina, Mississippi, Florida, Alabama, Georgia, Louisiana and Texas—sent delegates, although the Texans had to await the ratification of secession by the people of the Lone Star State. Lincoln read of the election of Jefferson Davis to be president of the Confederacy, and days later of Davis' inauguration with Alexander Stephens as his vice president. He also read that the Southern states were seizing the federal forts on their soil.

The progress of a president-elect en route to his inauguration was a once-in-a-lifetime event for many of the towns through which Lincoln's train passed, and at every stop people gathered and insisted that he speak. He was too good a politician not to oblige. "If the United States should merely hold and retake its own forts and other property, and collect the duties on foreign importations, or even withhold the mails from places where they were habitually violated, would any or all these things be 'invasion' or 'coercion'?" he asked an audience at Indianapolis. Then he waffled: "I am not asserting anything. I am merely asking questions."

At Philadelphia he learned that Allan Pinkerton, a detective hired by the railroad company to preempt sabotage, had heard rumors of an assassination plot in Baltimore, where secessionist sympathies ran strong. Lincoln at first resisted altering his schedule, but when additional evidence suggested real danger, he was persuaded. He disguised himself as an invalid and slipped through Baltimore in the dead of night.

He soon regretted that decision. Southern newspapers ridiculed his lack of courage; even Republican papers feared he had diminished himself on the verge of his inauguration.

All of Washington was on edge as Lincoln prepared to take his oath of office on March 4. General Winfield Scott, the army commander, stationed infantry, cavalry and artillery troops conspicuously about the capital, and special squadrons of policemen lined Pennsylvania Avenue. The great majority of the visitors who crowded the streets were from the Northern states—"judging from the lack of long-haired men in the crowd," an eyewitness observed. When the members of the House of Representatives were summoned to join the inaugural procession to the east side of the Capitol, their jostling for position escalated to curses, threats and near-fisticuffs. Chief Justice Roger B. Taney, whose decision in the *Dred Scott* case had elicited Lincoln's House Divided prophecy, visibly trembled as he stood near Lincoln on the rostrum.

Lincoln felt the tension as he looked out on the crowd. And he couldn't help reflecting that his caution had done nothing to ease the nation's crisis, which grew more acute by the day. Inaction had simply encouraged others to seize the initiative.

But now it was his turn—finally. He commenced by reiterating what he had been conveying in private: that slavery in the South was secure. "I have no purpose, directly or indirectly, to interfere with the institution of slavery in the States where it exists. I believe I have no lawful right to do so, and I have no inclination to do so."

Inauguration Day. With the unfinished Capitol as a backdrop, Lincoln finally addressed the nation's uncertain future.

Sadly, he continued, Southern radicals were not so tolerant. "A disruption of the Federal Union, heretofore only menaced, is now formidably attempted."

No disruption would be allowed. An unexpected steel entered Lincoln's voice—a tone few had anticipated and none in public heard. "The Union of these States is perpetual," he said. Secessionists would search in vain for constitutional authorization for their plan. "No government proper ever had a provision in its organic law for its own termination." If, as the secessionists contended, the Union was a union of states rather than of peoples, this afforded no easier exit, for, having been created by all the states, the Union required the consent of all the states to be destroyed. "No State, upon its own mere motion, can lawfully get out of the Union. . . . The Union is unbroken."

The Union of these States is perpetual. No State, upon its own mere motion, can lawfully get out of the Union. . . . The Union is unbroken.

And Lincoln vowed it would remain unbroken. "To the extent of my ability I shall take care, as the Constitution itself expressly enjoins upon me, that the laws of the Union be faithfully executed in all of the States."

The secessionists blamed Lincoln personally for endangering the peace of the Union; they had it just backward, he said. "In your hands, my dissatisfied fellow-countrymen, and not in mine, is the momentous issue of civil war. The Government will not assail you. You can have no conflict without being yourselves the aggressors. You have no oath registered in Heaven to destroy the Government, while I shall have the most solemn one to 'preserve, protect, and defend it.'"

These were fighting words. The secessionists had doubted Lincoln's resolve; his long silence had corroborated their doubts, to the point of encouraging their secession. But they could doubt him no longer. To speak of civil war was to make it possible.

Lincoln had never fought a civil war; none of his contemporaries had. He had only the vaguest notion of what it would mean or how it would be done. Yet if the secessionists persisted in their destructive ways, they would provoke a civil war.

He let his words hang in the March air above the Capitol grounds. Applause had interrupted him earlier; now the thousands were silent as they pondered his promise, and his threat. He gave both a moment to sink in.

Then he concluded more hopefully: "We are not enemies, but friends. We must not be enemies. Though passion may have strained, it must not break our bonds of affection. The mystic chords of memory, stretching from every battlefield and patriot grave to every living heart and hearthstone all over this broad land, will yet swell the chorus of the Union, when again touched, as surely they will be, by the better angels of our nature."

Critical Thinking

1. What events led to secession in South Carolina?

2. Could secession have been prevented?

3. Was the Civil War inevitable once secession was underway?

Create Central

www.mhhe.com/createcentral

Internet References

South Carolina and the Civil War
   http://library.sc.edu/digital/collections/civilwar.html

Industry and Economy during the Civil War
   www.nps.gov/resources/story.htm?id=251

North and South: Different Cultures, Same Country
   www.civilwar.org/education/history/civil-war-overview/
   northandsouth.html

The Civil War
   www.pbs.org/wgbh/aia/part4/4p2967.html

Timeline of Succession
   www.digitalhistory.uh.edu/learning_history/south_secede/timeline
   _secession.cfm

H. W. BRANDS is a history professor at the University of Texas and the author of 16 books. His latest is *Traitor to His Class,* a biography of Franklin Roosevelt.

Brands, H. W. From *American History*, April 2009. Copyright © 2009 by Weider History Group. Reprinted by permission.

Article   Prepared by: Wendy A. Maier-Sarti, *Oakton Community College*

Lincoln and the Constitutional Dilemma of Emancipation

EDNA GREENE MEDFORD

Learning Outcomes

After reading this article, you will be able to:

• Explain the elements of the emanicpation proclamation.

• Analyze the legality of the emancipation proclamation.

• Recount the response to the emancipation proclamation.

> The President shall be Commander in Chief of the Army and Navy of the United States, and of the Militia of the several States, when called into the actual Service of the United States.
>
> —U. S. Constitution, Article II, Section 2

On the afternoon of January 1, 1863, following nearly two years of bloody civil war, Abraham Lincoln set in motion events that would reconnect the detached cord of Union and that would begin to reconcile the nation's practices to its avowed democratic principles. Interpreting Article II, Section 2 of the Constitution broadly, the president used his war powers to proclaim freedom for those enslaved laborers caught in the dehumanizing grip of one of the Confederacy's most sacrosanct institutions. His bold move challenged prevailing notions of presidential prerogative and triggered criticism from his supporters as well as his opponents. While many abolitionists bemoaned the limited scope of the president's actions, alleging that he freed those persons over whom he had no control, while exempting from his edict those under Union authority, his more conservative critics charged that he had exceeded the powers the Constitution invested in the executive.

Lincoln anticipated the criticism. He knew that most abolitionists would be satisfied with nothing less than universal emancipation and that, contrarily, pro-South forces would find in his actions reason to brand him a betrayer of American liberties. Given that slavery evoked such polarization in the North, he realized that whatever action he took on the institution posed considerable danger to the goal of the war—preservation of the Union.

Although influenced by the practical considerations of containing the rebellion—that is, not losing any more slaveholding states to the Confederacy—Lincoln's greatest challenge regarding emancipation was to achieve it without violating constitutional guarantees. He understood slavery to be the cause of the war but he believed that the Constitution denied the president any easy solution for its eradication. Whatever his personal views on slavery (and there is incontrovertible evidence that he hated the institution on moral grounds as well as practical reasons), law and custom had deemed enslaved people property.[1] Because the Constitution protected property rights, Lincoln felt compelled to operate within those constraints. As war propelled him inexorably toward emancipation, he sought authority to do so within the framework that the Constitution provided.

The Civil War began as a struggle over national union, one half of the American people believed it indissoluble and fought to preserve it, while the other half wished to withdraw from it and secure their own identity. Northern attempts at appeasement and diplomacy having failed, war became the only recourse for a president convinced that secession was unconstitutional. Hence, in his first official act after hostilities commenced, Lincoln called up the state militias "to maintain the honor, the integrity, and the existence" of the nation.[2] The decision had not been an easy one. When he spoke before Congress in special session on July 4, 1861, he explained that.

"It was with the deepest regret that the Executive found the duty of employing the war-power, in defense of the government, forced upon him. He could but perform this duty, or surrender the existence of the government."[3]

Defense of the government ultimately led Lincoln to strike at the heart of the South's reason for challenging national union. It would prove even harder than prosecuting the war itself, because the Constitution—compromise document that it was—reflected the ambivalence of the framers over the issue of slavery. Lincoln had acknowledged "not grudgingly, but fully, and fairly," the constitutional rights of the slaveholder, but the treatment of slavery in the Constitution suggested to him that the framers had deliberately paved the way for the institution's eventual extinction.[4] The founding fathers and the earliest Congress

Article   Prepared by: Wendy A. Maier-Sarti, *Oakton Community College*

Why Was the Confederacy Defeated?

ALAN FARMER

Confederacy was huge making it difficult to blockade

Learning Outcomes

After reading this article, you will be able to:

- Articulate three reasons why the South was defeated.
- Draw connections between foreign trade partners and their stance on the American Civil War.
- Discuss economic weapons in war as an effective part of the overall strategy.

On 10 April 1865, General Robert E. Lee, having just surrendered to General Grant at Appomattox, wrote a farewell address to his soldiers. 'After four years' arduous service, marked by unsurpassed courage and fortitude', declared Lee, 'the Army of Northern Virginia has been compelled to yield to overwhelming numbers and resources.' According to Lee, the Confederacy lost the American Civil War not because it fought badly but because the enemy had more men and guns—indeed more everything. Historian Richard Current, reviewing the statistics of Northern (or Union) strength, concluded that 'surely in view of disparity of resources, it would have taken a miracle . . . to enable the South to win. As usual, God was on the side of the heaviest battalions'.

Yet not all historians would accept that the Union's superior resources were the prime cause of Confederate defeat. Many insist that the Confederacy lost—rather than the Union won—the Civil War. Did the Confederacy defeat itself or was it defeated?

The Union certainly had considerable advantages. There were 22 million people in the North compared with only 9 million in the South (of whom only 5.5 million were whites). The North had a much greater industrial capacity. In 1860 Northern states produced 97 per cent of the USA's firearms and 94 per cent of its pig iron. Even in agriculture the North enjoyed an edge. The Confederacy hoped to make good its lack of materials by trading with Europe, but the Union used its naval strength to impose an increasingly tight blockade. The Union was further aided by the fact that four slave states—Delaware, Missouri, Maryland and Kentucky—remained loyal to the Union. Nor were all the people within the 11 Confederate states committed to the Confederate cause. Pockets of Unionism existed, especially in the Appalachian Mountains. Slaves were also a potential fifth column. Throughout the war there was a steady flow of blacks fleeing to Union armies. The North converted first their labour and eventually their military manpower into a Union asset.

Nevertheless, in 1861 most Southerners thought that the Confederacy was favourite to win the war. The Confederacy's sheer size—750,000 square miles—was a major asset, making if difficult to blockade, occupy and conquer. Confederate forces did not have to invade the North: they simply needed to defend. The fire-power of the rifle-musket meant that battlefield tactics now favoured the defender. The Union, having no option but to attack, was bound to suffer heavy casualties. Southerners hoped that Northern opinion might come to question high losses. If Northern will collapsed, the Confederacy would win by default. Geography gave the Confederacy an important strategic advantage. In the crucial theatre of the war—North Virginia—a series of rivers provided a barrier to Union armies intent on capturing Richmond, the Confederate capital. Slavery, which might seem to be a Confederate weakness, enabled the South to enlist more of its white manpower than the North.

The Confederacy also had important psychological advantages. Southerners were defending their own land and homes—a fact that may have encouraged them to fight that much harder than Northerners, who were fighting for the more abstract pursuit of reunion. In 1861 most Southerners were confident that, man for man, they were better soldiers than Northerners. The ante-bellum South placed more emphasis on martial virtues than the North. In 1860 most of the military colleges in the USA were in slave states. The elite of the nation's generals had all been Southerners. Most military experts assumed that farmers, who knew how to ride and shoot, made better soldiers than industrial workers. Confederate victory in the first major battle at Manassas seemed to confirm this assumption.

At many stages, events on the battlefield might have gone differently. Historians stress different moments when the Confederacy was either unlucky or missed opportunities. Confederate forces might have been more pro-active after First Manassas. The Trent Affair could have brought Britain into the war on the Confederate side. Had Stonewall Jackson been up to par in June-July 1862 Lee might have triumphed even more spectacularly in the Seven Days battles. Who knows what would have happened had Lee's battle orders not fallen into Union hands in Maryland in September 1862?

The Confederacy had its chances in 1863. Given more inspired generalship, Grant might have failed to capture leadership/lack of

Vicksburg. Lee might have done better at Gettysburg, especially if Stonewall Jackson had not been killed at Chancellorsville. There were still good opportunities for the Confederacy in 1864. Lincoln's re-election in November 1864 very much depended on (belated) military success. The alternative was a victory for the Democrat party, parts of which were committed to peace. Perhaps President Davis might have taken up General Cleburne's proposal to redress the South's manpower shortage by conscripting slaves. In short, the Confederacy was not inevitably a 'Lost Cause'.

Superior leadership is often seen as the main reason for Union victory. However, in many respects, the Confederacy was well led. While President Lincoln's superiority to Jefferson Davis might seem self-evident, Lee could think of no one in the South who could have done a better job than Davis. Davis certainly worked hard and did his best to inspire Southerners. The Confederate government is often charged with failing to efficiently manage the country's economy and finance. The main criticism is that it printed too much money, thus fuelling inflation which ravaged the economy and lowered Southern morale. However, given the Union blockade, inflation was inevitable. Despite its economic problems, the Confederacy maintained over 3 per cent of its population under arms—a higher figure than the North. In terms of the management of military supply, the Confederacy could boast some organisational successes. Ordnance Chief Josiah Gorgas, for example, built an arms industry virtually from scratch and kept Confederate armies better supplied than had seemed possible in 1861. The main problem was the shortage—not the management—of resources.

The key aspect of leadership in the Civil War, as in any war, was military leadership. Many historians claim that Davis and Lee, Davis's most important military adviser and field commander, pursued a flawed military strategy. Davis chose to pursue what has been labelled an 'offensive-defensive' strategy. This consisted of placing conventional armies in an essentially defensive posture to protect as much territory as possible, and launching offensive movements when circumstances seemed promising. Lee emphasised the 'offensive' in 'offensive-defensive', seeking to find ways to gain and hold the initiative. His penchant for attack has been particularly criticised. Arguably a more defensive strategy would have conserved manpower, thereby enabling the Confederacy to prolong the war and perhaps exhaust Union will. Historians Grade McWhiney and Perry Jamieson argue that Lee's offensive strategy extracted a hideous price in battlefield casualties: the South literally bled itself to death in the first three years of the war. Emory Thomas claims that Lee learned the wrong lessons from General Scott's successful offensive strategy in the Mexican War. Thomas thinks Lee admired 'Scott's bold strategy and probably developed a confidence in attacking that made him miscalculate against an enemy well led and armed with rifles instead of much shorter-range muskets'.

However, it is unlikely that a purely defensive strategy would have succeeded. General Joe Johnston was the Confederate exponent of defensive warfare. Refusing to stand and fight, he surrendered huge chunks of land virtually without a struggle

in north Virginia in 1862 and in Georgia in 1864. This did not enhance Southern morale. Moreover, Confederate retreat often led to disastrous sieges and huge surrenders, for example Fort Donelson (1862) and Vicksburg (1863). Lee's battles in 1862–3 were certainly costly: from Seven Days to Chancellorsville his casualties were 65,000 (of whom 10,000 died). But this effusion of blood served a purpose. The key to success lay in winning victories that depressed Union and bolstered Confederate morale. Victories might also convince Britain and France to recognise the Confederacy. Lee, like all Civil War generals, recognised the advantage of fighting on the defensive. But he also knew that a purely defensive strategy would result in the Confederacy being picked off at will. The only hope in Lee's view (and surely he was right) was to retain the initiative and risk attack, hoping for a great Waterloo-type victory. As Prussia was to prove in the Seven Weeks War against Austria (1866) and in the Franco-Prussian War (1870–1), spectacular offensive victories could be won—despite the rifle-musket. On several occasions Lee's strategy almost won him an annihilating victory. When finally forced on the defensive in 1864–5, he had to fight the kind of war the Confederacy could not win.

The Confederate leadership has been taken to task for attempting to fight a conventional rather that a guerrilla war. Influenced by the Vietnam War, some scholars envisage small groups of Southerners striking at the enemy's extended lines of communication as frustrated Unionists sought to bring rebel soldiers to battle in the vast Southern hinterlands. Arguably Southern manpower would have lasted almost indefinitely while Union commitment eroded away. However, a guerrilla strategy in 1861 was inconceivable. A purely guerrilla-style war meant the loss of territory and thus of slaves, and this would have alienated most Southerners. A guerrilla war could erode Union will only as long as Southerners remained devoted to the cause. Irregular units could not have supplied battlefield victories of the magnitude Lee's army won in 1862–3—victories essential to national morale. Moreover, Davis needed to create a nation, with a successful national army, to win British and French recognition. Neither country would have recognised a fledgling Confederacy that relied on guerrilla units rather than on a formal army. Successful guerrilla wars have always benefited from dependable outside support, but no such support was available to the Confederacy. It should be said that there was considerable Confederate guerrilla activity in Florida, Tennessee, Virginia and Missouri (where it was particularly nasty). But when Davis called for an all-out guerrilla war in April 1865, there were no takers. Most Southerners recognised that a guerrilla war would simply extend the misery with little prospect of winning independence.

Some historians think Lee's strategic vision was limited to Virginia, where his influence concentrated Confederate resources at the expense of the West. The result was that the Confederacy lost the West and thus lost the war. Such criticism is unfounded. Lee was commander of the Army of Northern Virginia: Virginia was thus his rightful priority. If anyone was to blame for a Virginia-focused strategy it was Davis. In fairness to Davis, it seems highly unlikely that the Confederacy could have won the war by concentrating most of its forces in the

West where military conditions, especially control of the major rivers, favoured the Union. Virginia, the Confederacy's most important industrial state, had to be defended. In Virginia, geographical conditions very much favoured the defender. It thus made sense to send the best men and resources to the best army (the Army of Northern Virginia) and the best general (Lee!). Indeed Davis might be criticised not so much for his preoccupation with Virginia, but instead for dividing scarce resources more or less equally between East and West. However, Davis knew that the Confederacy could not survive long without both Virginia and the West. He had to try and hold both, with limited manpower and limited talent.

Many of the Confederacy's problems in the West stemmed from its poor commanders. The first overall Western commander, Albert Johnston, allowed Union forces to break through the Tennessee and Cumberland river defence line. Beauregard made plans not based on realities. General Bragg quarrelled with everyone and had a poor record. General Joe Johnston did little but retreat. General Hood was responsible for a series of costly defeats in 1864.

Nevertheless, claims that skilful Union and incompetent Confederate generalship explain the outcome of the war are not convincing. The Union did finally find the winning team of Grant and Sherman. Grant, often regarded as the war's best soldier, displayed his talent when capturing Fort Donelson (1862) and Vicksburg (1863). Overall commander from March 1864, he slugged it out with Lee in Virginia and won the war. Sherman's capture of Atlanta and his marches through Georgia and the Carolinas weakened the South logistically and psychologically. However, the Union army had more than its fair share of blunderers. Inept Union generalship actually gave the Confederacy a chance of victory. Even Grant and Sherman were far from supermen. Their 1864–5 campaigns were won because their forces were larger and better equipped than those of the enemy. Within a framework largely shaped by Davis and Lee, Confederate forces fought numerous battles, raised civilian hopes, stretched Northern will to the limit on more than one occasion but ultimately failed to achieve independence. This failure does not mean that the offensive-defensive strategy was flawed. There was no other rational strategy. Lee deserves to be held in high regard. Despite being outnumbered in every major campaign in which he fought, he won stunning victories. If other Confederate generals had fought as well, the war might have had a different outcome.

Today, many scholars insist that the Confederacy could have won if the Southern people had possessed the will to make the necessary sacrifices. There is a tendency to believe that once Southerners got past the heady summer of 1861, with victory at Manassas fading and the prospect of significant sacrifice looming, morale plummeted. As desertion and disaffection increased, Confederate resistance collapsed from internal stresses that rendered further struggle impossible. Historian Merton Coulter declared that the Confederacy lost because its 'people did not will hard enough and long enough to win'. Arguably, the Confederacy failed to generate a strong sense of nationalism. Accordingly, when the going got tough, Southerners found it tough to keep going.

In reality, however, Southerners had a strong sense of distinctiveness—a belief that they shared cultural values at odds with those of the rest of the nation. What particularly set them apart was slavery—the 'cornerstone' of the Confederacy. The strength of patriotic feeling in 1861 produced 500,000 volunteers for military service. Southern politicians, clergymen and newspaper editors, invoking memories of 1776, did their utmost to secure support for the Confederacy. The war, which gave Southerners a new set of heroes and which also created a unifying hatred of the enemy, strengthened feelings of national identity. So did military service. Historian James McPherson found evidence of very strong patriotism in the letters of Southern soldiers. Most believed they were fighting for freedom and liberty. Even during the awful winter of 1864–5 most soldiers faithfully discharged their duty. Thousands of courageous Confederate troops, for example, mounted impressive—but hopeless—assaults against well-positioned Federals in the battle of Franklin in November 1864. Historian Gary Gallagher suggests that the most nationalistic Southerners were young officers. Reared among the sectional controversies of the 1850s, they had few, if any, doubts about slavery, attributed base motives to Northerners in general and Republicans in particular, and supported secession. Once fighting began, their personal example in combat inspired their men and their achievements nourished patriotism and resolve among civilians. Devoted to the Confederacy, they remained outspoken advocates of continued sacrifice until the last days of the war.

Far from being a reason for defeat, the strength of Confederate nationalism explains why most Southerners fought as long and hard as they did. In the summer of 1864 Northerners almost threw in the towel when they suffered casualty rates that Southerners had endured for more than two years. 260,000 Confederate troops died in the war—a quarter of the white male population of military age. A further 200,000 were seriously wounded. The Confederacy's death toll was far greater than France's in the Franco-Prussian War. Nobody suggests that Frenchmen in 1870 did not have a strong sense of national identity. Yet France lost. Nationalism does not ensure invulnerability to those who possess it.

Given so much death and destruction, some scholars believe that Southerners came to doubt whether God was really on their side and that this helped corrode morale. This view is hard to substantiate. Southern Church leaders supported the Confederate cause until the bitter end. Most Southerners believed that God would ensure their success. Religious revivals swept through Confederate armies, especially in 1863–4. Many Southern soldiers equated duty to God with duty to the Confederacy. Rather than explaining Confederate defeat, religion played a vital role in sustaining Southern will. The notion that many Southern whites felt moral qualms about slavery, which undermined their will to fight a war to preserve it, is even less convincing. All the evidence suggests that most Southerners went to war to preserve their peculiar institution and remained committed to it to the end.

Recent scholarship has stressed that many groups within the South became disenchanted as the war progressed. Two-thirds of the Confederacy's white population were non-slaveholders who may have come to resent risking their lives and property simply to defend slavery for slaveholders. However, McPherson found little if any evidence of class division in the letters of Confederate soldiers. Large numbers of non-slaveholders were ready to fight and die for the Confederacy from start to finish.

'Historians have wondered in recent years why the Confederacy did not endure longer', wrote historian Drew Gilpin Faust; 'In considerable measure . . . it was because so many women did not want it to. It may well have been because of its women that the South lost the Civil War'. Severe hardship on the home front, Faust claims, led to a growth of defeatism which was conveyed by uncensored letters to Southern soldiers. Women told their men folk to put family before national loyalty. In reality, however, many Southern women remained loyal to the end, exhorting their men to stay at the front and fight. Increased privation, the experience of living under Federal occupation, and the loss of loved ones often reinforced rather than eroded loyalty to the Confederacy.

'The devils seem to have a determination that cannot but be admired', wrote General Sherman to his wife in March 1864. 'No amount of poverty or adversity seems to shake their faith—niggers gone—wealth and luxury gone, money worthless, starvation in view within a period of two or three years, are causes enough to make the bravest tremble, yet I see no sign of let up—some few deserters—plenty tired of war, but the masses determined to fight it out'. Sherman's subsequent actions underscored his belief that severe measures were necessary to break the dogged Confederate resistance.

There was some states rights obstructionism in the Confederacy: that was only to be—and was far less than might have been—expected. There were class tensions: there are in any state. There was war weariness: there always is. But even in 1864–5, letters, diaries and newspapers reveal a tenacious popular will rooted in a sense of national community.

As the war progressed, Lee and his Army of Northern Virginia embodied the Confederacy in the minds of most white Southerners. Lee's military success sustained Southern hopes. Contemporaries understood the centrality of military events to national morale and, by extension, to the outcome of the war. In his second inaugural address Lincoln spoke of the 'progress of our arms, upon which all else chiefly depends'. But for victories at Atlanta and in the Shenandoah Valley, Lincoln might well have lost the 1864 election. Lee won many, but in the end not enough, victories. The prestige and symbolic importance of the Army of Northern Virginia were such that few Southerners contemplated serious resistance after Lee's surrender at Appomattox, despite the fact that he surrendered only a fraction of Southerners under arms in April 1865. Appomattox was the end of the Confederacy.

When asked some years afterwards why the Confederates lost at Gettysburg, General Pickett replied, 'I think the Yankees had something to do with it'. The Yankees also explain why the Confederacy lost the war. The Union defeated the Confederacy: the Confederacy did not defeat itself.

Given the Union's strength, the Confederacy was always likely to be beaten. To win, the Confederacy had to wear down Northern will. A long bloody war was the best way to do this. The war was long and bloody but Northern will endured. The morale of Union soldiers was crucial. McPherson's study of soldiers' letters suggests that Northern soldiers were aware of the issues at stake and passionately concerned about them. In 1864 some 80 per cent of Union soldiers voted for Lincoln, proof that soldier morale still held strong. Federal victories from mid-1863 onwards helped sustain that morale. The Confederacy surrendered in 1865 because Union armies had demonstrated their ability to crush Southern military resistance. Defeat caused defeatism, not vice versa. A people whose armies are beaten, railways wrecked, cities burned, countryside occupied and crops laid waste, lose their will—and ability—to continue fighting. In war 'heavy battalions' do normally triumph. The Civil War was to be no exception. Unable to fight a perfect war, the stubborn Confederacy finally fell before the enemy's superior resources. The final epitaph of the Confederacy should be 'Expired after a brave fight'.

Critical Thinking

1. Discuss the three most important reasons the South lost the Civil War.

2. Why would some countries support the North while others supported the South?

3. What were three of the economic weapons used by the North and why did they apply those weapons in particular?

Create Central

www.mhhe.com/createcentral

Internet References

The Civil War: Goals, Strategies, and Consequences
http://users.humboldt.edu/ogayle/hist110/unit4/CivilWar.html

James McPherson Interview
www.neh.gov/about/awards/jefferson-lecture/james-mcpherson-interview

American President: Abrahman Lincoln: Foreign Affairs
http://millercenter.org/president/lincoln/essays/biography/5

The Unknown Contribution of the Brits in the American Civil War
www.smithsonianmag.com/history-archaeology/The-Unknown-Contributions-of-Brits-in-the-American-Civil-War.html

French Intervention in Mexico and the American Civil War
http://history.state.gov/milestones/1861-1865/FrenchIntervention

Farmer, Alan. From *History Review*, 2005, pp. 1–7. Copyright © 2005 by History Today, Ltd. Reprinted by permission.

Article   Prepared by: Wendy A. Maier-Sarti, *Oakton Community College*

Steven Hahn Sings the Slaves Triumphant

The Pulitzer Prize–winning historian recasts the Civil War as a black revolt that forged African-American activism.

GENE SANTORO

Learning Outcomes

After reading this article, you will be able to:

- Explain the role that African Americans had in ending slavery.
- Evaluate the impact emancipation had on African Americans.

Steven Hahn contends that blacks played a more active role in bringing an end to slavery than historians generally recognize. Indeed, in his latest book, *The Political Worlds of Slavery and Freedom,* he characterizes the Civil War as "the greatest slave rebellion in modern history." He argues that some Northern black communities may have functioned like Haitian or Brazilian "maroons"—independent sites peopled and governed by runaway slaves that were vital to sustaining black political and military struggles for emancipation.

Why Do You Call the Civil War a Slave Rebellion?

It's true that there was no big bloody uprising, like in Haiti. But the Confederates had no confusion about what the slaves were doing—fleeing north, refusing to work, demanding wages and so on. It was rebellious behavior, and they wanted government intervention to put it down. In *Black Reconstruction,* W.E.B. Du Bois writes about the "general strike" among slaves. You don't have to be a Marxist like him to see that he was really saying slaves were important political actors in the Civil War.

What about the Abolitionist Movement?

The public still has this idea that, with the exception of Harriet Tubman, white people are rescuing black people. But historians have learned that the abolitionist movement was made chiefly

of people of African descent. In the 1830s and 1840s in the Northern states, blacks had access to a public sphere of politics, and held conventions to press against discrimination and for political rights, which carried through the Civil War. They're the ones who subscribed to abolitionist newspapers. They set up and staffed the Underground Railroad. They knew where to go in order to be hidden and protected, or get employment.

The abolitionist movement was chiefly people of African descent.

What Made You Think Runaway Slaves Had a Key Role in All This?

In other slave societies, maroons, or runaway slave communities, establish independence, support revolts and become important politically. In the United States, it appeared that outside of Spanish Florida, the lower Mississippi and a few swamps, not much was going on that way. But then I started thinking about slavery and emancipation as a long national experience, not a sectional one, and I started to speculate.

How?

There were still slaves in the North at the time of the Civil War, even though they lived in states where theoretically slavery wasn't legal. Free blacks' status in the North could be contested; they could be kidnapped. Most people in the North, including Lincoln, supported the Fugitive Slave Law. So slavery was effectively legal everywhere. Then how do you think about the communities of African Americans in the Northern states? Historians write as if Northern and Southern blacks had little to do with each other, yet we know by the end of the antebellum period a lot of African Americans in the North were born in the South. What if some of these communities were like maroons? The people in them were fugitives from slavery who had to arm and defend themselves against paramilitary invasions, just as maroon communities elsewhere did.

For Example?

In Lancaster County, Pa., in 1851, there was a shootout between around 100 blacks and a Maryland slaveowner who was looking for four runaway slaves with his son and friends and a U.S. marshal. This is the kind of situation where the maroon analogy makes sense. Here are black people across the Mason-Dixon line in Pennsylvania, collected among themselves out in a rural area. Many of them are fugitives from slavery. They are armed. They have networks of communication designed to alert them to trouble. The slaveowners get deputized by the federal government.

How Did Slaves Push Emancipation?

When the war starts, the federal government doesn't really have a policy about slavery. Lincoln goes out of his way to assure Southern slaveholders that he will not tamper with, as he puts it, a "domestic institution." He tells Southerners that as the Union Army is marching through, if they need help putting down slave rebellions, the army will do that. Now, part of the reason is that he knows Northern sentiment is divided and he doesn't want to be distracted from saving the Union. But slaves have their own ideas about what's going on, and they act by running away to Union camps. They have local intelligence: Where's the Union Army? What's going on? Initially, the Union side doesn't want them and sends them back, so it's a risky undertaking.

What Changes the Situation?

Fairly early on, the Union side learns that the Confederacy is using slave labor to build fortifications. So the logic becomes, if we send them back, they'll be used against us. All of a sudden they're declared contraband of war, which still acknowledges they're property. But little by little, as the Union Army moves into the deeper South, slaves come in the hundreds and thousands. As the war drags on, they realize that black labor and, eventually, 200,000 black Union soldiers, will be important in saving the Union. So slavery becomes destabilized by what the slaves did.

How Does This Shape the Emancipation Proclamation?

Most people think it just establishes the idea of freedom and frees slaves in areas where the Union Army isn't. But they forget about the provision allowing blacks to enlist. This is a huge and amazing move, very different from the preliminary proclamation Lincoln issued in September 1862. Because of

African-American participation in the war, they were in a position to make claims afterward about citizenship and equality.

How Did All This Change America?

The Civil War completed the Revolutionary period's nation-building process. Look at the world of the 1850s. The sovereignty of the federal government was in dispute and local sovereignties were emphasized. There was a nativist movement looking to deprive growing numbers of immigrants of any political rights. Then look at the country in the late 1860s and 1870s, where you have the Reconstruction amendments, when the idea of national citizenship for the first time comes into being, when you begin a massive process of enfranchisement after a decade and a half of disfranchisement, including women's suffrage. Obviously this process was painfully slow, and met with serious pushbacks all along the way. But if the war had ended in an armistice instead of unconditional surrender, none of this would have happened for much longer. Slavery might have continued deep into the 20th century.

How Does Barack Obama Fit into This Picture?

Obama is clearly part of a new segment of African descent in the United States. As immigration laws changed in the 1960s and 1970s, more people from Africa and the Caribbean came here, some with a good deal of education and resources. He's also the product of the civil rights movement and affirmative action, which really contributed to the growth of a black middle class. That segment of the black population is much more integrated with other groups. So his election is a tribute to what the struggle for civil rights accomplished, but it could also reemphasize class distinctions. He is going to run into problems with African Americans who expect a lot of things from him, which as president of the entire country, he won't be able to deliver.

Critical Thinking

1. Why have African American's contributions to ending slavery been relatively overlooked according to the author?

2. What does resistance such as the slave rebellion indicate about the human spirit?

Create Central

www.mhhe.com/createcentral

Internet References

Lincoln on Slavery
   www.nps.gov/liho/historyculture/slavery.htm
African Americans and the Civil War
   www2.coloradocollege.edu/Dept/HY/Hy243Ruiz/Research/civilwar.html

Article   Prepared by: Wendy A. Maier-Sarti, *Oakton Community College*

A Slave's Audacious Bid for Freedom

DAVID W. BLIGHT

Learning Outcomes

After reading this article, you will be able to:

• Describe what happened to slaves if they tried to escape.

• Explain how critical and rare slave narratives were.

Mobile, Alabama, August 1864

One hot summer day in wartime Mobile, a city garrisoned by 10,000 Confederate troops, 17-year-old Wallace Turnage was driving his owner's carriage along Dauphin Street in the crowded business district when a worn harness broke, flipping the vehicle on its side. Thrown to the ground, Turnage narrowly avoided the crushing wheels of a passing streetcar. The stunned teenager shook himself off, then set off for the house of his owner, the rich merchant Collier Minge. Turnage was no stranger to hardship: he had already been sold three times, losing contact with his family. Ugly scars on his torso bore witness to many severe beatings and even torture. Yet his life was about to get even worse before it got better.

Born in Green County near Snow Hill, North Carolina, Turnage, the son of a 15-year-old slave woman named Courtney and an 18-year-old white man, Sylvester Brown Turnage, was thus one of the nearly quarter million slave children of mixed race in the 1850s, many the products of forced sexual unions. In the spring of 1860, Turnage's indebted owner had sold the 13-year-old for $950 to Hector Davis, a slave trader in Richmond, Virginia, leaving the boy to survive as best he could, orphaned in a dangerous and tyrannical world. One of Richmond's richest dealers in human property, Davis owned a three-story slave jail and auction house. By one estimate, slave traders in Richmond during the late 1850s netted $4 million per year (approximately $70 million in 2008 dollars). Davis often sold nearly $15,000 worth of slaves per week.

For the next several months, Turnage prepared his fellows in the "dressing room" for the auction floor. One day he himself was told to climb up on the block and sold to an Alabama planter, James Chalmers, for $1,000. Three days later he found himself on a large cotton plantation near Pickensville, Alabama, close to the Mississippi line.

It was mid-1860, a pivotal election year during which the American union was dissolving under slavery's westward expansion. Now a field slave, the young man had to adapt to another alien environment, falling prey to fear, violence, and loneliness. After several whippings, he ran away for the first of five times.

In the aftermath of the Civil War, Turnage wrote an extraordinary narrative, only recently discovered, of his path to freedom. In beautiful, if untutored and unedited prose, Turnage described a runaway's horrific struggle for survival. His fight with the slave system was one desperate collision after another, amidst the double savagery of slavery and war. Each of the first four times that he broke for liberty, he crossed the Mississippi line and headed north along the Mobile and Ohio Railroad, yearning, as he wrote, "to get home," which for him must have vaguely meant North Carolina. Each escape had been prompted by a violent encounter with an overseer. On one occasion, when the overseer approached him with a cowhide whip ready, Turnage stood his ground, "spoke very saucy," and fought long and hard, his foe nearly biting off his ear. For this resistance he was pushed facedown on the ground, his hands tied to a tree, and given 95 lashes.

During one bid for freedom, he traveled some 80 miles across the war-ravaged country, hiding among fencerows and gullies. Taken in by other slaves, betrayed by one couple, chased and mauled by bloodhounds, he struggled to outlast winter cold, starvation, and Confederate patrols. One sadistic slave-catcher, who held him in a cabin until his owner arrived, pistol-whipped and stabbed him, then pitched him into a burning fireplace in a drunken rage. Locked in neck chains and, at times, wrist chains attached to other fugitives, Turnage learned the logic of terror but also somehow summoned the strength never to surrender to his own dehumanization.

For all the miseries and dislocation of war, Turnage remained far too valuable for Chalmers to let escape. But after the fourth runaway in early 1863, the cotton planter sold him at the slave jail in Mobile, where he fetched the robust price of $2,000. Turnage labored in Mobile as a jack-of-all-trades house slave for the Minge family over the next 15 months until that August day in 1864 when the carriage flipped.

When Turnage arrived at the Minge house with news of the ruined carriage, his mistress excoriated him. He "got angry and spoke very short with her," and then fled "down into the city of Mobile," where for a week he "wandered from one house to another where I had friends." Hiding in haylofts and sheds, Turnage was discovered one day in a stable by a "rebel police-man" who pressed a cocked pistol to his breast. Dragged by the neck to the "whipping house," Turnage was soon confronted by his master, who ordered him stripped, strung up by his wrists on the wall, subjected to 30 savage lashes with a device "three leathers thick," and then told to walk home. On the way back, he took a different turn and simply walked out of Mobile, strid-ing at dusk through a huge Confederate encampment, undoubt-edly mistaken for a black camp hand.

For the next three weeks, Turnage traversed the snake- and alligator-infested swamps of the Foul River estuary, moving 25 laborious miles along the western shore of Mobile Bay, where on August 5, Adm. David Farragut's fleet won the largest naval battle of the Civil War. Turnage remembered seeing warships in the distance and hearing guns. In fear and desperate hunger, he crossed the Dog and Deer rivers, then somehow swam the fear-some Foul River, where he was "troubled all day with snakes." Today this extensive, beautiful wetland offers a gentle yet for-bidding waterscape; alligators crawl in their wallows, laugh-ing gulls squawk everywhere as delta grass—"broom sage" to Turnage—sways waist-high in the summer breeze.

After reaching Cedar Point, the southern tip of the main-land, he could make out the stars and stripes flying above a Union-occupied island fort. He made a "hiding place in the ditch" to protect himself from the swamp water and ducked Confederate patrols, growing "so impatient seeing the free country in view and I still in the slave country." The sun may have been blinding and his body all but spent, but Turnage's choices were clear: "It was death to go back and it was death to stay there and freedom was before me; it could only be death to go forward if I was caught and freedom if I escaped." This timeless expression of the human will to choose freedom at whatever risk manifests itself in most slave narratives.

Turnage was a desperate hero. After praying especially hard one night, he discovered that the tide had swept in an old rowboat, as if "held by an invisible hand." Grabbing a "piece of board," he began to row the rickety craft into the waves of Mobile Bay. A "squall" bore down on him, "the water like a hill coming with a white cap on it." Just as the heavy seas struck his boat, he heard "the crash of oars and behold there was eight Yankees in a boat." Turnage jumped into the Union craft just as his own vessel capsized. For a few long moments the oars-men "were struck with silence" as they contemplated the gaunt young man crouched in front of them. Looking back to the shore, he could see two Confederate soldiers glaring after him. As the liberators' boat bounced on the waves, he inhaled his first breaths of freedom.

The Yankees took him to the sand island fort, wrapped him in a blanket, fed him, and gave him a tent to sleep in for the night—likely the first acts of kindness he had ever experienced from white people. The next day they took him in a skiff to Fort Gaines on Dauphine Island, the long sandbar at the mouth of Mobile Bay. In that fortress, whose cannon-crowned brick walls stand intact to this day, Turnage was interviewed by Gen.

Gordon Granger, commander of all Union forces in the Mobile region, who was eager for intelligence about the city, which he hoped soon to capture. Granger offered Turnage the choice of enlisting in a newly raised black regiment as a soldier or becoming a servant to a white officer. Turnage opted for the job of mess cook for one Capt. Junius Turner of a Maryland regi-ment, whom he accompanied to the end of the war, marching into Mobile with the Union army in April 1865.

Sometime shortly after the war he traveled to North Carolina and retrieved his mother and four half-siblings. He moved to New York City, struggled to make a living as a common laborer, and managed to keep his family together until he died in 1916. He was married three times, losing his first two wives at a young age, and fathered seven children, only three of whom survived infancy under the grueling hardships of the black urban poor.

His memoir's final paragraph is a stunning, prayerful statement about the meaning of freedom.

Sometime in the 1880s, gripped by the dogged desire to be remembered, Turnage put down his narrative, which comes to an abrupt end after his dramatic escape at sea and liberation. But the final paragraph is a stunning, prayerful articulation of natural rights and the meaning of freedom: "I had made my escape with safety after such a long struggle and had obtained that freedom which I desired so long. I now dreaded the gun and handcuffs and pistols no more. Nor the blowing of horns and the running of hounds; nor the threats of death from the rebels' authority. I could now speak my opinion to men of all grades and colors, and no one to question my right to speak." As one of the "many thousands gone" prophesied in the old slave spiritual, Wallace Turnage crafted his own emancipation hymn.

Critical Thinking

1. Why did slaves risk horrible punishments in their quest for freedom?
2. Why were masters and others who enacted punishments against slaves never held accountable for their actions?

Create Central

www.mhhe.com/createcentral

Internet References

A History of US Slavery
www.gilderlehrman.org/history-by-era/colonization-and-settlement -1585-1763/origins-slavery
Runaway Slave Communities in South Carolina
www.history.ac.uk/ihr/Focus/Slavery/articles/lockley.html

Article   Prepared by: Wendy A. Maier-Sarti, *Oakton Community College*

A Graceful Exit

In one momentous decision, Robert E. Lee spared the United States years of divisive violence.

Jay Winik

Learning Outcomes

After reading this article, you will be able to:

- Explain why Lee chose to surrender rather than continue to fight.

- Describe why Lee felt surrender was the more honorable option open to him.

As April 1865 neared, an exhausted Abraham Lincoln met with his two top generals, Ulysses S. Grant and William Tecumseh Sherman, to discuss the end of the Civil War, which finally seemed to be within reach. Nevertheless, the president—"having seen enough of the horrors of war"—remained deeply conflicted. To be sure, the endless sound of muddy boots tramping across City Point, Virginia, and the heavy ruts left by cannon wheels marked Grant's preparations for a final all-out push to ensnare the Army of Northern Virginia. Yet Lincoln could not shake off his deep-seated fears that Robert E. Lee would somehow escape Grant's clutches or, worse still, that his worn but still formidable forces would melt into the western mountains to continue the war indefinitely as marauding guerrilla bands. Nor was this idle speculation. Lee himself had once boasted that if he could get his army into the Blue Ridge Mountains, he could continue the war for another "20 years."

Grant himself shared Lincoln's foreboding, later confessing, "I was afraid every morning that I would awake from my sleep to hear that Lee had gone . . . and the war was prolonged." At one point during their final meeting at City Point, a morose Lincoln pleaded, "My God! Can't you spare more effusions of blood? We have had so much of it." Indeed, what most haunted him now was the belief that the war might end only after some final mass slaughter, or that it would dwindle into a long twilight of barbarism or mindless retaliation, as had happened in so many other civil wars, thus unleashing an endless cycle of more bloodshed and national division. To reunite the country, Lincoln believed the conflict's close must be marked by something profoundly different: a spirit of reconciliation.

But after four years of bloodletting, could it? Distressingly, on the fateful morning of April 9, 1865, the decision ironically seemed to be more in Lee's hands than in Lincoln's. When the first glimmer of sun broke around 5 A.M., Lee's vaunted army was at last surrounded, and the aging general now faced a decision that would forever shape the nation's history.

With gunfire still rattling in the distance, Lee convened a council of war. The talk turned to surrender, whereupon one of Lee's top aides protested that "a little more blood more or less now makes no difference." Instead he suggested that the Confederates play the trump card that Lincoln most dreaded and dissolve into the hills as guerrillas. As Lee carefully listened, he knew that this option was not lightly to be ignored. Just days earlier, the fleeing Confederate president, Jefferson Davis, had issued his own call for guerrilla struggle. And hundreds of Lee's men had already vanished into the countryside on their own initiative, anticipating precisely that.

Could Lee have done it? Here, surely, was temptation. No less than for Davis, the momentous step of surrender was anathema to him. Moreover, the South's long mountain ranges, endless swamps, and dark forests were well suited for a protracted partisan conflict. Its fighters, such as the cunning John Mosby and the hard-bitten cavalryman Nathan Bedford Forrest, not to mention young Confederates such as Jesse James, had already made life a festering hell for the Union forces with lightning hit-and-run raids. If Lee had resorted to guerrilla war, he arguably could have launched one of the most effective partisan movements in all history.

If he had resorted to guerrilla war, Lee arguably could have launched one of the most effective partisan movements in all history.

In fact, in Missouri a full-scale guerrilla war characterized by ruthless reprisals and random terror was already under way with such ferocity that the entire state had been dragged into a whirlpool of vengeance. As jurist and political philosopher Francis Lieber ominously told Lincoln, "Where these guerrillas flourish, [they create] a slaughter field."

In hindsight, we can see that in a countrywide guerrilla war, the nation would quickly have become mired in a nightmarish conflict without fronts, without boundaries between combatant and civilian, and without end. It could well have brought about the Vietnamization of America or, even more distressingly, its Iraqization, disfiguring this country for decades, if not for all time.

But after careful deliberation, Lee rejected the option of protracted anarchy and mayhem, insisting that "we would bring on a state of affairs that would take the country years to recover from." By this one momentous decision, he spared the United States generations of divisive violence, as well as the sepsis of malice and outrage that would have invariably delayed any true national reconciliation.

But if this were perhaps Lee's finest day, so too it was Grant's. At the surrender at Appomattox Courthouse, Grant, heeding Lincoln's injunction for a tender peace now that the war was close at hand, treated Lee's defeated army with extraordinary generosity, not as hated foes but as brothers to be embraced. The most poignant moment of this most poignant of days came after the instruments of surrender were signed, and an emotion-choked Lee mounted his horse Traveler and let out a long, deep sigh. In a brilliant masterstroke, Grant walked out onto the porch of the Wilmer McLean house and, in front of all his officers and men, silently raised his hat to the man who just that morning had been his ardent adversary, saluting him as an honored comrade—a gesture quickly echoed by innumerable other Union officers.

This one small act would loom large in the months to come, rippling out into every corner of the South and setting a tone for the healing that was so critical if the country were "to bind up" its wounds, as Lincoln so eloquently put it. And lest anyone mistake the importance of reconciliation for both sides, Lee would later remark: "I surrendered as much to Lincoln's goodness as I did to Grant's armies."

Critical Thinking

1. Was Lee right in surrendering when he did?
2. How would the Civil War have ended had Lee not surrendered when he did?

Create Central

www.mhhe.com/createcentral

Internet References

Surrender at Appomattox
www.eyewitnesstohistory.com/appomatx.htm
Lee Surrendered
www.americaslibrary.gov/jb/civil/jb_civil_surrender_1.html
The Surrender
www.nps.gov/apco/the-surrender.htm
Lee's Surrender
http://ehistory.osu.edu/world/articles/ArticleView.cfm?AID=15

JAY WINIK, the author of *April 1865* (HarperCollins 2001) and *The Great Upheaval* (Harper 2007), serves on the governing board of the National Endowment for the Humanities.

Article   Prepared by: Wendy A. Maier-Sarti, *Oakton Community College*

How the West Was Lost

CHRIS SMALLBONE

Learning Outcomes

After reading this article, you will be able to:

- Describe how and why the west was settled.

- Critique American government response to Native American conflicts once western settlement expanded, displacing Native Americans.

- Analyze how western settlement led to the growth of America with a detrimental effect on Native groups.

At the beginning of the nineteenth century the United States neither owned, valued nor even knew much about the Great Plains. This vast tract of grassland which runs across the centre of the continent was described as the 'Great American Desert', but by the end of the century the United States had taken it over completely. As the 'new Americans' (many of them black) pushed the frontier to the west, they established their culture at the expense of that of the indigenous peoples, then known to the incomers as 'Indians'.

The great natural resource of the Plains was the buffalo, which migrated in vast herds. The peoples of the Great Plains hunted and ate the buffalo, made tepees from their hides and utilized most other parts to make tools, utensils and weaponry. Some of them, for example the Mandan and Pawnee, lived in semi-permanent villages; others, like the Lakota and Cheyenne, lived a nomadic life. When necessary, as in life or death situations of war or in securing food in the hunt or moving camp they could be very organized and disciplined, but normally life was very loosely structured. Different peoples or nations were distinguished by language or dialect and in variations of customs and beliefs. But all depended upon nature for survival and had a spiritual approach to it.

Before the arrival of the new Americans the native groups were often in conflict with neighbouring peoples for resources such as horses and land. The latter resulted in some movement in their patterns of settlement. Thus, the Cheyenne and Arapaho had divided into northern and southern groups in the 1820s. Some Cheyenne and Arapaho moved south, following reports of large numbers of wild horses and vast buffalo herds in the land south of the Platte River, while others remained north of the Platte near the Black Hills where they effectively became a separate group, closely allied with the Lakota. Other peoples,

such as the Pawnee, Crow and Arikara (or Rees), had become enemies of the Lakota when supplanted by them earlier in the century. The northern Cheyenne and Arapaho were an exception, most other peoples in the northern Plains were enemies of the Lakota. Indeed the name for them adopted by the new Americans, Sioux, was the Ojibwe word for enemy. In the mid-eighteenth century the Lakota had moved gradually westwards from what was to be Minnesota, defeating other peoples as they went and pushing them into new hunting grounds.

In 1840, when the Oregon Trail from Independence, Missouri to the Pacific was first used, the frontier of the United States was roughly at the line of the Mississippi-Missouri, only about one third of the way across the continent. Just two generations later, by 1890, the indigenous peoples had been supplanted and the western frontier no longer existed. Apart from one or two later additions, today's map of the United States was firmly in place.

To understand how this took place one needs to step outside the strict chronology of the events. The new Americans split the Plains environment and those who depended upon it into two. This began in the 1840s with the overland trails to Oregon and California, initiating the age of the Wagon Train, and was cemented by the completion of the transcontinental and Kansas Pacific Railroads in the late 1860s. A series of treaties were signed, confining the native Americans to ever-smaller areas, and every opportunity was taken for incursion into these areas by prospectors, hunters, and settlers, supported by soldiers.

Even before the trails were opened, trading posts were established at key communications points, such as at the confluence of the North Platte and Laramie rivers in Wyoming, where fur traders Robert Campbell and William Sublette built Fort William in 1834. In 1849 it was bought by the United States military to protect and supply emigrants travelling the Oregon Trail and renamed Fort Laramie. In the early 1840s relationships between the travellers and the native Americans on the trail had been good, but as the decade wore on relations became more tense, especially as numbers of the emigrants escalated with the California Gold Rush in 1849. Numbers of those seeking a quick fortune far exceeded those steadier individuals who wished to raise crops in the western coastlands of Oregon and California. As these numbers increased so did incidents between the two cultures. The settlement of the Plains did not become a problem for the native Americans until later, especially in the post-Civil War expansionist mood, when the 'sodbusters' were spurred on by the offer of free land through the Homestead Act of 1862. In the late 1840s the concern for the native Americans was that traffic down the Oregon Trail was keeping the buffalo from their traditional habitat in this area. As the numbers of incidents increased the government sought to alleviate the problem by attempting to keep the native Americans away from the trail. In doing so they used a method already used to legitimize riding roughshod over the eastern native Americans: the Treaty.

The various treaties between the United States and the indigenous peoples of the west were of as little value as they had been in the east. In 1851 the United States Indian agent Thomas Fitzpatrick invited all of the peoples of the Plains to a meeting in the vicinity of Fort Laramie. It was attended by members of the Lakota (Sioux), Cheyenne, Arapaho, Shoshone, Assiniboine, Crow, Mandan, Hidatsa, and Arikara nations. All these peoples still ranged widely across the central Plains, whereas the Comanche and the Kiowa, who did not attend the Fort Laramie meeting, were far in the south, in the vicinity of the Santa Fe Trail, and a separate treaty was signed at Fort Atkinson with them two years later.

By the 1851 Treaty of Fort Laramie, the government bound 'themselves to protect the aforesaid Indian nations against the commission of all depredations by the people of the said United States' and promised annuity goods for fifty years (later amended by the Senate to fifteen years). The native American chiefs guaranteed safe passage for settlers along the Platte River, and accepted responsibility for the behaviour of their followers in specified territories and recognized 'the right of the United States government to establish roads, military and other posts'. However, military posts already existed on the Oregon Trail: Fort Kearny had already been established in Nebraska as a stopping-off point and garrison in 1848, Fort Bridger in Wyoming as a fur-trading post in 1843, as well as Fort Laramie itself. Nor was the United States army a disciplined force: as emigrant William Kelley commented on the troops at Fort Kearny:

> A most unsoldierly looking lot they were: unshaven, unshorn, with patched uniforms and a lounging gait. The privates being more particular in their inquiries after whiskey, for which they offered one dollar the half-pint; but we had none to sell them even at that tempting price.

It is not surprising that conflicts arose with native Americans.

Also, noble words meant little when the arbiters of 'justice' attempted to mete it out in a summary manner. Only three years after the treaty, Lieutenant Grattan attempted to bully Conquering Bear's Lakota into giving up a visitor who was accused of helping himself to a lame cow. His troops were annihilated, which led to retaliatory action by the Army, when any available native Americans were punished, regardless of whether they had been involved in the original action. This approach reflected the Army's attitude generally, as indeed had Grattan's action in the first place.

However little value could be placed on the promises in the treaties, their terms stand as clear indicators of the new Americans perceptions of how to deal with what they called the 'Indian Problem', at any one point. The Treaty of 1851 was

an attempt to protect travellers on the Oregon Trail, which had become of high importance as a result of the discovery of gold in California in 1848. However, the commitment to protecting 'Indian nations' from 'depredations' by United States citizens was of far lower priority to the new Americans and was never properly enforced.

Similarly in a treaty signed in 1861 at Fort Lyon in the southern Plains, the Cheyenne promised to remain in the vicinity of the Arkansas River and not to interfere with the gold-miners along the Smoky Hill Trail from Kansas City to Denver attracted to the area from 1858 onwards. Yet only three years later, in November 1864, an estimated 200 peaceful men, women and children of the Southern Cheyenne and Arapaho were massacred by the Third Colorado Regiment of volunteers and regular troops at Sand Creek. The leader of the outrage, John Chivington, fed the bloodlust of his troops, and was fond of the chilling phrase which rationalized the killing of infants: 'Nits make Lice'.

The idea of limiting to set areas peoples accustomed to a free-ranging existence following their source of life—the buffalo herds—was as unrealistic as it was racist. The concept of the native Americans' land being restricted to a reservation dated from the earliest treaties, and was consolidated in the 'removal' of eastern peoples into Indian Territory (later Oklahoma) in the 1830s under the direction of President Andrew Jackson. The National Park concept is generally credited to artist George Catlin, known for his paintings of native Americans. In 1832 he advocated that the wilderness might be preserved, 'by some great protecting policy of government . . . in a magnificent park . . . A nation's Park, containing man and beast, in all the wild and freshness of their nature's beauty!' In 1864, Congress donated Yosemite Valley to California for preservation as a state park. The second great Park, Yellowstone, was founded in 1872, during the presidency of Ulysses S. Grant, who developed an 'Indian Peace Policy' at this time which aimed to 'civilize' them. By 1876 this policy had increased the number of houses sevenfold, the acres under cultivation sixfold, the ownership of livestock by fifteen times, and tripled the number of teachers and schools. The concept of the reservation was surely similar to that of National Parks and as such was recognition that the new Americans saw the native Americans as no more or less significant than the flora and fauna.

The native Americans unleashed a robust raiding campaign in response to the massacre at Sand Creek which interfered with the United States government's wish to expand and consolidate economically after the Civil War (1862–65). The Union-Pacific and Kansas-Pacific railroads were built across the Plains in the 1860s. To confine the Southern Cheyenne and Arapaho and to protect the settlers, travellers, railroad workers and miners, the United States government perceived the need for another treaty later in the decade and despatched a 'Peace Commission'. This resulted in the treaty of Medicine Lodge Creek, signed in 1867 between the United States Army and 5,000 Southern Cheyenne, Arapaho, Comanche, Kiowa and Kiowa-Apache. Under its terms the indigenous peoples gave up their claims to 90 million acres in return for reservations in central Indian Territory (Oklahoma). Yet just four years later, after a method of tanning the buffalo hides to produce a good-quality leather was developed, the buffalo-hunters moved in. They annihilated the buffalo, in a wasteful and devastating manner, in a few short years. In 1872-73 three million buffalo perished and by 1874 the hunters had moved so far south that the Treaty of Medicine Lodge Creek was a dead letter. All the land given to the Cheyenne and Arapaho had been stripped of the buffalo on which they depended. This was recognized by General Philip Sheridan when he said of the buffalo hunters:

> These men have done (more) in the last two years, and will do more in the next year to settle the vexed Indian question, than the entire regular army has done in the last thirty years.

The sorry remnants of the Southern Cheyenne and Arapaho united with the Comanche and Kiowa, and fought back in a last-ditch attempt at resistance: the Red River War (1874-75). Now without the animal that had long been their prime source of existence, they were harried and starved into submission. They were encircled in the Texas Panhandle by five columns of troops, who came at the native Americans from all directions, keeping them on the move, giving them no rest. The troops burned and destroyed whatever possessions they left behind, including tepees and winter food stores, as they hastily withdrew their families to safety. A small group of a few dozen warriors still roaming free despite constant harassment came into Forts Sill and Reno in Oklahoma in 1875, where they were humiliated, and seventy-one men and one woman, many indiscriminately chosen, were transported to prison in Miami, Fort Marion.

As the land available to the native Americans shrank, some chiefs refused to accept this and fought back against the Army. This allowed the new Americans to claim that the native American leaders could not control their followers and any agreements were therefore broken. This development supported the new American claim to Manifest Destiny whereby they justified their behaviour as the act of 'taming' a savage wilderness. Later commentators refined this argument to suggest that the native Americans had no cultural tradition of commitment to a permanent system of leadership and government.

It was undoubtedly true that the indigenous peoples functioned with loose social structures based on respect being given to an individual based on their qualities rather than on the office they hold, with no lasting obligation to follow their leaders' directives. However, the new Americans did not show themselves to be any more committed to acting upon agreements or attempting to enforce the rule of law. For as long as the land was seen as a useless desert, the new Americans were content to leave it to the native Americans. However, as soon as something of value was discovered—usually precious metals but, also the buffalo once the market had been established for their hides—the new Americans themselves violated the treaties with impunity. Thus when buffalo-hunters went to Fort Dodge in 1872 to ask if they could hunt south of the Cimarron, thereby violating the Treaty of Medicine Lodge Creek, Colonel Irving Dodge had replied,

> Boys, if I were a buffalo hunter, I would hunt where the buffalo are.

While in the southern Plains the native Americans were driven south, confined to ever-smaller areas and ultimately defeated, those in the north were more successful at repelling the invaders in the short term. The Lakota were themselves usurpers, for they had moved into the northern Plains in the late eighteenth century from the north and displaced peoples such as the Crow, Pawnee and Arikara, who remained so hostile to them that they proved willing to ally with the Army against the Lakota. As in the south, miners moved into the area, despite the Treaty of 1851 and this resulted in armed conflict. When gold was discovered in Virginia City, Montana, in 1862, Forts Phil Kearney and C.F. Smith were built to protect miners using the Bozeman Trail taking them north from the Oregon Trail. Helped by Crazy Horse, the Lakota chief Red Cloud led his Lakota and Northern Cheyenne warriors in a war in the Powder Valley of Wyoming in 1866-68 which culminated in these forts being evacuated and burned. A second Treaty of Fort Laramie (1868) followed, very much on terms dictated by the native Americans which reaffirmed the principles set out in the earlier treaty of 1851. It granted the Lakota a large area in Dakota including the Black Hills, important for hunting, a source of lodge poles and an area sacred to them: the United States army withdrew from the forts they had built and they were burned by the exuberant Lakota and northern Cheyenne.

Yet the advantage was to be short-lived; once again the discovery of gold by an expedition led by George Armstrong Custer in 1874, was to result in the rules being rewritten. Attempts to hoodwink the native Americans into selling the Black Hills in 1875 met with a rebuff: commissioners were told by Red Cloud that the asking price was $600,000,000, a figure so far in excess of the Commissioners' valuation that it rendered negotiation futile. Tactics rehearsed in the southern Plains were now re-enacted in the north. Lakota and Northern Cheyenne were given notice to 'come in' to Fort Robinson in Nebraska: those not doing so would be deemed 'hostile'. Three encircling columns under Generals Gibbon, Crook and Terry were assembled to harry and destroy. However, the Lakota chose to fight. This surprised the arrogant Custer who commanded Terry's troops but who underestimated his foe and chose to ride the glory trail in defiance of all logic. In the south the tactics of relentless pursuit had worked, not because of fatalities experienced by the native Americans, but because when their homes were attacked the priority of the warriors was to get their families to safety. Their abandoned possessions could then be commandeered or destroyed. The choice of Custer fitted with the expectation that the Lakota and northern Cheyenne would try to escape as had happened in the south. In September 1867 he had been court-martialled for deserting his command, ordering deserters to be shot, damaging army horses, failing to pursue Indians attacking his escort and not recovering bodies of soldiers killed by Indians; but it was his reckless direct approach appealed to his superiors.

However the Lakota and their allies proved more than a match for their enemies. At the battle against General Crook at the Rosebud River in June 1876, it was only a rearguard action fought by a Crow contingent supporting the Army which enabled General Crook to withdraw, and ten days later Custer's force was wiped out at the Little Big Horn by Lakota and Northern Cheyenne warriors.

When the news of Custer's defeat hit the newsstands in the east, the country was in the midst of centenary celebrations. A shocked nation recoiled; public opinion hardened and resources were found to put more troops in the field. The victors of the Little Big Horn were driven north into Canada.

While in most cases incursions onto land 'granted' to the native Americans in both areas was linked in both northern and southern Plains to the discovery of gold, the eventual supplanting of groups in the south was not. Here it was as a result of the native Americans fighting back after their source of life, the buffalo, had been decimated on the very land that had been promised to them less than a decade previously. The defeat in the south came at the end of a long line of losses that followed each discovery by the new Americans that the land of the Great Plains was not as useless as they had first thought. The native Americans were driven south by the slaughter of the buffalo. The buffalo had been wiped out by 1878 in the south, and two years later the hunters moved in on the northern herd, protected by the post-Little Big Horn United States military campaign against the victors. By 1884 few buffalo remained, and in 1885 they were virtually extinct. On the northern Plains, although the Lakota and their allies achieved some military successes, they were ultimately to suffer the same fate: the loss of land promised to them. They were driven further away from the heart of the Great Plains. The Oregon Trail and the railroad which carried travellers, information and goods to link east and west of the nation, was also the dividing line between north and south for the vast buffalo herd and the native Americans who relied on them.

The result for all native Americans of Plains was the same: confinement on reservations. A law was passed in 1871 which formally ended the practice of treaties which had considered the native Americans to be separate nations from the United States. Native American culture was undermined by the practice of removing young children from their families to be 'educated' in residential schools where they were beaten if they spoke their native tongue. Finally in 1887 a law was passed under which the president of the United States was given the power to divide up the reservations, which resulted in another boom-time for the land speculators. Gold, the bison and protecting travellers provided short term reasons for conflict, but ultimately in the clash of cultures, as Red Cloud, Oglala Lakota, observed:

> The white man made us many promises, more than I can ever remember, but they never kept but one; they promised to take our land and they took it.

Critical Thinking

1. Why did the American government readily displace and remove Native Americans, many of whom they had treaties and alliances with?

2. How did the railroads facilitate westward expansion?

Create Central

www.mhhe.com/createcentral

Internet References

Indian Treaties and the Removal Act of 1830
http://history.state.gov/milestones/1830-1860/IndianTreaties
American Indians
http://digital.library.okstate.edu/encyclopedia/entries/A/AM010.html
Native American History and Experience
www.usfca.edu/fac-staff/boaz/pol230/nov1.htm

Article   Prepared by: Wendy A. Maier-Sarti, *Oakton Community College*

'It Was We, the People; Not We, the White Males'

A suffragist's bold argument that women deserve to be citizens.

On November 1, 1872, Susan B. Anthony entered a barbershop in Rochester, N.Y., that doubled as a voter registration office and insisted she had as much right to vote as any man. Startled officials allowed her to register after she threatened to sue them. Four days later she cast a ballot for Ulysses S. Grant for president. She was arrested and charged with voting illegally. Before the case went to trial in June 1873, she gave the speech below in 29 nearby towns. A federal judge was unmoved and ordered the jury to find her guilty.

SUSAN B. ANTHONY

Learning Outcomes

After reading this article, you will be able to:

- Understand why Susan B. Anthony believed in civil rights for all Americans.

- Analyze the impact that Susan B. Anthony had on the women's suffrage movement.

Not Until When?

Years in which Major Nations Gave Women Equal Voting Rights:

New Zealand	**1893**
Finland	**1906**
Norway	**1913**
Canada	**1918**
Germany	**1918**
United States	**1920**
United Kingdom	**1928**
France	**1944**
Japan (with limitations)	**1945**
China	**1947**
Mexico	**1953**
Switzerland	**1971**

Friends and fellow citizens:

I stand before you tonight under indictment for the alleged crime of having voted at the last presidential election, without having a lawful right to vote. It shall be my work this evening to prove to you that in thus voting, I not only committed no crime, but, instead, simply exercised my citizen's rights, guaranteed to me and all United States citizens by the National Constitution, beyond the power of any state to deny.

The preamble of the Federal Constitution says: "We, the people of the United States, in order to form a more perfect union, establish justice, insure domestic tranquillity, provide for the common defense, promote the general welfare, and secure the blessings of liberty to ourselves and our posterity, do ordain and establish this Constitution for the United States of America." It was we, the people; not we the white male citizens; nor yet we, the male citizens; but we, the whole people, who formed the Union. And we formed it, not to give the blessings of liberty, but to secure them; not to the half of ourselves and the half of our posterity, but to the whole people—women as well as men. And it is a downright mockery to talk to women of their enjoyment of the blessings of liberty while they are denied the use of the only means of securing them provided by this democratic-republican government—the ballot.

For any state to make sex a qualification that must ever result in the disfranchisement of one entire half of the people, is to pass a bill of attainder, or, an ex post facto law, and is therefore a violation of the supreme law of the land. By it the blessings of liberty are forever withheld from women and their female posterity.

To them this government has no just powers derived from the consent of the governed. To them this government is not a democracy. It is not a republic. It is an odious aristocracy; a hateful oligarchy of sex; the most hateful aristocracy ever established on the face of the globe; an oligarchy of wealth, where the rich govern the poor. An oligarchy of learning, where the educated govern the ignorant, or even an oligarchy of race, where the Saxon rules the African, might be endured; but this oligarchy of sex, which makes father, brothers, husband, sons, the oligarchs over the mother and sisters, the wife and daughters, of every household—which ordains all men sovereigns, all women subjects, carries dissension, discord, and rebellion into every home of the nation.

Webster, Worcester, and Bouvier all define a citizen to be a person in the United States, entitled to vote and hold office.

The only question left to be settled now is: Are women persons? And I hardly believe any of our opponents will have the hardihood to say they are not. Being persons, then, women are citizens; and no state has a right to make any law, or to enforce any old law, that shall abridge their privileges or immunities. Hence, every discrimination against women in the constitutions and laws of the several states is today null and void, precisely as is every one against Negroes.

Critical Thinking

1. Analyze Susan B. Anthony's arguments for the rights of women.

2. How might a white male at the time responded to her?

Create Central

www.mhhe.com/createcentral

Internet References

The Official Susan B. Anthony House
http://susanbanthonyhouse.org/index.php

Susan B. Anthony
www.biography.com/people/susan-b-anthony-194905

The Trial of Susan B. Anthony 1873
http://law2.umkc.edu/faculty/projects/ftrials/anthony/sbahome.html

Susan B. Anthony
www.nps.gov/wori/historyculture/susan-b-anthony.htm

From *American History*, October 2010.

Article   Prepared by: Wendy A. Maier-Sarti, *Oakton Community College*

Foul Lines: Teaching Race in Jim Crow America through Baseball History

DAVID J. LALIBERTE

Learning Outcomes

After reading this article, you will be able to:

- Identify how minority communities created a stronger identity by adopting baseball during this time period.

- List five of the challenges that Jackie Robinson faced in his ascent into the major leagues.

Over the past few years, a troupe of actors has toured America recreating the "inspiring story" of the life of Jackie Robinson, the first African American of the twentieth century to play in baseball's major leagues. The opening scene of their play—the California Theatre Center's Most Valuable Player—shows a young Robinson nestled up to a radio box crackling a broadcast of a major league all-star contest; his mother's voice soon booms out from offstage, "Jackie, why do you insist on listening to that white man's game?" Later, performers recount the seminal events of Robinson's big-league inauguration, including enduring a bitter spring training in segregated Florida, persevering through spikings by players and taunting by fans, and, despite it all, excelling on the field and being named National League Rookie of the Year. At the play's end, the joyous star peers skyward in ethereal connection to his mother, and then proclaims 1947 the year that baseball became "a black man's game, too." Robinson, here a harbinger of a new, more perfect era, broadened the gates of America anew.[1,2]

There is much truth, of course, to this familiar narrative. Robinson did break baseball's color line, opening avenues of major league participation for America's black ballplayers and harkening to the coming dissolution of segregation in many aspects of American life. Yet Robinson himself, a past participant in the Negro Leagues, would have recognized baseball as "a black man's game, too" well before 1947. Part of this paper's aim is to reveal just how thoroughly black the national game was before Robinson's debut. But this paper is not just about black Americans. It is instead a broader examination of baseball and race during the Jim Crow era, an exploration of commonalities between peoples of color—Native Americans, African Americans, Japanese Americans, and Cubans—who played baseball in the United States from 1887 to 1947. In

viewing this larger picture, this narrative explores aspects of several intriguing historical episodes involving the national pastime—professional and amateur, competitive and recreational—rather than detailing the total sport participation for any particular ethnic group. My intention is to broadly assess baseball's dealings with race during this six-decade era in a relatively brief format valuable to non-specialists. In that light, this essay focuses on two significant themes: first, how the construction of baseball's color line prompted the paradoxical trends of racial exclusion—keeping many peoples of color out—yet also of racial maneuvering—allowing players deemed "white enough" in; and second, how Americans of color, in myriad ways, strengthened their ethnic communities by embracing the national game.[3]

Fortunately, many capable scholars have raised the historical study of baseball in particular and of sport in general to a position of respectability within academia over the past several decades, mirroring the broader emergence of cultural history as a whole.'[4] Still, efforts to integrate sport history into pedagogical discussions have seen relatively little fruition: *The History Teacher',* archives, for instance, contain only a small handful of articles even addressing sport and none published in the past twenty years.[5] Analysis of race, however, the socio-cultural centerpiece in sports integration stories, has received considerable attention on the instructional front, with several articles in this journal' dedicated exclusively to the topic.[6] The narrative to follow unites these themes of sport and race with a deliberate eye on potential young learners. Part of my continuing instructional hope is to challenge students with scholarly examinations they can not only digest, but might even enthusiastically approach. For some, that may mean discussing ballparks and shortstops alongside the more standard political fare of presidents, court decisions, and laws. Among sport history's potential benefits for the contemporary classroom, it seems to me, perhaps none is as great as this: turning a topic of intense, if hagiographic, student interest—sport—into one of legitimate scholarly analysis. Consider this essay a tool to move instructors in that direction.

For teachers, my goals here are . . . First, this narrative is designed to provide the introductory content knowledge needed to develop a colorful lecture, structure a spirited discussion, or create a student project on the topic. Second, the detailed end-notes accompanying the paper offer instructors a guide toward accessible recent scholarship penned on ethnic aspects of the sport; many of the sources listed there provide bountiful tangential information for the investigative reader. In all, I hope that this essay will challenge instructors to consider sports history—our national pastime's history, in particular—as a ripe and engaging field for student intellectual inquiry, and will provide those teachers venturesome enough to try with the means necessary to incorporate a topic on baseball and race into their U.S. History curricula.

Foul Lines

And so our story opens a full sixty years before integration, in September 1888, when a young mulatto African American, Moses Fleetwood Walker, jogged out onto a major league diamond in Chicago. Suiting up as a catcher for Syracuse of the International Association, the primary rival to the decade-old National League, Walker had produced solid onfield performances the past season, hitting .264 with 67 hits in 69 games played. But even his presence on the diamond provoked a torrent of racial abuse, most notably from the vociferous Adrian "Cap" Anson, captain of the Chicago White Stockings and obstinate white supremacist. Anson, who in preceding years refused to be photographed with black teammates, now greeted Walker with the shout, "Get that nigger off the field!", and then pulled his team from the playing grounds. With several other of the league's best players already threatening to leave the circuit if African Americans remained rostered, International Association leaders soon met in secret to agree that no more contracts would be issued to colored players. Although temporarily lifted during the league's reorganization the following two years, the approved color line excluding black players hardened rigidly following the 1889 season, the last in which African American players appeared in major professional baseball for fifty-eight years.'[7]

Ironically and perhaps most shockingly, this black exodus necessarily eliminated a popular practice amongst big league clubs of the era: having young black boys serve as mascots. Indeed, as early as 1875, a costumed African American youth named Albert Pierce paraded the foul lines for the St. Louis Browns organization, and for several seasons ending in 1889, Clarence Duval did the same for the Chicago White Stockings. Their repertoires included bringing bats and gloves to on-field players, dancing and singing for spectators, and twirling batons and performing theatrics to band-played music, but perhaps the most significant responsibilities for mascots of the time was to perform "hoodoo," the hexing of competing teams and the warding off of evil mysticism supposedly created by opponents. Historian James Brunson explains that late nineteenth-century mascots were often seen as curious amalgamations of entertainers, buffoons, and bewitchers, a role that many white Americans, increasingly convinced of their racial superiority, thought natural for black boys. Reality, however, proved the opposite true: when Duval was offered lucrative theatrical opportunities in the world of blackface minstrelsy, for instance,

he abandoned the White Stockings for the envisioned financial upsurge; Pierce never left the ballpark to reap his monetary rewards, betting heavily on Browns games and winning considerable dollars in the process. In this regard, these black performers likely proved savvier than white baseball audiences anticipated or perhaps ever recognized, transposing degrading circumstances to ensure future financial prosperity.[8]

By 1900, blacks—both players and mascots—were banished from the major leagues, though the "foul lines" of the national game would not remain unchallenged. Indeed, a handful of integrated and all-black professional nines arose throughout the late nineteenth and early twentieth centuries—including the Michigan State League's Adrian club in 1895 and a Pennsylvania minor league's Acme Colored Giants in 1898—although such squads almost always proved short-lived. Moreover, African Americans continued to appear on amateur rosters nationwide during this turn-of-the-century era, including on a 1910 town team in Honolulu, Hawaii; a 1914 YMCA ballclub in Buxton, Iowa; and on college squads at Harvard (1904) and at the University of Minnesota (1907). While undoubtedly dozens more instances of integrated play exist at the amateur level, even these brief examples demonstrate that racial demarcations ensconced upon the top major leagues proved more transgressable, though certainly still palpable, at lower competitive levels of the game. Clearly, integrated baseball existed across the country, albeit under much duress, a full half-century before Jackie Robinson—a fifty-year period filled with implicit and overt challenges by other peoples of color on this newly imposed color barrier.[9]

Notes

1. My sincere thanks to Robert Galler and to Samuel Regalado for their thoughtful critiques of this essay.

2. Mary Hall Surface and Gayle Cornelison, playwrights, *Most Valuable Player* (Los Angeles, CA: California Theatre Center productions, 2003).

3. On the history of ethnic groups in baseball, see Lawrence Baldassaro and Richard A. Johnson, eds., *The American Game: Baseball and Ethnicity* (Carbondale, IL: Southern Illinois University Press, 2002), which features historical essays on American ballplayers of African, German, Italian, Irish, Jewish, Slavic, Asian, and Latino descent. For a related analysis encompassing all sports, see George Eisen and David Kenneth Wiggins, eds., *Ethnicity and Sport in North American History and Culture* (Westport, CT: Greenwood Press, 1994), which includes writings on Canadians, Latinos, and American Indians in addition to chapters on Americans of Irish, German, African, Italian, and Japanese ancestry.

4. For excellent sport histories, see Benjamin G. Rader, *American Sports: From the Age of Folk Games to the Age of Televised Sports,* sixth ed. (Upper Saddle River, NJ: Pearson/Prentice Hall, 2009) and Elliot J. Gorn and Warren Goldstein, *A Brief History of American Sports* (New York: Hill and Wang, 1993). On the movement for cultural history, see Jean-Christophe Agnew, "Capitalism, Culture and Catastrophe: Lawrence Levine and the Opening of Cultural History," *Journal of American History* 93, no. 3 (December 2006): 772–791. The

best synthesis of all of baseball's past, ethnic and otherwise, in a concise, scholarly text continues to be Benjamin G. Rader, *Baseball: A History of America's Game,* third ed. (Urbana, IL: University of Illinois Press, 2008), which is an excellent starting point for those interested in an academic overview of the sport. Inclusion of baseball as a valid historical subject has now even reached the textbook industry: for high school editions, see Gerald A. Danzer, et al., *The Americans* (Evanston, IL: McDougal Littell, 2005), 654, and for college texts, see James A. Henretta and David Brody, *America: A Concise History,* fourth ed. (Boston, MA: Bedford/St. Martin's, 2010), 545–546 and James Oakes, et al., *Of the People: A History of the United States* (New York: Oxford University Press, 2011), 751.

5. The most recent discussion in *The History Teacher* on incorporating sports into the history classroom—in this case, the use of baseball cards as an educator's anticipatory set—is Thomas Mackey, "It's Nolan Ryan: A Historiography Teaching Technique," *The History Teacher* 24, no. 3 (May 1991): 353–356; for analyses more thoroughly dedicated to sports history's possibilities in undergraduate classrooms, see Paul J. Zingg, "Diamond in the Rough: Baseball and the Study of American Sports History," *The History Teacher* 19, no. 3 (May 1986): 385–403 and Robert F. Wheeler, "Teaching Sports History, History Through Sport," *The History Teacher* 11, no. 3 (May 1978): 311–322.

6. See, for example, these several recent articles: Jason Eden, "Answers to the Question: 'Who Developed Race?'," *The History Teacher* 44, no. 2 (February 2011): 169–177; Barbara C. Cruz and James A. Duplass, "Making Sense of 'Race' in the History Classroom: A Literary Approach," *The History Teacher* 42, no. 4 (August 2009): 425–440; Jonathan M. Chu, "The Risks and Rewards of Teaching Race," *The History Teacher* 37, no. 4 (August 2004): 484–493; Michael Johanek, "Race, Gender and Ethnicity in the United States History Survey: Introduction," *The History Teacher* 37, no. 4 (August 2004): 473–476; and Joel M. Sipress, "Relearning Race: Teaching Race as a Cultural Construction,' *The History Teacher* 30, no. 2 (February 1997): 175–185.

7. David Zang, *Fleet Walker's Divided Heart: The Life of Baseball's First Black Major Leaguer* (Lincoln, NE: University of Nebraska Press, 1995), 55; Jules Tygiel, *Baseball's Great Experiment: Jackie Robinson and His Legacy* (New York: Oxford University Press, 1983), 14. On African American

history more broadly, see Nell Irvin Painter, *Creating Black Americans: African American History and its Meanings, 1619 to the Present* (New York: Oxford University Press, 2006).

8. James E. Brunson III, unpublished article on black mascots conveyed to author at the 17th annual conference of *NINE: A Journal of Baseball History and Culture,* Phoenix, AZ, March 2010. Unfortunately, no published writings on the historical origins of sports mascots were uncovered in this research.

9. Janice A. Beran, "Diamonds in Iowa: Blacks, Buxton, and Baseball," *Journal of African American History* 87 (The Past Before Us—Winter 2002): 56–69; Steven R. Hoffbeck, ed., *Swinging for the Fences: Black Baseball in Minnesota* (St. Paul, MN: Minnesota Historical Society Press, 2005), 29, 44, 49, 61; Tygiel, *Baseball's Great Experiment,* 15. For broader context of the era's hardening racial hierarchies, see Marilyn Lake and Henry Reynolds, *Drawing the Global Colour Line: White Men's Countries and the International Challenge of Racial Equality* (New York: Cambridge University Press. 2008).

Critical Thinking

1. What were the ramifications of breaking the color barrier in Major League Baseball?

2. What were the real reasons behind the resistance to allowing African Americans to play in the major leagues?

Create Central

www.mhhe.com/createcentral

Internet References

Jim Crow Museum of Racist Memorabilia
www.ferris.edu/jimcrow/timeline/jimcrow.htm
The Road to Civil Rights
www.fhwa.dot.gov/highwayhistory/road/s14.cfm
Breaking the Color Line: 1940–1946
http://memory.loc.gov/ammem/collections/robinson/jr1940.html
Jim Crow, Meet Lieutenant Robinson A 1944 Court-Martial
www.archives.gov/publications/prologue/2008/spring/robinson.html
The Jackie Robinson of the NBA
www.ferris.edu/jimcrow/question/dec05/

Laliberte, David J. From *History Teacher*, vol. 46, no. 3, May 2013, pp. 329–334. Copyright © 2013 by David J. Laliberte. Reprinted by permission of the author.